PRAISE FOR *BONEFISH DREAMS*

"*Bonefish Dreams* is an entertaining treasure trove of information and stories, based on almost forty years of angling experiences, that covers all bases . . . where to find them, how to get there, where to stay, who to fish with, and what flies to use, just for starters."

—Bob Rich
Author of *The Fishing Club*, *Fish Fights*, and *Looking Through Water*, Hall of Fame angler, cofounder Bonefish & Tarpon Trust

"I would bonefish with Frank Foster anywhere he chooses because he knows the nuances that make this gamefish so rewarding, such that it just may be my final bucket list fish while on my deathbed! Read Frank's remarkable book, *Bonefish Dreams*, and you too will understand the 'why's'."

—Andy Mill
Author of *A Passion for Tarpon*, member of IGFA Hall of Fame, 1976/1980 Olympic downhiller, host of *The Millhouse* podcast

"*Bonefish Dreams* is a fun and entertaining read that left me with a smile on my face . . . and with the knowledge of a few places I had not visited . . . yet. If you love fly fishing for bonefish, get it."

—Chico Fernandez
Author of *Fly Fishing for Bonefish* and *Fly Fishing for Redfish*, member of IGFA Hall of Fame

"This book is filled with great stories and information about one of the world's greatest gamefish. If you love bonefish, you absolutely, positively MUST read it."

—Monte Burke
Author of *Rivers Always Reach the Sea*, *Lords of the Fly*, and *Saban: The Making of a Coach*

"*Bonefish Dreams* reads like an adventure novel, packed with characters, exotic locals, and almost 40 years of fly-fishing experience. If Frank Foster can cast a fly rod as well as he casts his words, he's a world champion."

—Paul Dixon
Fishing guide, media personality, Bonefish & Tarpon Trust Advisory Council

"*Bonefish Dreams* is a charming travelogue and a loving tribute to saltwater fly fishing that highlights anglers interacting with Mother Nature. It's as informative as it is enjoyable."

—Huey Lewis
Grammy-winning and Academy Award–nominated platinum recording artist, costar of TV fly fishing show *Buccaneers and Bones*

"*Bonefish Dreams* allowed me to learn a lot about fly fishing I never knew. And that's after living in Islamorada for twenty-five years."

—Paul Tudor Jones II
Bonefish & Tarpon Trust Lifetime Conservationist honoree, chairman National Fish and Wildlife Foundation, founder of Everglades Foundation

"Sign me up for one of Frank's trips! But if you can't go along, read this engaging, fun, lively and informative book. It's the next best thing to being there. He nails the full flats experience and you'll quickly understand the addiction of being a traveling bonefisher."

—Bill Horn
Author of *Seasons on the Flats* and *On the Bow*, vice chairman emeritus Bonefish & Tarpon Trust

"*Bonefish Dreams* is a fun read whether for anglers between trips to the flats or anglers with a flats fishing trip on their bucket list. This book is an entertaining collection of tales from an itinerant angler who has pursued bonefish and many other species in just about every place they swim."

—Aaron Adams, PhD
Director of science and conservation for Bonefish & Tarpon Trust, author of *Fisherman's Coast* and *The Orvis Guide to Fly Fishing for Coastal Gamefish*

"The stirringly entertaining stories in *Bonefish Dreams* triggered delightful flashbacks to my years of fly fishing for bonefish with some of the same guides on some of the same gorgeous flats. Frank's colorful storytelling and his helpful facts and tips make this book a flats fishing masterpiece!"

—Dr. Marty Arostegui
Member of IGFA Hall of Fame

"Through these pages you will learn that Frank Foster has covered a lot of water chasing bonefish. So, if chasing bones is high on your list this book is a must read. Although it's far more than another 'how to' book, you will come to know the ins and outs of bonefishing through Frank's vast knowledge as he takes you along on his passion-filled journey to parts unknown."

—Bill Bishop
Author of *High Rollers*

"Frank Foster has produced a cornucopia of bonefishing remembrances, lore and legend, tips and tricks, holy grail destinations, guide stories and celebrity interviews, fly patterns, angling techniques and so much more!"

—George Roberts
Author of *Master the Cast* and *Fly Casting in Seven Lessons*, former managing editor of *Tail Fly Fishing Magazine*

"Famous names drip from these pages. But they are people just like us who share a love and fascination with the fun and exotic fishing locations in this marvelous book."

—Norman Duncan
Professional engineer and inventor of the Bimini twist, the famous cockroach tarpon fly, and fiberglass push poles; renowned fishing guide and angler

"Excellent and entertaining! Frank Foster's *Bonefish Dreams* will inspire you to pick up your fly rod and dream about flats in exotic bonefish destinations. A must read for all fly fishing anglers."

—Luis Menocal
Former board member of Bonefish & Tarpon Trust, outfitter for domestic and international fly fishing adventures

"Join Frank Foster on an unforgettable journey into the world of bonefishing with vivid storytelling and expert insight. This book takes you to breathtaking locations, shares the thrill of the catch, and delves into the patience and patience behind the sport. Whether you're a seasoned angler or new to fly fishing for bonefish, this book is sure to inspire and captivate."

—Barry Krauss
Author of *Ain't Nothin' but a Winner*, former NFL linebacker, broadcaster, motivational speaker, artist, and international angler

Bonefish Dreams

FICTION BY FRANK FOSTER

Boca Moon

Boca News

Catch a Falling Knife

A Lady in Havana
(Writing as Ashley Morgan)

The Lookdown
(Short Story—*Ellery Queen Magazine*)

BONEFISH DREAMS
Stories, Facts, and Tips from Travels to the World's Best Destinations

FRANK FOSTER

STACKPOLE BOOKS
Essex, Connecticut

STACKPOLE BOOKS
The Globe Pequot Publishing Group, Inc.
64 South Main St.
Essex, CT 06426

www.GlobePequot.com

Copyright © 2026 by Tight Loops, LLC

All rights reserved. No part of this book may be reproduced in any form or by any electronic or mechanical means, including information storage and retrieval systems, without written permission from the publisher, except by a reviewer who may quote passages in a review.

British Library Cataloguing in Publication Information available

Library of Congress Cataloging-in-Publication Data available
ISBN 9780811778121 (paperback) | ISBN 9780811778138 (epub)

This book is dedicated to my family, all of whom have joined me in countless days on the water, rods in hand, at Boca Grande, and around our planet. I love and treasure each of them and the precious memories we created.

"In our family there was no clear line between religion and fly fishing."

—Norman Maclean

"If fishing is religion, fly fishing is the high church."

—Tom Brokaw

"The finest gift you can give to any fisherman is to put a good fish back, and who knows if the fish you caught wasn't someone else's gift to you."

—Lee Wulff

"If I only had one day left to fish? It would have to be chasing some bonefish around a flat."

—Lefty Kreh

About the Author

Before becoming a published author, Frank Foster was chairman and CEO of one of America's fastest-growing small public companies. After his company was acquired, he became a commercial real estate investor and developer and independent venture capitalist. Frank and his wife live in Central Florida and the mountains of North Carolina as he writes, fly fishes, enjoys his wine cellars, and plays golf with his treasured friends.

Important Note from the Author

I have committed to donating *100 percent of my author royalties* from the sales of this book to the conservation organization Bonefish & Tarpon Trust (BTT).

If you're unfamiliar with BTT, I hope you'll explore their website: www.bonefishtarpontrust.org. You will learn of their passionate commitment to preserving the precious natural outdoor cathedral God has given us and its priceless swimming inhabitants.

Why is this important?

May I respectfully suggest that it is our duty to be moral stewards of nature's gifts. In addition, sustaining the sporting life enjoyed by so many of us anglers is crucial as it generates commerce that economically sustains so many who serve the recreational fishing industry.

So, I hope you will kindly consider buying many, many copies of this book! They make wonderful gifts, and remember, I'm not making a cent from such sales. Instead, this book is my gift to the angling world and to the always-needy budget of Bonefish & Tarpon Trust.

Respectfully,
Frank Foster

Contents

About the Author xi

1 The Bonefish and the Martini 1
2 Star Struck 5
3 Humble Servant Bonefishing—Est. 1986 9
4 You Ought to Try 13
5 Fore in the Channel, Please! 16
6 Libations with a Legend 23
7 The Land of the Giants 30
8 Go East, Young Man, Go East 38
9 A Deflowering 46
10 And Now . . . The *Rest* of the Story 50
11 If It Walks Like a Duck 53
12 Lucy, I'm Home! 59
13 I'm Calling the Airline! 64
14 I Couldn't "Bear" It 71
15 Me and My Big Mouth 78
16 How About Leaving Me Alone 86
17 I Wonder If You'd Mind... 91
18 I Said Cast the Fly, Frank! 96
19 "Bair's-Tagonia" 105

Contents

20	Stopped for a Loss!	113
21	Lord Jim	123
22	*Now* You Tell Us!	134
23	Pittypat's Pursuit of Piscatorial Pleasure	139
24	Ray Charles	144
25	Where's the Fire?	146
26	I Want My Mommy!	153
27	More Magnificent Mothers	160
28	Mutton Mutterings	166
29	Conched Out? Not Yet!	170
30	Miss Liz	173
31	Cuba Without a Yo-Yo	180
32	Whither the Weather and When	186
33	It's Only Three Inches	188
34	I'm a Little Flighty!	192
35	A Potpourri of Piscatorial Prattle	195
36	Piscatorial Prattle Perpetuated	202
37	I Love You, Too, Frank!	207
38	'Cuda, Wuda, Shuda	218
39	On Vacation??	221
40	Prudent and Pithy Piscatorial Precepts: (a.k.a.—Some Nifty Tips for Fishing the Saltwater Flats)	225
41	Prudent Pithy Piscatorial Precepts Protracted: (More Handy Tips)	234
42	Save Me a Spot	240

Acknowledgments 244
Index 246

One

The Bonefish and the Martini

I'm a sick man.

Want proof? Well, I get about fifty days a year of guided fly fishing, go to the Bahamas four or five times a year chasing bonefish, and I've fly-fished in seventeen different countries. Instead of relying on an inheritance, my kids are going to have to get jobs! (Actually, they have wonderful careers and are a blessing in my life—but I think they're watching me pretty closely.)

I have other afflictions, one of which is a shortage of patience. I'm one of those guys who prays: "God, please give me patience…right now!"

My patience deficit surfaces when I pick up a new book because I have little appetite for prologues, prefaces, preambles, preludes, forewords, introductions, acknowledgments, and anything else that prevents me from getting immediately into the story or text.

But, despite those protestations, dear reader, I feel obliged to briefly acquaint you with what you may expect from this book. If you yearn for a provocative guidebook to saltwater flats fly-fishing opportunities around the globe, this book should resonate and inform. If learning about those opportunities via fast-paced stories and humor from a regular guy who's totally ga-ga about saltwater fly fishing (and fresh, actually) is in your strike zone, you may be stimulated and edified. Moreover, if you hunger for transcendent retreats into the vastness of God's pristine earthly creations and are drawn to vignettes of quirky, interesting, lovable people (along with some famous ones), you and this book may get along just fine. I will give you a peek over the transom into the souls of anglers revealing that they are competitive yet serene, fearful yet optimistic, and inculcated with an attitude of gratitude for simply being there. For many of them, any accounting of results becomes irrelevant measured against experiencing the high privilege of interacting with our world's glorious nature and its fascinating wild creatures.

In short, I have attempted through my hopefully entertaining experiences to present you with a worldwide guidebook to fly-fishing the saltwater flats that can either direct you to opportunities for your own travel or allow you to experience them through my stories and facts while receiving some possibly valuable instruction along the way.

To begin, it may be useful to tell you about how the saltwater flats-fishing industry began in earnest. That will require a quick history:

Back in 1958, a fellow named Gil Drake, along with the late A.J. McClane, long-time fishing editor of *Field & Stream* magazine, founded something called Deep Water Cay Club at the extreme east end of Grand Bahama Island. It was the granddaddy of Bahamian bonefish lodges. That's bonefish as in *abula vulpes*, the prized gamefish doggedly pursued by tiger-eyed fly-fishing anglers and often referred to as "the grey ghost of the flats."

I never met Gil Drake but I knew both his sons. Gil Drake Jr. became a renowned fishing guide in the Florida Keys and Everglades, and I fished with him. Gil Jr.'s brother Tommy Drake and I were elementary school classmates at Palm Beach Public School a very long time ago. I never understood why Tommy went to public school with me while Gil Jr., along with his classmate and now-famous sporting author Guy de la Valdene, attended the veddy, veddy fancy Graham-Eckes private school just down County Line Road from where Tommy and I went.

Back then I not only had never heard of a fly rod but had never even fished. My otherwise wonderful dad's idea of the outdoors was going out to get the paper in the morning. It took a thoughtful Sunday school teacher taking me fishing one day to plant a seed that later turned into an addiction.

He and I piled into a craft that was little more than an aluminum johnboat pushed along by something like a ten-horse Evinrude kicker he retrieved from the trunk of his car. We started by plowing right into the teeth of the often-nasty Palm Beach Inlet (my mother would have fallen out had she known this, but fortunately, a light breeze produced only gentle swells) looking for snook against a dock and the jetties. Drawing a blank there, we headed west toward Peanut Island and then north of the inlet where Singer Island was just being developed. It was winter, and my savvy teacher somehow knew that small grouper and not-so-small mangrove snapper had taken up temporary residence in some newly constructed canals. With spinning rods and live shrimp, we loaded that little boat with almost enough fish to submerge it, and I insisted on taking my catch home to clean myself. It was a huge mistake, but young boys often act like, well, young boys. I spent many hours ruining my mother's kitchen with fish scales and guts everywhere, all of which yielded barely enough filet meat to fit in a sardine can.

That experience stirred something in me. It's kept a rod in my hands all these years and ultimately obliged me to write this book. My aim with these accounts is not only to share my experiences and provide a roadmap for my fellow anglers but also attempt to divine what's really going on here: What is it that compels otherwise sane men and women to spend unspeakable amounts of money on equipment and travel? What is it that makes brothers and sisters of the angle sometimes risk their lives by flirting with dangerous weather, wildlife, and skin cancer? What is it that gets anglers back out on the water the next day after scoring abysmal results (maybe even getting skunked) the preceding day?

Soon after I had caught my first bonefish on a spinning rod at Chub Cay in the Bahamas' Berry Islands, my wife and I heard about Deep Water Cay Club and made a number of trips. Reservations were made through an office in West Palm Beach run by the delightful Deanna Fairbanks, whose son Cole is currently an expert Boca Grande tarpon and snook guide. I've tarpon fished with Cole several times. An accomplished tier, Cole invented a unique black-and-gold fly for me that bonefish slurped up with impunity. He suggested I name it, and since I thought it looked like a polecat, that's what it became.

In addition to being the granddaddy of Bahamian bonefish lodges, Deep Water Cay Club was also the Cadillac of such venues. The accommodations were plush, the Bahamian fare in the dining room was first cabin, and the guests were pampered. All of which is why their display ads in the fishing magazines bore what I always thought a unique, catchy headline: *"The Bonefish and the Martini."*

I should stress that this is *not* a book about Deep Water Cay Club. Instead, it's a book about *all* the Deep Water Cay Clubs, along with independent guides and their fisheries, lodges and their proprietors, motherships, interesting people—at home and abroad—and the stories they helped to create. In addition, you'll find ensuing chapters dripping with facts about the destinations I discuss and instruction that I hope will help you expand your angling horizons and open new opportunities for memorable fly-fishing experiences on the saltwater flats.

Two

Star Struck

I have so many friends who are immersed in participation sports like golf, tennis, pickleball, and even croquet. But when I mention fly fishing, their eyes glaze over, and they politely say something like, "Oh, yeah, I've done a little fishing. But you're going to fly somewhere on an airplane to do it?"

I know their thoughts: They are dumbfounded at the time and money I spend to fly long distances to do what they figure is plopping down on my derriere while trying to squeeze the marrow out of some kind of "pole" as I stare for hours at a bobber praying it will suddenly disappear below the water's surface. I can almost hear my buddies asking each other, "How does he get a smelly stringer of fish home on the airplane?"

These dear friends of mine are blissfully unaware of only casting when a fish is sighted, of catch-and-release methodology, and how complex and technical is my sport. They have no conception of the athleticism, hand-eye coordination, keen vision, and stamina required of fly-fishing anglers. "Stamina?" they would ask. They have no knowledge of long wades of the flats, a multi-hour tussle with a 150-pound tarpon, or full days of using the walk-and-wade method to fly fish a river or a stream.

As for athleticism and hand-eye coordination, picking up a fly rod for the first time and trying to make a cast of eighty feet to a moving target like a bonefish would be a humbling jaw-dropper for my friends.

Now, it's possible many of you share my addiction to fly fishing. Exploring the root cause of this addiction requires an investigation that may be helped by drawing contrasts with some other sports.

For example, I play golf and I used to play handball and tennis. Pickleball may be in my future but more likely not. So, let's use golf. It's a sport that cannot happen unless a golf course architect evaluates a piece of property—acreage that is likely pristine and magnificent or it would not be considered for a new course. With the aid of an armful of topographical maps, the architect invites into his brain a vision of how to utterly massacre a slice of God's immaculate creation. Then comes moving thousands of cubic yards of earth, possibly dynamiting natural rock formations, and creating something that, while highly pleasing to the golfer's eye, puts a serious strain on the water table to keep it lush and green.

Now, I'm certainly not criticizing the game of golf. It would be hypocritical since I enjoy playing it myself and it's a marvelous, genteel sport for gentlemen and ladies with important history. Moreover, building and maintaining golf courses along with tournaments and equipment sales provides livelihood and pleasure for a great many folks—all good. But for my purposes here, golf provides contrast and perspective to help explain a sport that thrills me to my core—fly fishing. To that point, if I were on a small plane experiencing a mayday with both my golf clubs and my fly rods aboard and something had to go over the side…yep, the clubs.

The reason for this is simple. Both sports require hand-eye coordination, athleticism, and practice. Both require lots of expensive equipment. Both are very technical. But fly fishing offers expanded dimensions in two profound ways.

First, golf is static rather than interactive and man-made rather than in concert with nature. A player stands over his golf ball, which is inert, and with skill and luck, he or she strikes that ball effectively. But fly-fishing vodka-clear flats means interacting visually with the fly caster's moving target. And that target is not man-made but a feral creature of God's creation. An angler who engages with that creature in a game of deception can experience his or her blood being stirred beyond measure.

Let's use bonefish as an example to help those who have never held a fly rod while hunting on the flats. Here's how it works.

An angler standing on the bow of a flats skiff with perhaps sixty to eighty feet of fly line stripped out and onto the deck is poled by his guide across a flat where the water clarity is "read-a-newspaper-on-the-bottom" clear and the depth as little as a foot. Bonefish are always moving as they grub on the bottom looking for their lunch. Once a fish is spotted, an angler must have the athleticism of a football quarterback in calibrating the factors of wind and the speed of the target so that the cast will properly "lead" the moving fish. That assumes the angler's "casting thoughts" (like swing thoughts in golf) allow executing the cast with the required length and accuracy.

With fly fishing, no bulldozers are required to prepare a place to do it. Instead, its business is conducted in nature's outdoor cathedral that existed long before the first fly rod was designed.

And what a cathedral it is that God gave us. Every trip to the flats is an all-day free pass to the world's most stupefyingly fascinating aquarium. Bonefish, barracuda, permit, sharks, needlefish, snapper, shad, boxfish, ocean tolly, stingray, crabs, spotted leopard ray, and three species of turtle are just some of the intriguing wild critters that provide a visual smorgasbord whether from the bow of a flats skiff or while wading the diaphanous, skinny water of the saltwater flats.

That's not to mention the birds. Ospreys, heron, frigates, egrets, the exquisite flamingo, and its almost-lookalike, the roseate spoonbill. Shorebirds abound as well, including plovers, avocets, and turnstones.

The saltwater flats experience is voyeuristic. Species we see are preoccupied with their own agendas and have two goals:

The first is to get food.

The second is to avoid becoming food.

So, the self-absorption of wild creatures like bonefish makes them very approachable so long as the angler employs stealth. There is something unthinkably scintillating about presenting fake food—a fly—to a wild critter who does not realize you are close enough to observe the details of its movements. If your casting and stripping of the fly are properly executed and you correctly strike the fish when it takes, the exhilaration of the hookup and the ensuing wail of a smoking fly reel is rocket fuel for the addiction I have described. It means you've come tight with a sight-fished trophy and all is right with the world.

But guess what? All is right with the world anyway. No matter if you botch the cast, step on your fly line, your fly gets refused, or…well, even if you get skunked, it is a blessed privilege to just be there trying. Because it's largely about the "there." Yes, almost every venue for fly fishing is a montage of God's creation that is resplendent, complex, peaceful (or violent), and generous with its visual gifts. On the flats, the eye is presented with an ocular buffet of flora, fauna, birdlife, and swimming wild creatures that leave even a fishless angler eternally grateful for the privilege of looking, without touching. Of being at peace, without pursuing.

My favorite of these visual gifts may be one I am privileged to experience when either poling or wading bonefish flats that are near the ocean.

I am hopelessly in love with starfish.

In fact, sometimes I miss casting to a bevy of bones because I'm distracted by a lovely, reddish-orange starfish lying motionless on the bottom of the flat. While they are still when we see them, they do "walk" along the bottom using their tube feet. Starfish are not really fish—scientists call them sea stars, and not all of them have five legs. But all starfish I've seen have had five legs and were compellingly beautiful.

I remember wading Moore's Island in the Bahamas once with my best angling buddy (my sweet wife, Patti) and seeing one gorgeous starfish after another.

"I want starfish at my funeral," I said.

She gave me one of her loving glances that always dissolves me.

"I'll see that you have them," she said.

Three

Humble Servant Bonefishing—Est. 1986

It was the middle of June in 1986 when my wife's cousin, Doug, and I—he was also one of my best friends and fishing buddies—drove down to Miami and spent the night. The next morning, we boarded his secondhand forty-foot sportfish boat that was built many years earlier by a company called Pacemaker. To this day, it is the only such craft I've seen bearing that brand.

Off we went in an easterly direction headed for Bimini, the Bahamian island closest to the Florida mainland that was made famous by Ernest Hemingway's *Islands in the Stream*. We had the good fortune, despite our vintage, off-brand craft, to safely cross the often-nasty Gulf Stream. We were accompanied by my friend's partner in the boat, a commercial mortgage broker from Miami who, originally from Ohio, had worked his way through the University of Miami by collecting wages and mammoth tips as a mate on also mammoth sportfish boats. This guy was a walking encyclopedia of bluewater fishing.

Our attempts to emulate the great angler Hemingway drew a blank. Endless trolling while deeply inhaling diesel fumes (don't worry, this is the last you'll hear of billfishing in this book, as this trip was my bluewater swan song) produced nothing but a few twenty-five pound barracudas when we trolled a little too close to the reefs.

My friend's boat partner had a bit of the devil in him. When we were in the fighting chairs and dozing from the combination of beer and the aforementioned diesel fumes, he would deliberately veer toward a reef, causing a 'cuda to knock down an outrigger and jolt us out of our slumber to an apparent marlin bite that was only another barracuda. We would rail at him for this display of treachery only to have it recur when we next dozed off.

Not having raised a billfish at Bimini, we continued east to the Berry Islands and a wonderful place called Chub Cay. If you don't know Chub, its flats and yacht basin are adjacent to The Pocket, a name for the extreme northwestern corner of something called The Tongue of the Ocean. In a matter of a few hundred yards, the water depth goes from flats depth at Chub to the Tongue's 6,600 feet! Look at a chart or a map and you'll see what I mean. This phenomenon has a good bit to do with the very large size of Chub Cay bonefish as, often, the closer to the ocean the flat, the larger the bonefish.

Not surprisingly, Chub Cay is a very hot billfish destination with regular tournaments. At the time we went, Chub had its own private fishing club, but we docked on the transient side of the marina and dined in a separate non-member restaurant for the riffraff like us.

Although this book is about flats fishing, I must insert here that we did raise a 190-pound marlin from The Pocket on a trolled artificial bait. And like the mindless fools we were back then, we brought the fish in, hoisted it up on the Club's scale, and weighed it, thereby slaughtering a beautiful animal.

I had never even seen a fly rod, much less held one, but had read about bonefishing in the sporting magazines. My interest piqued, we asked if there were any bonefish around Chub Cay and if there were any guides. I never dreamed that, in the years to come, I would make an almost countless number of trips to Chub with my fly rods to experience their marvelous flats that may hold the largest bonefish in the Bahamas.

Yes, we were told, there is a bonefish guide available. My friend and I booked a half-day trip with David Lightbourne, and I still fish with him and his nephew, Ramon (Razor) Adderley, to this day. David didn't have much of a skiff back then, but it sufficed. His push pole was hand-carved from a red pine tree, and in the absence of anything even approaching a poling platform, he poled while standing on the stern of his boat. Having no bonefish tackle, we used David's spinning rods which were similar in age and condition to the Pacemaker boat we used to traverse the mighty Gulf Stream.

I don't remember if our bait was shrimp (difficult to obtain in the Bahamas back then) or a piece of conch David had mutilated with his bicuspids before penetrating it with a hook. We began at the superb flat right off the Chub Cay airport. We were about fifty yards offshore as David poled us toward the west with a falling tide. It was a sunny, mid-June day under a few cottony clouds with little if any wind. It was my first exposure to the horizontal temples of God's creation—the saltwater flats that, for my money, have it all over fancy aquariums in metro areas. The skinny-water, vodka-clear flat we poled provided a personal running video of marine life that was novel and mesmerizing if all one did was clutch one's rod and watch.

"Here they come," said David.

I was on the bow first. "Here *what* comes?"

"Point your rod at ten o'clock. You don't see that?"

I peered at the water and saw what he was talking about—my first look at bonefish. It was a squadron of eight formidable black shapes in tight formation. They slid languidly across the luminescent white sand bottom mimicking mini torpedoes tracking their target. In a moment, I realized the target was us!

"Cast it out there in front of them," David said.

Some readers of this book may have never experienced hanging on to a fishing rod curved to the breaking point in strained agony, helpless in submission to the initial hundred-yard run of a seven-pound bonefish accompanied by the sound of the drag on a fishing reel wailing in plaintive protest until the creature causing the commotion decides to take a breather from streaking in the opposite direction. It occurred to me that the exhilaration delivered by this interaction with a wild critter must be similar to what turns drug users into incorrigible addicts. I became hooked that day, causing me to spend a good portion of my life trying to capture that feeling as often as possible.

In the years to follow, having moved to fly rod, I began to go to the Bahamas four to five times a year—Grand Bahama, Abaco, the Berry

Islands, Andros, Bimini, Sale Cay, Carters Cays, and Grand Cay. Not to be mired in a Bahamas rut, I've also hustled after bonefish (along with tarpon and permit) in Mexico, Cuba, the Seychelle Islands, Turks and Caicos Islands, and the Florida Keys.

Perhaps 40 percent of my trips have included my best fishing buddy I mentioned, who is also my roommate. That would be my adorable wife Patti, who never practices her casting, does not know a 5-weight from a 12-weight rod, or otherwise possesses any interest in the technical aspects of fly fishing. But she nevertheless throws a beautiful tight loop, makes precise, delicate presentations, and catches the hell out of all the species, including very large tarpon. The only thing that has eluded her is the fussy permit, but she's working on that.

The rest of my trips have been with many fellow gentlemen anglers whose friendships I treasure. I'm always the organizer and manager of our trips, handling everything from booking lodges and guides, transportation to and from, gear lists, and everything else. Before each trip, I email a trip memo that I always sign this way: *Your Humble Servant—Bonefish Frank*.

So now you know what's behind: Humble Servant Bonefishing—established 1986. Naturally, I had some interesting tee shirts made. Interesting because of what else is printed on them. But I'll save that for another chapter.

Four

You Ought to Try…

After the life-changing experience at Chub Cay tussling with my first bonefish, it was several years before I made the transition to fly fishing. Buying my first fly rod was easy, but figuring out how to cast it was unspeakably difficult. Initially, I could throw a piece of cooked spaghetti further than my fly line. But, after lessons, practice, watching videos, reading books, getting coached by guides, plus a lot of fishing over the years, I finally got to where, on a good day, I could cast eighty feet into a fresh breeze and turn the leader over. Now, that's nothing to brag about when compared to some folks I've fished with (such as my buddy Dave Perkins, an owner of Orvis), but it has been enough to keep me constantly heading to the airport with my fly rods, brimming with the excitement of a child.

So, in the period soon after that first Chub Cay bonefish and transitioning to fly rods, Patti and I still went bonefishing with spinning rods. And guess where one of those trips was? Yep, Deep Water Cay Club. We made our reservations with Deanna Fairbanks and packed our *own spinning rods* for the trip.

SPIN OR FLY?

Those of you contemplating the pursuit and capture of your first bonefish on the flats may be wondering...spinning or fly rod? Well, a spinning rod is much easier to cast. And if you're fishing with some kind of meat on a bare hook—shrimp or conch—you stand a better chance of a hookup. Why? Because bonefish have a keen sense of smell and, even if your cast is WAY off target, they can pick up the scent of the meat, come to it, and—voila!—you're hooked up.

So, you say, if that's the case, why fool around with that frustrating fly rod?

Perhaps the main reason is that the additional challenge of fly fishing carries its own attraction along with a greatly enhanced level of satisfaction when successful. Trust me, after you've learned at least some of the intricacies of flycasting, casting a spinning rod becomes as blah as blah can get. This is partly because casting a fly rod involves both hands—much more interesting. And if you're a righty, your left hand becomes very involved not only with casting and hauling but also catching. Because, until you have your hooked fish "on the reel," your left hand serves as the drag system for your fly reel.

Another reason for learning to cast a fly rod is the unfair advantage it gives you over using a spinning rod. Bonefish are always on the move. In fact, when fly rods first began to be used to pursue cruising, always-moving bonefish, some folks would say using one was "cheating." Here's why they said that: Often, what is shaping up as a perfect cast with either a spinning or a fly rod falls to the water far from its target because the fish you were aiming for made a U-turn while your cast was already airborne. Arrgh! When this happens with a spinning rod you must *furiously* reel all the line back in to recast, which may be too late. Remember?—Bonefish are always moving. With a fly rod, on the other hand, the angler can, with a vigorous haul, pick the entire fly line off the water and, in one cast, place it back in the path of the bonefish before the target has swum out of range.

> On top of all that, folks, compared to a lump of meat threaded onto a hook, expertly tied bonefish flies sure are prettier! All of this may explain why it's very rare these days to see someone do as I did on that early trip to Deep Water Cay Club and show up at the lodge with spinning rods.

The first morning of this early-in-our-"career" trip to Deep Water Cay Club with our spinning rods is a clear memory. As is customary with most bonefish lodges, the guests walk from the lodge to the dock to meet their guide and his skiff for the day's fishing. Anglers tote their rods and other gear while the guide or staff handles a cooler with the day's lunch and beverages.

So, here came Patti and me to the dock with our spinning rods and the first fellow guest we saw was a chap carrying several fly rods who was attired as though he had just exited an Orvis store and bought everything in it.

Our eyes met.

He began to look us up and down.

His gaze stopped on our spinning rods.

Now, understand that this guy was a perfect stranger. We had not met at dinner the night before; he must have been a late arrival.

Grasping his fly rods, he glared derisively at our spinning rods before sharing this little gem:

"You ought to try going out there with a fishing rod sometime."

Thankfully, he turned away before I had a chance to say something I would later regret.

But at that moment, I vowed this to myself: If I ever did take up fly fishing, I would never, ever become a fly-rod snob like this guy.

Well, you know what happened. I became one!

Five

Fore in the Channel, Please!

Once I started chasing bonefish with a fly rod, I began traveling to various Bahamas locations and elsewhere to the tune or four to five times a year, either with Patti or my gentlemen angler friends.

One spring, Patti and I realized we had not been to Deep Water Cay Club in quite a while. The Club had another in its string of owners then, which meant booking with them and not that sweet lady, Deanna Fairbanks.

As with most bonefish lodges, all the guests dine together at a communal table each evening. At Deep Water Cay Club, though, it's at multiple communal tables. That's because they had among the largest capacities of any bonefish lodge I know of; I believe at that time they could accommodate twenty-four rods (guests).

There were multiple tables for eight. The first few nights, Patti and I ended up with professional golfer Fred Funk and his buddies from Jacksonville where he lived. This was shortly before he won the Players Championship. It so happened we were acquainted with Fred's mother-in-law and that jump-started our dinner conversation.

Fred Funk was an absolute riot. He was beyond congenial in that he had a bit of a boyish silly streak we shared and appreciated. Example: When we asked where he went to college, he replied with a broad grin, "Why, Funk U., of course!" This exuberance continued on the dock after our dinners where he would conduct a nightly raucous shark-fishing contest. We thoroughly enjoyed his company and were sorry to learn he was only in camp for half our planned stay.

We were amazed by what happened next. When we returned from fishing the next afternoon, we were told that another pro golfer, Davis Love III, had just arrived. He was accompanied by then PGA Tour Commissioner Tim Finchem, on-course NBC-TV commentator Mark Rolfing ("What's he got, Rolfie?"), and another gentleman.

Well, with all due respect to our new best friend Fred Funk, we felt Davis Love was more of a celebrity and, particularly accompanied by his heavy-hitter companions, would prefer his privacy. Accordingly, during cocktail hour, Patti and I shrank away to a small corner of the patio overlooking the ocean and kept to ourselves as we assumed the staff would seat us at one of the other dining tables, certainly not Davis Love's.

So, Patti with her rum drink and I with my bottle of Bahamian Kalik beer were minding our own business when none other than Davis Love came bounding up to us, hand extended.

"Hi, I'm Davis Love," he said.

"Frank and Patti," we said, each of us taking his hand. (Those of you who frequent lodges know that last names become futile with a large number of guests).

"Why don't y'all sit at our table?" he asked.

We looked at each other for about two beats and nodded.

"Sure," I said.

Well, we ended up dining with Davis Love, Tim Finchem, Mark Rolfing, and that other guy (Mark told me he was one of those people who sponsored young players financially on the PGA Tour) for the next three nights. Our time with them was convivial and pleasing. It turned out Davis and I had a mutual friend in Lakeland who shared a bowhunting interest with him.

But, as they say on the TV commercials, wait, there's more.

Deep Water Cay Club was what I call a "bonefish factory." By that, I mean it was a large operation that was run as a tight ship and afforded its anglers little or no flexibility in fishing hours, mainly because the guides were ferried from the cay across the channel to McClean's Town each day at a certain time.

REEL 'EM UP!

Fishing hours can be a touchy subject at some lodges. It can be an issue for an angler because of how daunting traveling can be to the fishing. Even if you fly private, it's demanding, but dealing with TSA, connections, customs each way, and just making sure your reservations are in order can drain the stamina of an enthusiastic angler. And remembering all your gear is nerve-wracking because if you don't bring what you need to some places in the world, you'll rarely find it there.

So, enthusiastic anglers like me can get very frustrated with lodges that have rigid, inflexible fishing hours. Here is an example of what can happen in those cases: You and your guide are, say, bonefishing on the west side of Andros (an hour's boat ride from the lodge) near the big-bonefish flat called The Land of the Giants at three o'clock with beautiful weather and surrounded by...well, giants. You're about to cast to a "hog," and your guide says, "Reel it up. Gotta be back at the dock no later than four."

"Aargh!!" you say to yourself.

To be clear, there are some anglers who are perfectly fine with this and, by mid-afternoon, have had enough fishing anyway. They're already starting to taste that ice-cold Kalik accompanied by freshly fried conch fritters.

But almost all my angler friends feel as I do, namely, that it's a long way and a lot of trouble to travel to a place with a beautiful flat loaded with fish only to have to leave it in the middle of the afternoon to sit at the lodge and drink wine. After all, we can have a drink anytime we want to at home. Moreover, I live on a spring-fed freshwater lake in Central Florida, and I can tell you I have yet to see a tailing bonefish there!

So, here's a suggestion.

First, when you arrive at your lodge, talk to the manager or head guide about this. If fishing hours are flexible that's great. But if they are rigid, you might consider broaching the subject and making arrangements to fish later than the normal hours if the situation so dictates. This may cost you a little extra money but can be well worth it. Explain that the flexibility you seek can work both ways. In other words, if at two or three o'clock you and your guide are poling endlessly under a thick cloud cover and seeing nothing, volunteer that you'd be perfectly willing to wrap it up early.

Now, this is facetious, but I have always said that the ideal bonefish guide, at lunch time, has his push pole in one hand and his lunch sandwich in the other—and keeps fishing!

But here's one only a little more serious: Particularly as the day gets short, never, ever look at your watch or mention to either the guide or your angling partner the time of day!

Because of the inflexible and, to me, rather short fishing hours at Deep Water Cay Club, the next afternoon around four, following our return from the flats, I found myself wade-fishing with Davis Love on the ocean side of the cay. This resulted in a less-productive outing than if either of us had been alone. Why? We were both too polite. Better put, we were each *obsessed* with fairness.

Along would come a bonefish, and he'd say, "You take it."

I'd say, "No, you take it."

"I insist."

"No, I insist."

And so it went until one of us finally decided to make a cast. I seem to recall that we each caught a decent bonefish before it was time to shower and grab a Kalik.

But there is still more. Following the next day's fishing, Davis and I shared a casting lesson with a now-legendary guide who was then still working for Deep Water Cay Club. His name is Omeko Glinton—everybody calls him "Meko"—and he developed the renowned "Meko Special" bonefish fly that is used all over the world. Meko, born just across the channel from Deep Water Cay in McClean's Town, comes from fine stock as he is the grandson of the patriarch of all Bahamian bonefish guides, David Pinder Sr. Meko subsequently left Deep Water Cay Club and became the head guide at nearby North Riding Point Club before leaving there to open his own lodge that he now successfully operates. By the way, if you want to learn more about the history of Deep Water Cay Club, the Pinder family, and Gil Drake, there are some excellent books by acclaimed authors Guy de la Valdène and Chris Dombrowski that I highly recommend. Go online, and you'll see.

It should be noted here that, not surprisingly, Davis Love III could cast circles around yours truly. In fact, why he thought he needed a casting lesson from Meko was beyond me. But I sure needed one. I still remember the main tip Meko gave me—to keep my rod-handle thumb 180 degrees from my target. It made it easier to pull off the "power snap" with one's thumb that the legendary Joan Wulff describes in her casting videos. It was a big help.

When the lesson was over, Davis asked Meko to demonstrate his own casting. Like so many Bahamian bonefish guides, Meko can cast the entire fly line and a good portion of backing *with either hand.* Every time I see this done—something I only dream of being able to do—I try to decide if I should be inspired or humiliated. I confess it's often the latter.

Well, not only did I believe "DL3" did not need a casting lesson, in typical "giver, not a taker" fashion for him, he did something for Meko that Meko was counting on.

He gave him a golf lesson.

Turns out Meko was trying to learn the game. His enormous bag of shag balls and a few clubs looked like they were willed to him by somebody of Walter Hagen's era and then left outdoors ever since.

The golf lesson ensued, after which Meko, likely recalling the request to show off his casting, said to Davis, "How about showing us how *you* do it?"

Davis paused a beat or two trying to sort out the request. He then walked out on the main dock of Deep Water Cay Club with the shag balls and Meko's far-less-than-state-of-the-art driver. Meko had some tees, and Davis was able to ratchet one into the dock between the planks and tee up a few of the shag balls.

With no practice swings, DL3 began to send shag balls into a 300-yard orbit out into the channel separating Deep Water Cay from

McClean's Town, causing me to gently say, with a grin, "Fore in the channel, please!"

Kind and considerate, Davis Love is the quintessential gentleman. We corresponded for a while after our time at Deep Water Cay Club. He wanted me to come to Sea Island and play Ocean Forest Golf Club with him, but we never could work out a time. I saw him recently on the practice tee at Fredrica Golf Club in Sea Island where my scratch golfer son and I were playing as the guest of a friend. We had a nice reunion. Sadly, he told me he rarely picks up a fly rod anymore.

As we visit other saltwater flats-fishing destinations in the chapters that follow, I will provide a hearty menu of facts to assist you in either deciding to visit or help you if you go. I wish it were possible to do the same for Deep Water Cay Club but, sadly, as I write this, it is closed indefinitely.

In 2019, the cay became ground zero for the horrors of Hurricane Dorian's 185-mile-per-hour winds. The lodge complex was mostly obliterated along with the private homes that had been built by then. So, it's unclear when, if ever, the Club's famous guests will return. Davis Love, Fred Funk, and Mark Rolfing weren't the only ones. Over the years, the Club has been a favorite of the likes of Ted Williams, Curt Gowdy, Lefty Kreh, Michael Keaton, Tom Brokaw, Liam Neeson, Huey Lewis, and others.

Deep Water Cay Club had a succession of owners that succeeded the founder, Gil Drake. I don't know them all, but a group of partners from Memphis led by a wealthy chap named Mason Hawkins had it for a long time. Then it was an ownership group from coastal Georgia that decided to change the character of the place by developing the real estate on the cay, thus the very nice private homes.

For quite a while, the owner has been Texas lawyer, rancher, and conservationist Paul Valdiek, who, after assuming ownership of Deep Water Cay Club, invested $44 million between the Club facilities on the cay and an elaborate marina at McClean's Town right across the channel from Deep Water Cay. While I have no verification, it seems to be common knowledge that Valdeik's financial partner was a lady from Europe who is purported to be the Bayer Aspirin heiress. Again, without verification, I was told by a former manager of Deep Water Cay that the heiress has bought each and every one of the homeowners out of their property on an as-is basis at prices that exceeded their original investment. Sounds somewhat preposterous, but my source is a credible one.

I have further understood from various sources that the cay is for sale but at a very high price that has attracted little interest thus far.

Deep Water Cay Club was unique. It offered a plenitude of posh and was, to my knowledge, the only private island-based Bahamian bonefish lodge with its own landing strip (it accepted private jets) and Bahamian Customs office. The guides were legendary, the Hells Bay skiffs top-notch, and the staff superb. I miss it. Maybe someday it will pull a "phoenix" on the angling community. Let's hope so.

Six
Libations with a Legend

Assume for the moment that you are as passionate about golf as I am about fly fishing and you are told that you can sit for a beer and a chat with the world's very first champion golfer.

You'd need a time machine to whisk you back to 1860 because you'd be sitting down with Willie Park Sr., who, on October 17 of that year, bested Old Tom Morris for the very first Open Championship at Prestwick Golf Club in Scotland.

Since fly fishing for bonefish hasn't been around as long as golf, I needed no time machine for recently sharing a Kalik (he had a Sands) with the fly-fishing equivalent of Willie Park Sr.

The gentleman I interviewed is a Senior, as well. He's Grand Bahama's David Pinder Sr., the patriarch of all Bahamian bonefish guides, the grand master, the icon, the living legend.

David Senior, as he is called, is ninety-two now and not as physically robust as he once was. But upstairs? He's still got it, as evidenced by the lucid memories that rolled off his tongue, delivered with the pleasing musicality of his delightful Bahamian patois.

I sat across from the legend in the living area of the Freeport condo my angling partners and I used while fishing with David Sr.'s grandson, the rock star bonefish guide, Meko Glinton. It had been decades since I fished with David Senior at Deep Water Cay Club. But smooth, charismatic old fox that he still is, he professed to remember me. Instead of traditional khakis from his guiding days, he was clad in some kind of plaid sport shirt, buttoned at the neck, and although indoors, perhaps having something to do with his cataracts, wore large sunglasses that made him bear an eerie resemblance to the late Ray Charles. Topping everything off was a cap bearing the Bonefish & Tarpon Trust logo.

David Senior spoke in soft, measured tones underscoring his obviously thoughtful, considered answers and would occasionally display his teeth, a little yellow these days, and the trademark, unmistakable wide gap between his incisors.

Here is my interview with the legend.

So, you grew up in McClean's Town?
"Yessir. It's about as far east as you can get on Grand Bahama. We lived in a two-room house. There was twelve of us brothers and sisters sleeping mainly on the floor. Daddy, who was born in Eleuthera, was a sponger before he became a pastor."

Did you fish as a boy?
"Everybody did. The water was our second home. When I started guiding, I didn't have to go and learn the water. I already knew where all the flats was, where the brown water was, what the tides was doing, and where the fish was. Because fishing was our living. We fished to eat. We sold what we caught and ate it too."

I'll bet you fished with a Cuban yo-yo.
(He smiles) "You mean a hand line? Oh, yeah. Everybody done that. And I still do. You can cast a lot further with it than most people think."

You're still fishing on your own at ninety-two?
(He smiles again, this time accompanied by a soft chuckle) "Yessir, I am."

So, how long did you work at Deep Water Cay Club before you retired?
"It was over forty years."

And how did you get started?
"In April of 1956, a couple of other boys and me had been hired to move some rocks when Mr. Drake came by and…"

That would be Gil Drake, the founder of Deep Water Cay?
"Yessir. I was a little bigger than them two other boys so Mr. Drake chose me to come and work for him and help him build Deep Water Cay. It was hard work. We had to move lots of building materials over from McClean's Town to Deep Water Cay in small boats that was barely seaworthy. Like I say, it was hard, but we got it done, and the Club got built. He paid me fifty cents an hour and soon hired me full time. Two years later, I was guiding full time."

But what about the bonefishing?
"Every time we'd cross the sound in them boats hauling materials, Mr. Drake had one eye where we was going and his other eye on schools of bonefish that would tail on the flat right across the sound from the Club. He'd ask me if I thought I could catch them. I told him I knew I could catch them because I've caught plenty of them on a hand line. But I wondered why anybody would want to catch one when there are so many other kinds of fish that eats as good or better without having to worry about all the bones. Well, he told me about his plans, went and got me a spinning rod and some shrimp he'd done brought over from Palm Beach, and we caught a lot of bonefish, the two of us. Soon after that I started guiding his friends. They'd come over from Florida and stay on their boats because the Club wasn't finished yet."

So, who taught you how to be a bonefish guide?
"There wasn't nothing to teach. I'd grown up on all the flats and knew where everything was. Every mangrove bank, channel, and sandbar. And I sure enough knew where the bonefish was. My skiff was an old keel

dinghy I pushed along with a shaved, red pine push pole. I already knew bonefish were skittish, so alls I had to do was sneak up on them poling that old boat and tell the angler to cast his spinning rod with his piece of shrimp on a hook out in front of the fish and wait. It wasn't that hard because, back then, the bonefish was everywhere. There's still plenty of bonefish here today, but back then, you couldn't run the boat hardly anywhere without seeing them. Sometimes we'd catch eighty to ninety fish a day."

Have the sharks cut the number of fish down?
(Shakes his head) "There was just as many sharks back then. But today the sharks is better trained. You know what I'm talking about, they hang around a bonefish skiff waiting for an angler to release a fish."

So, tell me about the fly rod coming along.
"That wasn't until five or six years after the Club opened. A few anglers was starting to catch them that way in the Florida Keys, and it made its way over here. I loved it and still do. It's a much more interesting way to catch a bonefish, and it's got advantages over a spinning rod. I taught myself how to cast and then fine-tuned things so's I could start teaching my anglers. Some of the anglers who started doing it were really bad at casting. Standing up there in in the back of the boat poling, I was getting hooked all the time. In the early days with the fly rod, I'd wear a baggy jacket when I poled so the fly would snag the jacket instead of me. That jacket ended up full of holes from fish hooks."

Being the pioneer, you must have trained a lot of other guides.
"No, not really. Remember, I had four sons working at Deep Water Cay Club with me—David Jr., William, Joseph, and Jeffrey. I only trained them, but they went on to train lots of other guides. They sort of passed it on."

What were your three favorite flies?
"My favorite fly was one that anglers don't seem to use much any more, and I ain't sure why. It's the Pink Puff. My other two were the Gotcha and the Crazy Charlie."

Did you prefer fishing a bank that is a windward or a leeward shore?
"Well, the leeward shore is easier for casting and easier for poling. But, I'll tell you, I always found more fish on windward shores. I think it was because there was a better chance of the wind stirring up food for the bonefish."

You're famous for not wearing polarized glasses.
"It may be why I have cataracts now, but I always thought I could see the fish better without them. But I always told my anglers to wear them."

Biggest bonefish you guided a guest to?
"One day up in Thrift Harbour, we caught a fifteen-pound bonefish. We weighed her on a scale, putting the scale's hook in her mouth and holding her up to read it. These days we ain't supposed to do that because Bonefish & Tarpon Trust has proved it cuts way down on the fish's chance for survival. I'm sorry I did it, but back then, we didn't know any better."

Would you say that's your best fish story from your forty years at Deep Water Cay?
"No. I'll tell you one that says even more about our bad conservation in the early days. The Club had a rule back then that you'd never see today. Each guide could kill one bonefish a day to eat. You probably know bonefish are good eating if you're willing to deal with the bones. We caught an eleven-pound bonefish, and I decided I'd take her home. But there was something different about this fish. Even though I knew she'd died, she wouldn't stop wiggling. That's the best way I can describe that situation—that fish just wiggled. Well, when we got back to the dock, I gutted this eleven-pounder and found a one-pound bonefish in her stomach. I put that small fish in the water, and it swam a little ways. I never knew for sure if it survived."

It's a different world from a conservation standpoint now, isn't it?
"Yessir, and it needed to be. I really like the new approach of not even touching bonefish to release them. I guess you know you can do that by

just holding the hook only or using one of them tools. Now, when you do touch a fish, it don't matter if you wet your hands first because at least some of his slime will come off. That's bad enough but at least some of that slime will also go in the water. That's what the sharks smell, and they come running looking for their lunch."

If you had to name your number-one casting tip, what would it be?
"Concentrate more on powering your backcast. It gets overlooked, and too much emphasis is on not going back more than two o'clock. It's like a golf swing—if your backcast is a little longer, you can build up more line speed."

I hate to ask you about Dorian.
"I went to Freeport, where things were not as bad. It probably saved my life because I didn't have no house when I finally got back to McClean's Town. That Dorian was a bad lady. She didn't work out so good."

You remember Deanna Fairbanks, right?
"She was in the Club's Palm Beach office and booked the guests. She was a nice lady, and I liked her son, Cole, who was over at the Club a lot."

I heard repeat guests would send her flowers hoping she would book them with you.
(A broad grin this time) "I may have heard something like that."

Do you remember when the Prime Minister visited McClean's Town to honor you?
"Can't forget that. It was all about the impact fly fishing for bonefish was having on the economy. But I shouldn't have got all that credit. It was a team effort with everybody at Deep Water Cay Club."

You've had quite a life. Any regrets?
"No sir, none at all. When I think of Gil Drake and A. J. McClane and what they did for me and my family—my four sons guided at Deep

Water Cay Club, my daughter and son-in-law done worked there for years, other family did too—I sometimes wonder what would have happened without all that. Yessir, that day Mr. Drake came by when I was moving rocks and hired me for fifty cents an hour was the luckiest day of my life."

SEVEN

The Land of the Giants

Way before that Deep Water Cay Club trip where we encountered Fred Funk and Davis Love, I was completing my transition from spinning tackle to fly rod, and it was time to catch my first bonefish on fly. Bahamas, here I come.

Naturally, I took my best fishing buddy (Patti) on a trip to what was the hot ticket of bonefish lodges, the Andros Island Bonefish Club. The locals, along with many in the close-knit community of fly-fishing anglers, either called it by its acronym, AIBC, or just "The Bonefish Club."

I booked that trip through the legendary George Hommel. He and equally legendary Billy Pate (numerous world records for tarpon on fly) owned World Wide Sportsman in Islamorada, then a rather small fly shop with a fishing travel business. I treasured knowing George; what a class act. In addition to being Billy Pate's partner and then selling his business to Johhny Morris and Bass Pro Shops, he was a famed fishing guide who always guided George H. W. Bush when he came to the Keys. I was referred to George Hommel by my friend, private equity giant and Bonefish & Tarpon Trust co-founder Roe Stamps. That was a great call because I acquired my initial assemblage of fly rods and reels from George, and if I had a problem with one of the old Billy Pate reels, George would fix it with his own hands and never even charge me for shipping.

George Hommel was big fan of Andros Island Bonefish Club. Not long after it opened, it was frequented by most of the big names in fly fishing, including George Hommel, Lefty Kreh, Stu Apte, Billy Pate, A.J. McClane, and Mark Sosin. AIBC was where Jim McVay invented the now world-famous Gotcha bonefish fly. All these people knew each other, sometimes fished with each other, traded information, and enjoyed mutual respect and admiration.

Indeed, the fly-fishing world is close-knit. I often say I have never met a guy or a gal carrying a fly rod case who was a jerk. On the contrary, the standard is gentlemanly, considerate behavior. Brothers and sisters of the angle are the first to volunteer help to their angling colleagues, whether friend or perfect stranger. This is as simple as offering a fly or two to a fellow angler or as significant as frequent Bahama-bound anglers stepping up with serious financial help for island hurricane victims.

That kind of giving occurs because anglers genuinely love the people who facilitate pursuing their passion. They know these folks share the same respect and appreciation for God's wild creatures they pursue and their awe of the natural venues in which they are privileged to conduct these pursuits.

The Bonefish Club's owner and head guide was local Bahamian Rupert Leadon, one of the most charismatic people I've ever known. Over the years, we had a great friendship that lasted until he was claimed by a sudden heart attack in 2012. Rupert tragically died on a plane as it sat on the runway trying to depart the Fresh Creek airport for Nassau and the hospital.

Rupert was an enormous black gentleman whose physique resembled that of an NFL defensive end. His biceps seemed about the size of my thighs. He had the most fluid, athletic walk I've ever seen; it made me think of a lion stealthily moving in on a zebra.

There was a trip with Rupert I'll never forget. We arrived back at his dock after the day's fishing to an almost dead-low spring tide that was in its final stages but still running hard. This made the distance between the deck of the skiff and the higher dock much greater than usual. Somehow, in disembarking from the skiff, a miscalculation left me momentarily suspended in mid-air between the skiff and the dock. I was nanoseconds from falling into the rushing tide when somehow an enormous arm became attached to my puny bicep. Rupert, *with just one hand*, lifted me back in the skiff to safety for another go at climbing onto the dock.

"That first step's a big one, Frank," he said with a wide grin.

That capacious grin of Rupert's illuminated everything and everybody within a fifty-foot radius. After the day on the flats was over and the Kaliks were being downed, he would often "play the saw" for his guests. It was amazing, really; I've never seen anything like it since. I'm talking about a carpenter's saw he would rapidly bend and move in such a way as to generate sounds that turned it into a very entertaining musical instrument. He learned it from his dad.

CAPTAIN RUPERT

Rupert Leadon was born in Fresh Creek on the east side of Andros Island and, as a younger man, worked at the defense contractor Autec's plant nearby. He was a diesel mechanic and somehow acquired the nickname "Gas Boy." Later, he worked at the Andros Town Yacht Club and began taking visitors on fishing and lobster trips. It wasn't long until he discovered the rapidly growing sport of catching Andros's very large bonefish on a fly rod. An entrepreneur at heart, Rupert figured out how to buy from the Bahamian government an old, formerly British sisal plantation near Behring Point on the North Bight and, starting with a machete, built his bonefish lodge.

"Andros Island is the richest island in the world. We're the untamed spirit of the Bahamas. We need to bring people back to fish here." —Rupert Leadon

I always thought Rupert Leadon was probably the best bonefish guide in the Bahamas. To avoid offending some of my other great guide friends who are just as good, I'll clarify that by saying, at least in my opinion, there were none better. He was among the first guides—and not nearly enough of them do it today—to say to his angler when he first sees a fish, "Point your rod." Then he would say, "more left, more right"—whatever—until the angler saw the fish too.

Although I fished with Rupert many times, on that first trip to Andros Island Bonefish Club he assigned us his son, Brian, for our first couple of days of fishing. While a little grumpy, he was a superb guide. On our first day, we ran to the west side, and as soon as we cleared Loggerhead Creek and turned north, he quickly brought the skiff off a plane because we were surrounded by large bonefish. My lousy casting then was only exceeded by my ineptitude as a rookie fly-fishing angler as I broke off the first two fish I hooked. I had not yet gotten the hang of letting my left hand be "the drag" until I cleared the line to the reel and let the reel take over.

Knowing we were beginners, Brian would see a fish and, if we were lucky enough to get the fly in front of it, he said, "Strip. Strip. Strip... Stop. *Long* strip!" That last command was in lieu of telling us the fish had eaten the fly, which he knew would likely result in the dreaded trout set (lifting the rod prematurely and losing the fish). "Long strip" was, of course, the desired strip strike that is preferred in salt water.

On subsequent trips with Rupert I learned all the hot spots and honey holes by the names he had assigned to them. These names are still used today by guides all over Andros.

The most famous is The Land of the Giants. It's an enormous pure-white sand flat on the west side of Andros just across from a bay marked on the nautical charts called The Wide Opening. Its name could not be more apt. All my double-digit bonefish have come from Chub Cay, but I have hooked and lost even bigger ones at The Land of the Giants. And I have angler friends who have taken fish from there weighing in the teens.

There was also The Last Resort near a blue hole. And Barbara's Cove was named after a lady angler who came to fish with Rupert four times per year and bought him his big Action Craft skiff.

Rupert provided me with some firsts.

In addition to introducing me to honey holes on the west side of Andros, Rupert was the first to insist I try a Bahamian Kalik beer instead of the Heineken I had ordered the first time I stood at his bar. I've ordered no other brand since.

I ate my first bonefish (and only, I think) with Rupert. He was an ardent conservationist, but on rare occasions, a bonefish will fail to survive being caught. Such was the case one day and Rupert brought it back to the lodge for cooking. Bonefish is quite delicious, but the bugaboo is…yes, the bones. I've heard that Bahamians know how to jerk on the fish a certain way that makes all the bones lay in one direction and—eureka!—it's easily edible. But I've also heard the story is a myth. I ate a few bites that day, picking out the bones, and it was pretty yummy.

Rupert was the first to show me the flamingos on the west side of Andros. They took flight as we approached, and I gasped at the visual delight it brought me. Pictures of flamingos do not do them justice; in person, they are beyond exquisite.

It was not far from Flamingo Central that Rupert showed me my first west side of Andros tarpon in Cabbage Creek. While Andros's west side tarpon are not abundant, they are found there in larger numbers than anywhere else in the Bahamas. It was while poling the Cabbage Creek flat near shore looking for bonefish that we found a laid-up silver king on the edge of the channel that weighed fifty-ish pounds. Thanks to George Hommel preparing me, I had in the rod rack a Sage 9-weight equipped with a purple tarpon fly flecked with red. I hurriedly handed my bonefish stick to Miss Patti while Rupert fetched the tarpon rod.

Rupert talked me through our presentation strategy.

"So, you see the fish is looking into the current, right?"

We were poling toward the east on the southern bank of Cabbage and into the falling tide that was sucking the water out of Cabbage at an ever-increasing velocity.

"Yeah, into the current," I replied.

"Now listen to me, Frank. Don't cast the fly right at that fish."

"Why?" I asked.

"Because the current will take it before he can see it. And, anyway, if he sees the fly land, he may not eat it."

"Okay, so…"

"Here's what I want you to do. Cast the fly way up-tide of him, a good twenty feet, and maybe five or ten feet across the line he's laying on. Then strip the fly gently, just staying in touch with it with your left hand, so it kind of swims with the current and ends up in his face. You do that and he'll eat it. Guaranteed."

At that comment, I thought my new 9-weight rod was going to slip right out of my hand owing to the copious moisture that had instantly visited my palms. I was younger then and therefore not alarmed by my suddenly raging pulse.

"Okay, got it," I managed to squeak out. "So, when do I cast?"

"Now!" was the answer, not delivered with a modicum of patience.

I somehow made the cast just as instructed. And somehow the fly indeed swam right to the laid-up tarpon. And, just as promised, the majestic fish turned slightly towards me, opened his cavernous yap, and sucked in my fly!

All good, right?

Well, it was until stupid, inexperienced angler me committed the dreaded sin of striking the tarpon before he had finished eating my fly and turned away with it, which would have allowed me to come tight.

As the elegantly beautiful silver king swam away, my new 9-weight became momentarily on high alert, somehow sensing its exposure to a violent encounter with my knee. Fortunately, my temper extinguished itself a moment after it ignited. I apologized to Rupert, who silently picked up the push pole and started looking for the next one.

FEEDING THE FISH

There was a reason Rupert was concerned about that tarpon seeing my fly land. He knew it would be game over. Andy Mill, in his massively wonderful book *A Passion for Tarpon*, explains that tarpon are lazy, opportunistic feeders and will not go out of their way to chase food. But if they happen onto a juicy morsel that literally appears in their face (like your fly), they will often eat it. The operative phrases here are "happen onto" and "in your face." Anglers going from bonefishing to tarpon fishing must endure a period of adjustment at the beginning of their trip in which they try to forget the benefits of landing their fly close to a bonefish.

The goal in presenting a fly to a tarpon is to land it plenty far enough from the fish, to one side or the other, to allow the angler to begin stripping the fly in such a way that it converges with the path of the fish and replicates the phenomenon of the tarpon "happening onto" an attractive meal that is "in its face."

But casting to daisy-chaining tarpon is different. There the goal is to land the fly right next to the chaining fish while being sure to cast to the right side of the chain if they are going clockwise and the left side if counterclockwise.

Forty years after Rupert Leadon built it, Andros Island Bonefish Club is still successfully operating under the management of Rupert's son, Shawn Leadon. It's convenient to travel to, very moderately priced compared with some of the other Bahamian lodges, and the guides are rock solid.

JUST THE FACTS

Lodge Name: Andros Island Bonefish Club

Location: Behring Point, Andros Island, Bahamas

Nearest Airport: Fresh Creek Airport (MYAF)

Drive from Airport to Lodge: Twenty-six minutes

Getting There: Numerous commercial flights to Nassau and either Le Air scheduled flights to Fresh Creek or charters. Watermakers Air direct from Fort Lauderdale or private charter.

Capacity: Twenty-four guests

Fly Shop: Modest with a few flies and some hats

Rate for Five Nights Lodging, Four Days Fishing: $3,040 (2025 rates)

Includes: Guided fishing, all meals, transfer from airport, lodging, double occupancy, shared skiff

Does Not Include: Tips, alcoholic beverage, VAT, airfare

Website: www.androsbonefishing.com

Author's Comments: "The Bonefish Club," as it is still called, is an institution that continues to thrive and please anglers worldwide. Although some minor upgrades have occurred over its forty-year history, the lodge itself remains rather basic, if not Spartan, but can always be counted on for tasty Bahamian vittles and expert guiding. The club is located on Cargill Creek, and the skiffs are but a few steps from the lodge—no trailering necessary. Probably not the place a gentleman angler would take his non-angler wife but, hey, The Bonefish Club is all about the fishing, and it's held up very well despite the heartfelt absence of Rupert Leadon playing the saw at night.

Eight
Go East, Young Man, Go East

I know, I know. Horace Greeley said go west. But notwithstanding two well-run operations based in Freeport, most bonefish anglers arriving on Grand Bahama Island head east where, with Deep Water Cay Club closed, currently three bonefish lodges are operating.

One is North Riding Point Club. Semi-private and owned by former Treasury Secretary Robert Rubin and his well-heeled buddies both at home and abroad, it's expertly managed by Paul Adams who once did the same thing at Deep Water Cay Club. And do you remember the rockstar guide, Meko Glinton? He guided at North Riding Point for quite a while but now has his own operation called Meko Experience. Finally, there is East End Lodge, and more about that shortly.

From Freeport, it's about an hour east by lodge vehicle or taxi to McClean's Town, where the mainland of Grand Bahama Island ends. Deep Water Cay Club lies just across the channel from McClean's Town and, when still open, had its own landing strip and customs agent. But many anglers who visited Deep Water Cay flew to Freeport and took the one-hour drive to McClean's Town followed by a short boat ride across the channel to the cay. Patti and I have used both methods.

However, in the few days leading up to September 1, 2019, no one was arriving anywhere on Grand Bahama. Instead, many were scrambling in desperation to get off the island before Category 5 Hurricane Dorian descended with 185-mile-per-hour winds. After making landfall on Elbow Cay on Great Abaco and then obliterating Marsh Harbour, the killer storm continued northwest across the Bight of Abaco. Next stop: McClean's Town.

In 2010, McClean's Town was said to have a population of 391. One way or another, almost all those warm, lovable people lived off the sea, be it subsistence fishing, selling their catch to a bonefish lodge, or working as an employee of one of the lodges. But on September 1, 2019, that population number was tragically reduced by Dorian, whose violence caused a twenty-foot storm surge at McClean's Town. It was estimated that 60 percent of Grand Bahama Island was underwater, and there were seventy-seven known deaths with 246 souls never found. Since McClean's Town and nearby Deep Water Cay were ground zero (the storm punished the settlement for twenty-four hours), it must be assumed the tiny settlement's losses were a large percentage of the total. On the Internet, it is possible to see drone footage of cars, trucks, and portions of houses far offshore after the storm passed.

McClean's Town's survivors, while thankful to be alive, were left destitute by Dorian, many with no place to even sleep after so many homes simply vaporized in the storm's fury.

In the wake of this, many of us regular Bahamas anglers who have developed a great affection for the islands and its people sprang into action. We enlisted the participation of some generous anglers and non-anglers who owned their own airplanes and then we contributed and raised money for aviation fuel and hurricane relief supplies, much of which was purchased from places like Home Depot and Lowes and flown to both Grand Bahama and Abaco. Multiple flights took place. Groups with which I was associated were certainly not the only ones doing this sort of thing as the outpouring was gratifying beyond words and made a huge difference.

But there were others who were much closer to the tragedy at or near ground zero who greatly distinguished themselves in the relief effort and, just as important, in the rebuilding effort. One was North Riding Point Club's general manager, Paul Adams, who, with the help of the partners in his semi-private lodge, raised a very, very substantial amount of hurricane relief money, perhaps dwarfing the amounts raised by many.

But another was a man from Jupiter, Florida, named Robert Neher, who owns a chain of UPS stores in South Florida. He and a Bahamian partner own something else—East End Lodge located right at McClean's Town. That partner is Cecil Leathen, also East End's head guide. If you're not familiar with the lodge, it is located right on the water, and anglers walk all of 200 feet or so to the modern, floating dock each morning to board their skiff. From that dock, one can gaze across the channel at the closed Deep Water Cay Club before casting off to fish the exact same fishery made famous by "the granddaddy of bonefish lodges" when it was open.

Robert Neher recalled being on his first vacation in eight years when the storm struck.

"I was sitting beside a pool looking at my cell phone radar watching the storm pass right over my lodge with 200-mile-per-hour wind gusts and all I could think of was: This is my community. These are my friends."

As with Deep Water Cay Club, Hurricane Dorian all but leveled East End Lodge, causing it to close and ending the livelihood of its guides and staff. The area was without power for a year. But that's when Robert Neher sprang into action.

The first thing he did was start a GoFundMe that raised $300,000 for not only his guides and staff but also other disenfranchised McClean's Town residents. Next, he actively participated with and coordinated folks like me and others who organized and funded relief flights. But what he did next was the clincher.

Robert, adroit businessman that he is, had perhaps the most favorable insurance coverage of Bahamian assets I have ever heard of. He confided in me the amount of the settlement check he received for the losses at this lodge, and it was, well, substantial. As a frequent almost forty-year client of Bahamian lodges such as East End and a business guy myself, I am aware that operating a fishing lodge is a very tough business and how attractive simply cashing the check and moving on might have been.

But that is not what Robert Neher is about. Instead, driven by his affection for the people of McClean's Town and concern for their livelihood, he and Cecil Leathon rebuilt East End Lodge bigger and better, adding six new single-angler rooms and building a larger, better dining room and bar. Robert and Cecil are now able to employ even more McClean's Town folks than before the storm. Always one of the top Bahamian bonefish lodges, East End is now open again and better than ever. Along with some of my gentlemen angler friends, I was privileged to be the first guest after Rob and Cecil reopened.

> "People needed a lot of things. But the main thing they needed was a job." —Robert Neher
>
> "If we didn't come back, the whole community is gone. We have a lot of employees and for the folks who are sixty and seventy years old, there was no hope for them. We have to do this for the town." —Cecil Leathen, Co-owner and Head Guide, East End Lodge

The fishing was surprisingly good after East End reopened. Perhaps it was because of the lack of fishing pressure for so long and the fish seeing a fly for the first time in ages. But there are long-term concerns about the fishery because of what Dorian did to the mangroves. When we first ventured to the flats, the scene was almost macabre as the mangrove trees on cay after cay were denuded of their leaves and presented as skeletal shapes that bore an eerie, metaphorical reminiscence of gruesome scenes from concentrations camps. Being smothered in salt water to their tops for so long left sixty-nine square miles of mangrove trees the color of slate; we saw a bunch of grey sticks instead of the lush, healthy tropical greenery of island after island of red mangrove plants.

But Robert Neher is not one to wring his hands over a problem. He was all in as an essential partner collaborating with Bonefish & Tarpon Trust, the Bahamas National Trust, and some other Bahama- and US-based resources to attack the problem with an ambitious and aggressive mangrove restoration project. It began with a shipment of 15,000 propagules and 7,500 seedlings in November 2020 and has resulted in

110,000 new mangrove plants on Grand Bahama and Abaco! In fact, the locals from guides down to school children are being trained to collect propagules and raise seedlings. The very talented scientist Justin Lewis, the Bahamas Research Manager for Bonefish & Tarpon Trust, is directing the project, and we were privileged to meet and get to know him on several of our East End trips.

> "We are very lucky that the underwater habitat is still intact. The seagrasses came through the storm surprisingly well and the fish are still very healthy."
>
> —Justin Lewis, Bahamas Research Manager, Bonefish & Tarpon Trust

> "The mangroves are our first line of defense. With enough time, they can rebound on their own, but now we're trending toward more frequent large storms. We see the enormous task in front of us, but we have to help our natural environment to come back."
>
> —Jewel Thompson-Beneby, Bahamas National Trust

I'm not sure how many trips I've made to East End Lodge, both before and after Dorian, but they are many. I have been there with Patti and with my angler buddies, but perhaps the most special trips there have been with other angling companions—my son, Skip, and my two grandsons, Matthew and Will, all on separate trips. The grandson trips were particularly special since they caught their first bonefish on the fly rods I had given each of them. Despite the perhaps questionable casting instruction they got from me, they both did very well.

That first trip after East End reopened was a special one as well. I remember one day fishing with my great friend Rich Fulton from

Orlando. Our guide, whose name I will not mention, is a thirty-year veteran of Deep Water Cay and East End. He's as talented and expert as any flats guide in the world, great fun to be with on the water, and, perhaps most important, he consistently finds fish. But he has an condition that prevents him from ever getting out of the skiff and into the water to wade or whatever. It's the "whatever" that came into play one day with my angling partner Rich.

We were fishing in a superb place called Thrift Harbour, and the excellent guide to which I refer put me on a single cruising bonefish that we caught and measured to nine pounds. I put my rod back in the holder, and Rich scampered up to the casting platform just in time to strip out before we came upon a school of three very, very large fish. As we poled closer, we saw why they looked so big—they were permit!

Rich made a great cast, let the fly sink a long time, and the lead fish tipped up on it and inhaled it. The ensuing tussle was no brief affair. Our guide poled us to the shallowest spot possible as Rich worked the fish to close quarters as it became apparent that he was fighting a permit that would go every bit of twenty pounds. Naturally, Rich was intent on landing such a trophy fish and was prepared to do whatever it took to do so. Not wanting to casually lean over the gunwale to grab the large permit by the tail, Rich got in the water and prepared to tackle this monster like an NFL linebacker, if necessary. Not yet realizing our guide never exited the skiff for any reason, Rich asked him to join him, an invitation that drew no response.

That's when it got interesting. Out of nowhere came a lemon shark that was in the five-foot range and became Rich's competition for his gorgeous permit. I grabbed my "shark stick" (a retractable Orvis wading staff) and joined Rich in the water beside our skiff. It all happened very fast, but Rich and I together stomped, beat the water with the stick, yelled, whatever. The shark thankfully retreated, and I got back in the boat as Rich grabbed the permit by the tail, slung it in the skiff, and then clambered in himself, one eye on the still-lurking lemon shark.

But this may be the best part of this little fish story. The standard issue permit fly is a crab pattern with lead eyes that allow the fly to sink fast. I was shocked when I learned what fly Rich's huge permit ate: A tiny, feather-light #6 bead-eye Gotcha!

I have fond memories of my times at East End Lodge and great respect and admiration for Robert and Cecil and for their wonderful staff. And, by the way, one of my favorite pictures from East End is of my grandson, Will, sitting on the first step of the lodge's front porch with his arm around Rob's lodge dog Teddy.

A VALUABLE TOOL

It should not surprise that the thoughtful and considerate Robert Neher would come up with an ingenious answer to a problem anglers face. That problem is pesky, corrosive salt water and how harshly it treats an angler's equipment. It will attack everything up to and including the zipper on your rain jacket. Most anglers rinse their reels and rods with fresh water at the end of the day's fishing, in fact, many lodges, including East End Lodge, have their staff do this for their guests.

But a frequent blind spot with many anglers when it comes to the corrosive power of salt water is the fly box. Many anglers (and I have been as guilty as anyone) will remove a just-fished fly from their tippet, dripping with salt water, and place it back in their fly box.

If you don't see the problem with this, you have never experienced what I have on too many occasions and that is hooking a very nice bonefish (or large mutton snapper) only to have the line go limp because a corroded hook simply dissolved under the stress of the fight.

Robert and Cecil's East End Lodge is the only one I have ever seen provide their guests, with compliments, a nifty little thing called a "fly dryer," which I assume was designed by Rob. It's made of something like rubber, is perforated for air flow, is about four by six inches, and its flexibility allows a slit on one side to open like jaws when squeezed. You'd just have to see one if you haven't. It's a very clever and effective device in which you place your just-used flies so they can dry before returning to your fly box.

Just the Facts

Lodge Name: East End Lodge

Location: McClean's Town, extreme east end of Grand Bahama Island

Nearest Airport: Grand Bahama International Airport (FPO)

Drive from Airport to Lodge: One hour

Getting There: Bahamasair and American Airlines. Connections from Nassau on Western Air. Charters from South Florida.

Capacity: Twelve guests

Fly Shop: Moderately robust. Good fly selection, some tackle, modest inventory of shirts and hats. Excellent selection of rods and wading boots for guests at no charge.

Rate for Five Nights Lodging, Four Days Fishing: $5,160 pp, shared room and skiff, VAT included (2025 rates)

Included: Guided fishing, all meals, lodging, appetizers, Wi-Fi, house wine with dinner, airport transfers

Not Included: Guide and staff tips, beverages from bar

Website: www.eastendlodge.com

Author Comments: Rob and Cecil didn't just defiantly rebuild East End Lodge after Dorian's savagery, they substantially improved it. For one thing, in deference to aging, snoring angler guests, they added six single rooms. And they expanded the main lodge with larger common areas and a new bar that allows guests to enjoy a water view while sipping their Kalik or special rum drink. Speaking of the water, the footprint of the complex is the same and still requires guests to walk only two hundred feet or less from their room each morning to the modern, safe, floating dock where their skiff is moored. East End offers critical elements sought by any angler: Access to a superb fishery with expert guides and dependable Bahamian cuisine. While deliberately not "over the top," the physical plant is solidly luxurious and lady-friendly. And if an angler's lady does not fish, the staff arranges other things to do either on the gorgeous surrounding water or in nearby Freeport, where shops abound. Like almost all Bahamian lodges, the staff is cheerful, efficient, and just plain lovable. East End Lodge: Always a good choice.

Nine

A Deflowering

On a trip with my son to Andros Island Bonefish Club, I called Rupert Leadon, booked the trip, and he assured me that my son and I would fish exclusively with him.

Well, when we arrived, everything had changed.

ESPN was there filming a fishing show, and they were requiring Rupert, as the lodge owner and head guide, to be in the show. Consequently, my son and I fished with Rupert's brother, Dennis, most of our days and with Rupert Jr. (Nick) one day.

This was quite a few years ago as evidenced by the fact that this series of shows, called *In Search of Fly Water*, was narrated by the late, legendary sportscaster Curt Gowdy.

The "star" of the show—the angler—was a lady named Karen Graham. It's not necessary to describe her pulchritude. Suffice it to say she was a former Estee Lauder cover girl and that sort of covers that. Karen was a bright and charming gal who was originally from Mississippi and went to Ole Miss before moving to New York to teach French, after which she became a model.

But when we met her, she was no longer in the modeling business but operating a fly-fishing school in the Catskills. Obviously an expert trout angler, she had never laid eyes on a saltwater flat until this trip.

My son and I had no knowledge of show business, and we found it interesting that it took the entire time of our stay for the cast and crew to film a day's fishing. This was apparent when we noticed that Karen, with angler and guide Rupert, came to breakfast each morning wearing the exact same clothes as the day before.

Returning from the flats each afternoon, Karen would repair to her room to spend the necessary time to become dinner-table beautiful. But that first afternoon, Rupert headed directly for the long bar at his lodge. After his third Kalik, he said, "That woman can't cast ten feet. She ain't never gonna catch a bonefish!"

Not only was that comment terribly unfair to Karen, but it was also grossly premature. She was a world-class trout angler but new to long saltwater casts that require double hauling with an 8-weight rod instead of delicate presentations with a 5-weight. We learned that, starting with the second fishing day, she easily took to the double haul, and with the longer casts it provided, she began catching very nice fish for the show.

DOUBLING DOWN ON THE DOUBLE HAUL

The double haul. A profusion of instruction is available to help beginning and intermediate anglers learn it. Defined, it's a false casting technique of vigorously pulling on the fly line with one's non-rod hand to create resistance and therefore boost line speed.

Why double haul? Because the extra line speed results in more distance on the cast.

The plethora of instruction to which I refer is in books, videos, podcasts—you name it. But I'll pass on something I've never seen in any of this material that may help double hauler wannabe's join the club:

When beginner anglers ask me to teach them the double haul, I suggest this: Start by not worrying about releasing any line as they practice hauling. Instead, as a drill, strip out around thirty feet of line and hang on tight to it with the non-rod hand while making false casts using the double-haul motion and not letting any line out. I further suggest: While doing this drill, look back at the extended backcast each time.

This drill for beginners eliminates the variable of letting line out with each false cast (too much to deal with at first—wait until later). I tell them to just grab the line with their non-rod hand and, while false casting, haul on the back and forward cast for all they're worth but don't let line out. Then, if the beginner looks back at the loop of each false cast while continuing over and over the hauling motion with the non-rod hand, it locks into the fledgling angler's muscle memory the feel of both the hauling motion and the timing of the backcast.

Most new anglers to whom I've suggested this say it's been a big help.

Something else my son and I learned about filming television fishing shows (I believe it's the same with movies) is that scenes are not necessarily filmed in sequence. This became very clear when, on the last day we were there, the very *first* scene of the show was filmed.

Here it's necessary to interject a brief primer on the elocution of most Bahamians because they pronounce certain consonants entirely differently than most Americans. For example, the "th" sound, as in the word "three," they pronounce as if it were spelled "sree."

But the consonant that is important for this little story is "v." The Bahamians pronounce it as though it were a "w." They would pronounce the movie *Victory at Sea* as "*Wictory at Sea*."

Here is the opening scene of the show as we saw it filmed that last day at the lodge:

Rupert was on the dock waiting beside his skiff for Karen to appear from the lodge for the "first" day's fishing. On cue, Karen emerges. She's in her best Orvis flats clothes clutching a couple of fly rods as she makes her silky, feminine but obviously athletic walk toward Rupert.

Rupert, beaming, greets her.

"Good morning, Karen!" he booms. "I understand you've never caught a bonefish before. Well, let me assure you that, after today, you will no longer be a wirgin!" ("Wirgin," not "virgin.")

All of us spectators were a little shocked, regardless of the elocution, but also hysterical with muffled laughter. I saw the ESPN producer at the airport on our way home and asked him about the scene.

"If you cut that scene, you are the biggest wuss," I said.

He grinned. "Don't worry," he said. "It's definitely in the show."

Well, months later when it aired, guess what? The scene had been cut.

TEN

And Now . . . The *Rest* of the Story

If you are old enough to remember the legendary radio newscaster and commentator Paul Harvey, you are familiar with his famous byline, "And now...the *Rest* of the Story." Well, here is the rest of the story about our Estee Lauder cover girl turned fly-fishing instructor, the lovely Karen Graham.

A mutual friend told me that one Saturday morning a Boca-Grande snook-fishing acquaintance was watching ESPN on television while diving into scrambled eggs in his Tampa breakfast room. He was very wealthy and recently divorced.

On his TV screen appeared the show *In Search of Fly Water*, featuring Karen Graham as the angler, and at the sight of Karen on the screen, scrambled eggs started falling out of my acquaintance's mouth. He was stunned and mesmerized by the physical appearance and lilting Southern voice and manner of the former model he was watching. It was apparently a case of love at first sight, electronically!

I'm told our ESPN viewer began working on a plan to meet Karen personally and pursue her romantically. He decided the best approach would be to book at her fly-fishing school in the Catskills. He did so and traveled there tingling with anticipation and excitement. But when he arrived, he learned that Karen was away and her partner in the school was teaching the class in which he had enrolled. Worse, the partner was a bearded, former Penn State offensive lineman.

And Now... The *Rest* of the Story

I'm told our smitten TV watcher returned to Florida, drilled down deeper, and learned everything he could about Karen. When he came to the part about her being a sister in the Chi Omega sorority at Ole Miss, he knew he had a lead worth tracking because he knew that the wife of a friend went there at about the same time. A little detective work put him in a position to contact Karen and mention some recognizable names for credibility.

Karen had been married to the owner of the Stardust Casino in Las Vegas and then had a relationship with TV personality David Frost but was single when our love-struck caller rang. He decided to be very aggressive: He asked if he could pick her up in his plane and fly her to his ranch out west. She quizzed him a bit on his background and told him to call her back the next day. He did, she accepted his invitation, and they ultimately got married!

While they were married, Patti and I saw them at a party, and I had quite a pleasant reunion with Karen reminiscing about my son and I being at The Bonefish Club for the filming of her show. She was still stunningly beautiful and just as intellectually powerful as I had found her during our communal dinners with the other guests each night at The Bonefish Club.

So, as Paul Harvey would have said: And now you know...the *rest* of the story.

ARE YOU A PALMIST?

Memories of Rupert Leadon bring back this: He was the first guide to caution me against a particular angling technique I still see used. Let me explain by saying that I play a little golf. I'm only an average player, but one thing I pride myself on is my pace of play. Unfortunately, some of my golf partners play very slowly, and I think this comes from watching the pros on television. You've seen it: Those guys look at every putt from four sides and take an eternity discussing each club selection with their caddy, ad nauseum.

Well, similarly, something I occasionally see on TV fishing shows, in my opinion, improperly influences some anglers and that is the technique of "palming the reel." For those who don't know what I mean, when fighting a large fish, the drag system built into the reel allows line to be pulled from the reel by the fish. These reels have a dial that allows the angler to either loosen or tighten the drag. But placing one's hand, or palm, on the reel while the fish is struggling against the reel's drag applies extra pressure and, in effect, momentarily further tightens the drag on the reel.

I've seen anglers palm the reel when a fish is making its initial long run to try to slow it down by applying extra pressure. That always makes me remember doing this on one of my first trips with Rupert when he said, "Get your hand off that reel! You'll break that fish off! Let the drag do its job!"

Palming the reel does have its place. It's when you have a big fish at close quarters after a long fight. You may even have already tightened your drag and palming the reel at very close quarters can indeed be a useful way to apply extra, *final* pressure to your fish. But it is still necessary to take care not to use too much palm or you can still experience a break off. Now, particularly when fighting a large tarpon at close quarters, there is an additional technique that puts pressure on a fish and that is clamping the fly line (wouldn't want to do it with the backing if it's still out) against the butt section of the rod with your hand. You can still use that clamping hand as a "drag" by releasing the line with your hand when the fish bolts on you. Very effective with a large fish.

Thanks for the memories, Rupert. You are missed!

Eleven
If It Walks Like a Duck...

On one of my trips to the Bahamas on a mothership to fish for bonefish, weather forced us to divert to an alternate location—Great Harbour Cay in the Berry Islands.

Please allow me to describe "The Curious Case of Great Harbour Cay."

The natural tropical luminosity of the cay is unmatched, particularly the shimmering beaches and vast, alabaster flats. Seeing this, a Canadian developer in 1967 invested $38 million ($250 million today) developing residential lots, a spectacular clubhouse, a first-class marina to accommodate large yachts, and an eighteen-hole golf course designed by Joe Lee who, after designing 125 others in seven countries, declared Great Harbour Cay one of his favorites.

But when we pulled into the marina...oh, somewhere in the early 2000s...it was run-down, the clubhouse was basically in ruins, and the golf course's fairways looked more like wheat fields.

It's sad and curious because, while I wasn't there to see it, after everything was built in the 1960s, it was THE hot ticket for the worldwide glitterati. Frequent guests and visitors were Cary Grant, Brigit Bardot, Sinatra with his Rat Pack, the Rockefellers, Ingrid Bergman, Douglas Fairbanks Jr., Hugh O'Brien, and Telly Savalas (who always arrived by helicopter). Jack Nicklaus even had a house there given to him by the developer in return for his promotion of the golf course. Players like Julius Boros and Lee Trevino played in tournaments there.

So, what happened?

From what I understand, the developer's residential lots were quickly snapped up by buyers who were mainly speculators looking to flip their investment for a quick profit. Very few of them built homes, and there was, therefore, little financial base from which to have a property owners association to contribute to sustaining the place. When the developer pulled out, there were power outages, fuel shortages, and an infrastructure decline.

When I was there, the Bahamian government was stepping in to restore the infrastructure. I understand the airport runway is now in excellent shape, nine holes of the golf course have reopened, and the rest of the cay is making a strong comeback.

Make no mistake, Great Harbour Cay bonefishing, and particularly the permit fishing, is outstanding, and the patriarch of their guides is the great Percy D'Arville, with whom we were fortunate enough to fish. One evening, on the television in the salon of the mothership, Percy graciously played for us an instructional video he had created. It was on bonefishing and featured Percy demonstrating what he referred to as the "blue heron walk," which we, much later, renamed the "duck walk."

Here's what it was all about:

Wade-fishing for bonefish can be very challenging because of the difficulty in stealthily approaching either a school of fish or singles and doubles. Wading anglers often find bonefish that are out of casting range. What to do? Wade closer to them, of course. But that's not as easy as it sounds. It has always amazed me how a school of bonefish somehow, without spooking, stays just out of casting range as the angler wades toward the fish. They obviously know we are there, but how?

I have seen many anglers try to cope with this by simply wading faster. And, in my early days of trying to learn the sport, I committed the same error. The usual result of the faster wading is the fish maddeningly remaining the same distance from the angler. And if the angler gets particularly rambunctious with his or her wading, the fish spook and go racing off as if they had stolen something.

Many guides suggest coping with this frustrating situation by simply staying put and remaining quiet in the hope that the fish will eventually wander within casting range. But this approach can yield unpredictable and spotty results.

Percy, in his video, demonstrated a way to stealthily close the gap between wading angler and bonefish—his ingenious and fascinating blue heron walk. In his video, Percy gently lifts his foot out of the water, then points his toe downward almost vertically in an exaggerated fashion. His foot then silently reenters the water to complete the step. Then comes the other foot for another toe-pointed, silent reentry and so on. Percy's scheme aims to emulate an Olympic diver's goal of a silent, "un-splashy" entry into the water. Anyone who has studied a blue heron stealthily and slowly advancing on its prey would see the striking similarity between that and Percy's technique.

Those of us on that trip never forgot that video, and when those anglers now accompany me on a trip, I see them using Percy's technique (which we renamed as the duck walk), as do I. The technique is rather difficult to pull off when dealing with water that's a little deep but is very, very effective in shallow wading. In fact, if the water being fished is shallow enough, the gap between lazily feeding bonefish and the angler can be closed fairly rapidly.

That was the only time I ever fished Great Harbour Cay. But, with the cay making a nice comeback, there is now a new bonefish lodge there—Soul Fly Lodge—and I hear very good things about it. Percy D'Arville guides for them. And I'll bet he's still doing the duck walk.

SAY WHAT?

So, let's return to the fundamental problem that the duck walk was designed to solve: the difficulty of stealthily wading within casting range of bonefish without detection.

Could it be that bonefish can hear? My answer to that is…I have always thought so.

I recall fishing on the west side of Andros with Rupert Leadon's brother Dennis and casting to a single bonefish that, I swear, looked as big as a supertanker in the water. My casting was still a work in progress then but I miraculously put the fly in front of this clearly double-digit fish whereupon Dennis spat out, "Strip!"

Well, that did it. Game over. At Dennis' words, that bonefish, very happily feeding until that instant, streaked off like a Ferrari aiming for a hot zero-to-sixty time. Further to this point, the Cuban guides fishing the Gardens of the Queen area, when approaching a particularly juicy bonefish presentation opportunity, will say, "No speaking please!"

So, while I'm sticking with that story, the science may not back me up:

"The misunderstanding likely results from a property of sound waves—they typically don't travel from one medium to another, from water to air, for example."

—Dr. Aaron Adams, Chief Scientist of Bonefish & Tarpon Trust, from his book, *Orvis Guide to Fly Fishing for Coastal Gamefish*

But it's not only voices that prove bonefish can hear. Accidentally dropping something in the boat or closing the cooler lid less than gently will kill a presentation opportunity as fast as if you'd heaved a lighted cherry bomb at the fish.

"Low frequency sounds…travel farther than high frequency sounds. This means the noise made by dropping a reel onto the deck of the boat is detected almost immediately by fish within a significant radius of the boat."

—Dr. Aaron Adams, from his book, *Orvis Guide to Fly Fishing for Coastal Gamefish*

I still see some of my angler friends standing on the casting platform of our skiff fishing while wearing various kinds of shoes. I'm reluctant to offer many suggestions to my fishing companions as I don't want to be bossy. I think they feel the need to wear shoes to protect their feet from the sun, but I always fish barefoot after heavily lathering the tops of my feet in excellent, waterproof sunscreen.

Fishing barefoot is desirable for two reasons. One is that wearing shoes makes it impossible to feel your stripped-out fly line on the casting deck and it's therefore so easy to step on it while casting. (That's when you fight the urge to break your fly rod in half over your knee after losing that big 'un.) The other reason is that shoes are noisy and, once again, yes, nearby fish can hear them clunking.

Orvis once had a product that resolved this issue—they sold casting socks! I had some and thought it was a great product. They were made of very thin white silk so you could still feel the fly line with your feet while getting extra sun protection. However, they did look a little odd and caused some good-naturedly derisive comments from my fishing companions. Sadly, I lost my pair of casting socks, and Orvis stopped making them. When I asked my fishing buddy Dave Perkins why his company stopped making them, he replied with a bit of a smirk that his dad (Leigh Perkins) and I were the only ones who liked the product!

Just the Facts

Lodge Name: Soul Fly Lodge

Location: Great Harbour Cay, Berry Islands, Bahamas

Nearest Airport: Great Harbor Airport (GHC)

Drive from Airport to Lodge: Four minutes

Getting There: Commercial flights to Nassau connecting to Le Air. Direct from Fort Lauderdale on either Maker's Air or Tropic Ocean Airways.

Capacity: Eight guests

Fly Shop: Yes, a rather complete one

Rate for Five Nights Lodging, Four Days Fishing: $5,075 (2025 rates)

Included: Meals, guided fishing, open bar, airport transfers

Not Included: VAT, tips, airfare

Website: www.soulflylodge.com

Author Comments: Soul Fly Lodge opened in October 2021. I have not yet been able to get there but look forward to doing so. The setting appears magically tropical, and the lodge was once the Carriearl Hotel and the former residence of "Mr. Celebrity" Earl Blackwell in the heyday when one might bump into Cary Grant on the beach. It appears more "resorty" than many lodges as it is close to the beach and sports a lovely pool and accommodations—no doubt a lady-friendly spot that would be embraced by a non-angling companion. The dining room is open to the public on weekends, but I've experienced that at fancy places like Delphi Club with no problem. As for the fishing, I was thoroughly satisfied by it when on our mothership visit. To me, it makes one think of Christmas Island with vast, pure white flats, particularly around the Ambergris Cays area that is literally infested with husky, Berry Islands bonefish and, far more important to many anglers, large permit.

Twelve

Lucy, I'm Home!

By now you know I am mainline addicted to fly fishing, particularly sight-fishing on the saltwater flats where there is virtually no blind casting as the angler does not cast until he or she sees a fish.

Further to that, after a glass of wine, I'll sometimes tell this one:

"Patti asked me the other day which I love more…her or fly fishing. I thought a minute and replied…saltwater or fresh?'"

Feeding my habit with around fifty days per year of guided fly fishing has brought me great satisfaction and fulfillment. But while I cherish my wonderful fishing memories, I equally treasure the lasting, special friendships that have come from years of fishing with my favorite guides and lodge operators in the Bahamas and other places around the world.

A distinctive attribute of many Bahamian bonefish guides is the commonality and pure Bahamian flavor of their surnames. Prime examples are Lightbourne, Adderley, Pinder, Leadon, Rolle, Lowe, Sawyer, Bain, and Burrows.

I've been fishing with Ricardo Burrows in Sandy Point for over thirty years. To say we have become dear friends is an understatement. Sometimes, when we are in the company of new acquaintances, one of us will point to the other and speak a favorite phrase: "Different color, different mother, still my brother." And we mean it with all our hearts.

RICKY

Born in Sandy Point, Ricardo Burrows still lives and guides there. For those asking, "Where is Sandy Point?" it is the southernmost tip of Great Abaco Island. More recognizable names on Abaco are Marsh Harbour and Treasure Cay, and some anglers are likely familiar with lodges on Abaco, like Blackfly Lodge, Abaco Lodge, and the Delphi Club.

Ricardo got his schooling right in Sandy Point but, as a young man, gained fame in all of the Bahamas as a point guard leading the Sandy Point basketball team to sixteen All-Bahamas championships in a row. Ricardo is built like an NFL running back and moves as fluidly as a leopard creeping up on an unsuspecting impala. He and his charming wife, Monique, are pillars of the Sandy Point community and their church.

Some Bahamian bonefish guides are difficult to understand in conversation. It's because, while English is the language of the Bahamas, the version Bahamians speak is sometimes referred to as "Bahamianese" or sometimes "Bahamian Creole" (there is no French involved, as is the case with the Creole spoken by Haitians). This can be problematic for an angler being poled across a flat and listening for instructions from the guide on where a fish has been sighted, where to cast, when to start stripping, and so on.

But with Ricardo Burrows (and many other guides), this has never been an issue as Ricardo's English is like that heard on any street corner in the United States. He does, of course, say his "Vs" as though they were "Ws." (As did Rupert Leadon on Andros when he told Estee Lauder cover girl Karen Graham that after he guided her to her first bonefish she would no longer be a "wirgin.")

But when in conversation with locals, Ricardo can slip into "Bahamianese," and I can barely understand a word! It's an amazing and entertaining phenomenon. And while Ricardo speaks American and Bahamian English fluently, I occasionally fished with his late dad, "Graveyard" Burrows, and he may as well have been speaking Portuguese. Interestingly, Ricardo learned bonefishing from his first job guiding at Pete and Gay's Guesthouse and ended up teaching his dad the craft.

After his Pete and Gay days, Ricardo and Monique, with some financial help from the late Rick McCreery and his wife, Joan, built Rickmon Bonefish Lodge (Rickmon—Ricardo and Monique, right?). The lodge is now in the hands of Colorado-based Eleven Experience and is being redeveloped. Eleven, as it's called, is owned by retired Blackstone billionaire Chad Pike and operates land-based lodges all over the world plus a couple of motor yachts rigged for mothership flats fishing. And good-guy Cameron Davenport runs their fly-fishing programs worldwide. I have been a repeat customer on Eleven's motherships in the Bahamas for bonefish and the Marquesas Keys for tarpon. As I write this, Ricardo operates his bonefishing from a smaller lodge adjacent to the old Rickmon Lodge. Very comfortable, it's called Tailing Bones Lodge and can accommodate four anglers in single rooms with private bath and features Monique's marvelous Bahamian cuisine.

Ricardo has some nicknames, the main one being "Brownie," which is what most folks in Sandy Point call him. Sometimes I call him "Captain Brownie." His dad gave him that handle at birth when he popped out of his mom's womb as…yep, a brown baby. Wife Monique, however, calls him "Ricky." It was fairly recently that it finally occurred to me to ask Ricardo if, when returning from a day on the flats, he calls out to Monique: "Lucy, I'm home!"

Since Ricardo is younger than I, it was unclear to me if he'd ever even heard of Desi and Lucy, but his face quickly displayed all his pearly whites as he said, "Oh yeah!"

Patti and I have fished with Ricardo countless times, and I have taken many of my gentleman angler friends to Sandy Point. Close to the ocean and with flats as resplendent as any in the Bahamas, it's five diverse fisheries.

There are the "town flats" close to Sandy Point. Then there is the area of mangrove banks to the north all the way to and including

Crossing Rocks. Then there is the area south of Sandy Point called Cross Harbour that includes several large creeks. There is Gorda Cay that the government leases to Disney for their cruise ship visits. Finally, there is the magical Moore's Island that is perched right next to the ocean and, along with Gorda Cay, features some monster bonefish along with frequent encounters with permit and large mutton snappers.

Ricardo and I have been fishing together so long we have our own code names for certain fishing spots. One is "the bank that holds no fish," which is Ricardo's favorite flat but has been largely unproductive for me. There is also "Perry's Cove," a place wonderful guide and friend, Perry Adderley, always goes to first when he arrives at Moore's Island. There is also the graveyard, the airport, and others, but a favorite is a place we call "duck walk." It's a relatively small pure-white sand flat on the east side of Moore's Island. It got its name because it's the first place Ricardo saw me execute the "duck walk" I learned from Percy D'Arville at Great Harbour Cay.

WHERE ARE THEY?

Ricardo and I have done plenty of duck walking over the years as we are both partial to wading. He is a student of the game, but I never realized to what extent until I saw the following passage in an article that mirrored Ricardo's approach to finding fish around dead low tide.

> "During low tide, bonefish often rest in flat-side channels waiting for the next flooding tide. From their perspective, why expend energy unnecessarily? In the hour or so on either side of the low tide, stalk the edges of flats, searching for bonefish laid up, or cruising slowly in slightly deeper water.
>
> "Bonefish are experts at using the tides to their advantage, which allows them to maximize their benefits in the tradeoff between feeding and avoiding predators. I guess you'd expect this from bonefish—they've been perfecting this for millions of years. Like many predators, bonefish try to get away with as little travel as possible in their search for a meal. There is no reason for them to expend energy swimming long distances if there is no need. This is why when bonefish retreat from a flat during low tide, they often do not stray far."
>
> —Dr. Aaron Adams,
> Director of Science and Conservation,
> Bonefish & Tarpon Trust

Thirteen

I'm Calling the Airline!

I have taken a number of anglers to fish with Ricardo Burrows at Sandy Point when it was their first visit there and first time fishing with Ricardo. Three of those times stand out.

One involved an angler who was also new to me, a casual acquaintance who had asked to accompany me on one of my bonefish trips. He was a decent angler and caster and good company.

At least until this happened:

We were wading in Blackwood Creek, south from Sandy Point. We were into some nice bonefish, but the sharks were driving us berserk. When wading, I sometimes ask my guide to carry my barracuda rod in case we see one, and Ricardo had it in hand. There was a lemon shark, about a five-footer, that, after inhaling three of our hooked bonefish in a row, finally wore out his welcome with Ricardo who stripped line off my 'cuda rod and casted to this pesky shark and hooked it. Some number of minutes later—it wasn't that quick a fight—the shark was subdued, and Ricardo "hung him out to dry" on the top of a mangrove bush, doing the birds a favor. He then declared, "He won't be eating any more of our fish, now let's catch some big bones!"

To my shock and surprise, my new angler friend took issue with what Ricardo did. But it had nothing to do with the slaughter of the shark. Instead, he said to Ricardo, "What the hell are you doing messing around catching that shark? You're supposed to be taking care of us, not fishing on your own. Don't you understand that?"

Ricardo was speechless but managed to mumble something about trying to help us with our bonefishing. But that didn't stop it.

"I'm serious!" the angler said. "You're supposed to be taking care of us!"

In over thirty years, it's the only time I have ever seen Ricardo angry. But he kept his cool, only saying that he can come out and fish anytime he wants to, that he was just trying to be helpful. But he did say this:

"Let's go to the boat."

Which we did and headed back to the lodge early. When Ricardo and I were alone, I didn't wait for him to say anything. Instead, I volunteered:

"You better get a good look at that guy because it's the last time you'll see him here with me."

Another first-timer to Sandy Point, my great friend Bill Gutermuth, was on the skiff with me when the weather allowed us to cross to Moore's Island on our very first day of fishing. We were fishing on the east side of Moore's, north of the large creek, and I was on the bow.

A very large single bonefish appeared about 100 feet away coming at me—the dream shot. My fly was a mantis shrimp pattern, and the dream shot became my dream come true as the huge fish tipped up on my fly and snarfed it. Game on.

I knew it had to be a leviathan because we found ourselves poling after this fish that was making my reel scream like it was in the dental chair without Novocain. Way, way in the backing four times.

When we finally had the fish at close quarters, I was feeling really good about the possibility of landing him.

Then it happened.

Out of nowhere, a single lemon shark appeared—huge, maybe six or seven feet—that became very, very interested in my trophy bonefish.

Then I saw something I've never seen before or since. Dropping his push pole to the deck with a clatter, Ricardo almost flew out of the skiff and, in his bare feet, began sprinting, to the extent it was possible in the foot-deep water, toward my hooked fish and therefore to the shark. He caught up to them both and began kicking the shark with his bare feet in an attempt to dissuade it from eating my prize. I must say this again: It was something I've never seen before or since.

Alas, Ricardo's valiant effort was for naught. But thankfully the shark ate my bonefish and not one of Ricardo's feet. All that was left was the head of the bonefish, mantis shrimp fly hooked in his lip, and Ricardo brought it back to the skiff. Ricardo still had a BogaGrip from the old days before Bonefish & Tarpon Trust cautioned us all to stop using them. He lipped the head of our fish with the BogaGrip and held it up to read the scale.

Just the head weighed seven pounds!

Ricardo said there was no doubt the entire fish would have weighed somewhere in the teens. Bill Gutermuth stood next to me wearing a wide grin and said, "When can we book our next trip here?"

JAWS

Most bonefish anglers and guides find sharks…well…annoying is far too mild a term. Maddening? Infuriating? Here's what Dr. Aaron Adams, Director of Science and Conservation of Bonefish & Tarpon Trust, told me when I interviewed him:

"Frank, we're doing some interesting studies on shark predation in the Florida Keys. But they are a protected species in the Bahamas. You have no doubt seen this as an angler—while wade-fishing for bonefish alone, you may not see so many. But as soon as a skiff with anglers moves in nearby…here come the sharks that become trained to lurk around skiffs hoping for a released fish to eat. Until the Bahamian government might decide to allow some harvesting of sharks, your only recourse is to vary your fishing spots in an attempt to disrupt the predictability the sharks may be benefitting from."

The third newcomer to Sandy Point that comes to mind was also a newcomer to fly fishing. He is one of my dearest friends and also one of my real estate partners. He wanted to learn to catch bonefish so, after spending a fortune at the fly shop getting outfitted and taking a series of casting lessons, here we were with Ricardo at Sandy Point.

Our first afternoon of fishing was wading near the lodge on a flat called Key Point. At my request, Ricardo stayed with my friend and I got way off to the side. My goodness, the fish were everywhere; they just kept coming and coming. I must have landed over a dozen very nice fish that afternoon.

Meanwhile, my friend struggled mightily as his casting lessons were not working at all. I felt so bad for him as fish after fish came right at him and he simply could not get the fly to them. His frustration mounted, and I once looked over and saw him in a mock exercise of breaking his rod over his knee.

The day over and back at the lodge, he was fuming.

But at me!

"Why did I ever let you talk me into trying this? This is the most ridiculous sport ever invented. I'm calling the airline because I'm going home in the morning and see if I can sell all these damn fly rods you made me buy!"

I calmed him down and explained that it takes time to get the hang of casting and let's see what tomorrow brings.

The next morning presented us with a sky that was the color of slate and, over Gorda Cay, loomed a menacing cloud bank that was way beyond grey; it was close to ebony. In view of that, we stayed close to the lodge and waded again.

Once again I asked Ricardo to dote on my friend and impart all the guiding skills he could muster, but this time, I stayed close with them. We almost immediately encountered some nice tailing bonefish. They were very happily feeding away, oblivious to our stalking presence, which allowed us to creep very close to them and provide a shorter casting range that much better suited my rookie friend.

He made a cast, and the fly miraculously landed precisely in the perfect spot. One of the tailers saw the fly and pounced on it like a kitten on a ball of string, making a large disturbance in the process. My friend emitted unintelligible grunts of delight as his rod assumed a severe curve while he hung on and we all listened to the sweet music of a fly reel surrendering its line and backing to a heavy quarry. As my friend worked the fish closer, Ricardo splashily waded toward the fish and grabbed the leader. He was taking no chances with this, my friend's first bone. It was a handsome six-pounder.

Ricardo's splashing and the disturbance the fish made when he ate the fly did not seem to faze the other contently tailing fish. My friend casted again. He caught another fish. I tried to remain calm, but inside, I was nothing short of jubilant.

This fish were still there, and I looked over to see my friend stripping out line to cast again. I had been keeping my eye on that vicious-looking black cloud over Gorda Cay and warily watching its inexorable advance toward us. My friend had been laser-focused on his newfound success as a bonefish angler.

But Ricardo had not overlooked the storm.

"Reel 'em up, guys, we gotta get outta here," he said.

I'll never forget my friend's response.

"But they're still tailing!"

My dear friend had gone from "I'm calling the airline" the night before to, the next morning after catching some tailing bonefish, being willing to risk his life to keep doing it.

SAFETY FIRST

We pulled into the lodge that day just as the wind from that anvil-topped storm began to whip, making the air suddenly feel like January on a Chicago sidewalk. Moments later, the sights and sounds were those of a battlefield as the squall's rage erupted in a meteorological tantrum of lightning bolts, horizontal rain, micro bursts, and ear-shattering thunder claps.

Ricardo's call was the correct one.

Boating Magazine has studied boaters and thunderstorms extensively, including insurance claims over a ten-year period showing that lightning strikes on boats occur at the rate of about one in 1,000 in any given year. They also discovered that 33 percent of all claims are in Florida and 29 percent in the Chesapeake Bay area.

But what to do when a storm interrupts an angler's fun by appearing when the skiff is not moments away from the lodge as we were that day?

Boating Magazine says to take down everything with any height, like antennas. And certainly take anything like graphite fly rods and lay them horizontal on the lowest deck. They say stow all electronics, preferably in something like a microwave oven, if there happens to be one on board (that one won't work on a flats skiff!).

And they say to avoid holding onto metal objects like railings, particularly two of them at one time. Apparently, some boaters in a storm will man the helm with a wooden spoon to avoid contacting metal!

I was once bonefishing with Ricardo outside of Blackwood Creek down in the Cross Harbour area. The sky did not seem especially dark but suddenly we noticed the graphite fly rods on the skiff were performing their best impression of Linda Ronstadt's "Blue Bayou." Yes, a little tune. We got up on a plane to run home but got boxed in by what were actually two storms. We spent the next hour laying prostrate on the deck of the skiff next to our rods. Never forgot it.

JUST THE FACTS
Lodge Name: Ricardo's Tailing Bones Guest House

Location: Sandy Point, Great Abaco Island, Bahamas

Nearest Airport: Marsh Harbour (Leonard M. Thompson Intl.—MHH)

Drive from Airport to Lodge: One hour

Getting There: Delta flies nonstop from Atlanta, and there are many options from South Florida and Nassau.

Capacity: There are four sleeping rooms with en suite bath that are normally used for single anglers. But each of the rooms have king beds so, on a couple's basis, the lodge could accommodate more guests.

Rate for Five Nights Lodging, Four Days Fishing: $4,250 (single room, shared skiff)

Includes: Guided fishing, all meals, lodging, transfer from airport, VAT

Does Not Include: Tips, alcoholic beverages, airfare

Website: www.tailingbonesguesthouse.com

Author Comments: Ricardo Burrow's small, quaint Tailing Bones lodge is not where you will find down pillows, Egyptian cotton, and turndown service that includes a little chocolate on your pillow each night. That's not to say it's not very nice, very comfortable, and even lady friendly. But with Ricardo, it's all about the fishing and wife Monique's perfectly delicious Bahamian fare like lobster, cracked conch with peas 'n rice, and that to-die-for Bahamian mac 'n cheese (how do they do it??). I've already described the fishery, and Ricardo, now sort of the patriarch of Sandy Point bonefishing, has all the top guides at his disposal. So, even if his lodge is full with anglers in each of his single rooms and all want to fish solo…well, as they say in the Bahamas…no problem, Mon! Ricardo's location could not be more ideal. While the lodges closer to Marsh Harbour must trailer their guests thirty to forty minutes to Sandy Point, Ricardo's guests are already there when they wake up each morning. It's a hearty breakfast and then a walk all of 100 feet to their skiff for the day's fishing. Ricardo also has a unique approach to fishing Moore's Island while based there that he offers on request. Tailing Bones…Ricardo named it right!

Fourteen
I Couldn't "Bear" It

I fell in love with Chub Cay in the Berry Islands after that first trip in 1986, and when I learned to catch bonefish on a fly rod, I began to go often. I mostly fished with David Lightbourne, but it was another guide, Joe Louis, who caught me my first double-digit bonefish.

Joe and I were wading a huge, pristine, white-bottomed flat just off Fish Cay. Three large bones were cruising out of a small mangrove patch near shore coming right at me—the dearly beloved dream shot. I put the fly in front of them, and one of them picked it up. That fish then embarked on a Herculean effort to reduce my Orvis reel to a handful of smoldering, melted metal. Its long runs took me four times way, way in the backing before I finally got the upper hand.

This was before the conservation organization Bonefish & Tarpon Trust wisely discouraged anglers from using the BogaGrip, a device that grabs fish by the lip and allows the angler to hold them up and weigh them. This fish tipped the BogaGrip scale at just under eleven pounds, but perhaps the most intriguing part of this little fish story is this: Of the three fish I casted to, as is often the case, the little one ate it!

It's one of the reasons I have always said Chub Cay's bonefish are the Bahamas largest. My experience has been that a six-pound bonefish at Chub is not particularly remarkable.

When I first started going to Chub Cay back in the 1980s, I was charmed by the purely native flavor of its whimsical quaintness. It was old-timey postcard Bahamian with small "villas" perched right on a pristine beach that was also a bonefish flat. But that flat rather quickly deepens before eventually falling off the wall and becoming thousands of feet deep as it morphs into the nearby Tongue of the Ocean. In those days, the enchanting villas, surrounded by gently swaying palm trees, were one-story, two-bedroom affairs of frame construction painted either classic Bahamian pink, canary yellow, or baby blue.

The clubhouse for the members, on the other hand, was of coquina shell construction (pink, naturally) and called The Harbour House. The current club members' names were listed on a board in the foyer. One name I remember seeing on that board was that of Jack Nicklaus.

This was all on the members' side of the Chub Cay marina while on the transient side—for John Q. Public—were some slips, a small "roach motel," and a previously mentioned little restaurant for low-life transients, as was I on my first visit in 1986. The only thing that took from the vintage charm of Chub Cay those days was that there was no way for the marina to flush its water in and out with the tides as the ingress and egress was a narrow cut. Consequently, seaweed and refuse would build up on the water's surface in the back corner of the marina. It was unsightly, and it stank.

This situation was remedied when Chub was acquired for redevelopment by my old college chum Walt McCrory, a lawyer from Fort Lauderdale. Good-guy Walt and I married sorority sisters and occasionally kept in touch. On one of those occasions, he told me of the grandiose plans he and his partners, one a construction guy and the other a boat show impresario, had created for Chub.

The plans included dynamiting the rock on the side of the marina opposite the entrance to provide tidal flushing and resulting water clarity. They then planned to completely rebuild the marina as a state-of-the-art, floating-dock affair that could accommodate yachts to 200 feet. Those charming villas were to be relocated elsewhere on the cay to be used as employee housing. And, finally, the Harbour House (the clubhouse and dining room) would become the ship's store as they planned a grand clubhouse with dining, sleeping rooms, and an infinity pool.

I Couldn't "Bear" It

All of this happened except for the completion of the clubhouse, but Walt's plan depended on a real estate play using the land made available by relocating the villas. Sadly, the financial crisis of 2008 destroyed the market for the housing they planned to sell and Chub went into receivership.

I still went to Chub and fished with David Lightbourne during this time, staying at privately owned rental properties that pre-dated my pal Walt McCrory's redevelopment project. Those property owners were members of Chub Cay Club and would always arrange for us to dine at the Harbour House on the member's side of the facility. We had some wonderful dinners there, always served by two great waiters, Remedy and Charlie, wearing their colorful Androsia shirts. As diners on the members' side, we were required to wear long pants, a bit of an oddity in the Bahamian out islands.

Things could be challenging at Chub when it was in receivership. We rented gas-powered golf carts from the Club for transportation between our rental house and the dock and the Club. They were in terrible condition, and fuel was always scarce. More than once, David Lightbourne brought us fuel for our golf cart, or we would have had to walk all over the cay.

Then, thankfully, along came Mr. Bishop.

George Bishop is a billionaire oilman from Texas. Before Chub went into receivership, "Mr. Bishop," as he is known on the cay, happened by in his blue-hulled sixty-foot Viking sportfish boat. He was intrigued by the place, began asking a zillion questions of the receiver-appointed general manager, and, ultimately, bought Chub Cay. His reign has been the embodiment of the most efficient form of government—a benevolent dictatorship—and it is now a delightful place to visit either as an angler or as a vacationer to the Bahamas. Mr. Bishop's able general manager, David Renaud, is largely responsible for this pleasant circumstance.

Mr. Bishop finished all the construction projects, including the new clubhouse, which is breathtaking. It has lovely sleeping rooms and excellent cuisine still served by Remedy and Charlie. The marina usually looks like an upscale boat show with palatial motor yachts up to 200 feet, exotic sportfish boats and center console offshore fishing boats, some with as many as five outboard engines hanging from their sterns, each boasting 300 horsepower.

One of those yachts we saw frequently was a 120-foot Westport called *Sea Bear*. Jack Nicklaus' golf handle given to him by the sports media was "The Golden Bear," thus the name of his ship.

A frequent guest on *Sea Bear* was my late friend Andy Bean, who was pretty tight with Jack. Andy sadly left us at the tender age of seventy, but he won a dozen or so times on the PGA Tour and not infrequently finished high in the Masters and British Open tournaments. I knew him more as an angler and often mused that Andy might be more intense about fishing than his vocation of golf. This was perhaps evidenced by his email address, which was andy@evergladesnook.

It was when Andy was riding high in professional golf that Patti's cousin, Doug, and I would go to the Everglades snook fishing with Andy and his childhood friend, Brant Martin. We would stay at a little place in Chokoloskee but often have dinner at the historic Rod & Gun Club in sometimes-infamous Everglades City. We would rarely see each other on the water, but I remember one day we rendezvoused for lunch. Andy was wearing a brand new Tarponwear fishing shirt that day with a price tag usually tolerated only by well-heeled anglers. It was incandescently hot, and between bites of his sandwich, Andy proceeded to take out his knife and slice the long sleeves off his new, expensive shirt, transforming it in moments to a sleeveless model.

My buddy and I looked at each other wondering why we couldn't have been PGA Tour golfers making enough money to give no thought to trashing a shirt that goes for as much as 180 dollars today.

Mr. Sea Bear himself—Jack Nicklaus—and his totally charming wife Barbara frequently visited Chub Cay on their yacht and were always gracious to everybody, including us. Jack spent his days at Chub Cay doing the same thing I was there for—chasing those big bonefish around the various flats like The Sand Bank, Fish Cay, Frazier's Hog Cay, Sandy Cay, Cockroach Key, Crab Key, and sometimes out west to an area called The Bushes.

On one of our trips to Chub during the receivership days, Jack and Barbara were there on the *Sea Bear*. I was having terrible tummy

I Couldn't "Bear" It

problems accompanied by a low-grade fever, which I later learned was diverticulitis. But while there, I just wanted all the Pepto-Bismol I could swallow so I could finish the trip. This was the pre-Mr. Bishop time when everything, including fuel, was scarce. Therefore, no Pepto on the mostly bare shelves at the ship's store.

On our way in from fishing one day, we saw Jack and Barbara at the dock. Barbara kindly went onboard the *Sea Bear* and very graciously came out with a large quantity of Pepto-Bismol for yours truly, and it did indeed get me through the rest of the trip.

That particular day had been dreadful owing to weather in which the wind blew about twenty to twenty-five miles per hour, the sun never appeared, and there were passing squalls. Despite that, Patti and I managed to land two or three bonefish resulting from some very hard work and a lot of old-fashioned luck.

While Barbara was so graciously fetching my Pepto, Jack began to talk about what a miserable day it was, both weather and fishing, and volunteered that they got skunked. He then asked how we did, and I told him that, despite the horrendous conditions, we eked out a couple or three fish.

The globally familiar countenance of Jack Nicklaus clouded over with skepticism. "You caught three?" he said. When I nodded, he added, still seeming incredulous, "On fly?"

My answer to that one was to smile and "air cast" an imaginary fly rod, separating my hands as I emulated the double haul.

He shook his head back and forth and repeated that they had been blanked.

What came to my head at that moment was to say, "So, are you trying to say you didn't catch Jack?"

Thankfully my filter kicked in, and I kept my trap shut. But I did tell the story to my dear old friend and fraternity brother who is good buddies with the Golden Bear.

My friend told me I should have gone ahead and said it.

I suppose I should burn the photograph I have of that first double-digit bonefish I captured on the Fish Cay flat at my beloved Chub Cay because

I used the dreaded BogaGrip to determine its weight. But that was way before anglers had the benefit of studies by scientific research organizations like Bonefish & Tarpon Trust that told us of our crimes against nature.

A 2007 study at the Cape Eleuthera Institute in the Bahamas assessed the effects of a lip-gripping device on bonefish. Two control groups of bonefish were held vertically in the air and horizontally in the water for the same amount of time, and the injuries to fish held horizontally in the water were far less severe. But what was astounding is that the fish in the control group held with bare, clean hands showed no damage at all. The types of injuries inflicted by lip-gripping devices could affect the bonefish's ability to feed.

BOGAGRIP—NON!

According to the 2007 study's lead author, Dr. Andy Danylchuk, a professor of Fish Conservation at the University of Massachusetts Amherst and a Bonefish & Tarpon Trust (BTT) Research Fellow, these types of injuries could impact a bonefish's ability to feed. "It's easy to visualize how severe injuries to the mouth can impact handling prey, like crabs and shrimp, not to mention force bonefish to channel energy to heal wounds and fight infection," said Dr. Danylchuk. "Although we didn't document any short-term mortality (less than forty-eight hours), if we care about the future of bonefish, anglers shouldn't use a lip-gripping device when handling them."

JUST THE FACTS
Name of Lodge: Chub Cay Club
Location: Berry Islands, Bahamas
Author Comments: If you're wondering what happened to the other details about Chub Cay Club, they do not appear because they have become irrelevant. At least irrelevant for yours truly as, sadly, Chub Cay became a pure private club as of January 2025. Now, if you're up

for a $50,000 initiation fee and $5,000 in annual dues, you can still book and go there to fish. As for me, were I to join, I might feel as if I had to go there all the time, and there are too many other destinations I also love. So, if you are indeed interested, Chub is looking for members. Their website is www.chubcay.com.

FIFTEEN

Me and My Big Mouth

Although I left for good as a toddler, I've always loved the city of my birth—Miami. It has become perhaps the most cosmopolitan city in America. I enjoy going there because the optics of its tropical kaleidoscope are stimulating, it is culturally diverse, and its drum beats incessantly with the sound of thriving commerce and progress.

My dad was a Miami guy. He was city tennis champ and went to Miami Senior High before heading off to the University of Florida with his best high school buddy, George Smathers, who later became a United States senator. Like other "Florida crackers," such as dearly departed famous angler and television personality Flip Pallot, my dad pronounced Miami as "MY-AM-UH."

Which brings me to another South Florida landmark, the one folks call "Boca." That would be the city of Boca Raton or, translated to English, Mouth of the Rat. But, friends, that is not the *real* "Boca" as it is a newcomer, established in 1925 as a result of the Florida land boom.

Indeed, the *real* "Boca," established soon after 1885 when phosphate was discovered near the banks of the Peace River, is on the southWEST coast of Florida. That would be Boca Grande. Yes, it translates to Big Mouth.

So, what did phosphate have to do with Boca Grande?

A look at a Florida map will reveal a huge body of inland water north of Fort Myers and south of Sarasota called Charlotte Harbor, which empties to the Gulf of Mexico and refills multiple times each day as the tides flow. Boca Grande Pass is the conduit for this tidal flow. (Such watery avenues are called "passes" on the west coast of Florida but "inlets" on the east coast.)

Boca Grande Pass is unique in that it is not only wide but naturally about seventy feet deep, which is why it is still referred to as Port Boca Grande. A loading dock was built for ships to call from all over the world along with a railroad from inland-Florida onto the barrier island that terminated at Boca Grande Pass. This railroad allowed mined phosphate to be shipped overseas.

And it allowed something else: The wealthy could come to the quaint village of Boca Grande in their private rail cars to visit the Gulf-front estates they built and enjoy spectacular tropical beauty and pleasant winter temperatures.

It was about this time that Boca Grande tarpon fishing became popular. Back then, it was done with rowboats that a steamer towed uptide in Boca Grande Pass and released to drift live baits downtide across huge pods of tarpon. The heavy tackle was primitive by today's standards, but many lady anglers in their Victorian, high-collared dresses tussled mightily with the treasured gamefish, scientific name *Megalops atlanticus*.

Perhaps the most prominent families to establish themselves in Boca Grande with Gulf-front estates were the DuPonts and the Crowninshields. But in those days, Boca Grande also hosted the likes of Henry Ford, Thomas Edison, the Rockefellers, the Astors, and Vanderbilts. The very cheeky Gasparilla Inn was built in 1911 and, still owned by descendants of the DuPont family, thrives to this day.

Patti and I had a house on Boca Grande for many years. Perhaps not surprisingly, the island is the setting for my first two novels, *Boca Moon* and *Boca News*.

One winter we decided to see what it would be like to spend the night and dine at the Gasparilla Inn. At that time, a coat and tie were required in the dining room, and before dinner, we had a cocktail in the bar. It was fascinating to see multi-generation, blue-blood families, the ladies classily garbed and the gentlemen, from the silver-maned grandfather down to the prep-schooler, in their navy blazers with various yacht or country club embroidered crests on the breast pocket. They had all been coming from up north at the same time during the winter, year after year.

When it was time for our reservation, we sallied forth to the dining room and presented ourselves to the maître d'.

"We're the Fosters," I said.

"I know," he said.

"Oh?" I mused. "How did you know?"

"Because I know everybody else."

The DuPonts were not the only famous folks to frequent Boca Grande, then and now. Katharine Hepburn wintered there for many years, and Lana Turner, Robert Redford, Harrison Ford, Michael Keaton, Tom Brokaw, and Jimmy Buffet (nearby Cabbage Key spawned his famous "Cheeseburger in Paradise") have often been seen on the streets. These days in Boca Grande village you may very likely bump into Nick Saban, Dabo Swinney, or Tucker Carlson, as they all have Boca Grande homes. (It is said that longtime football rivals Saban and Dabo occasionally dine together.) If you book at the Gasparilla Inn and play the golf course, you stand a good chance of seeing avid golfer and part-time Boca Grande resident Brit Hume. As prominent a family as any to frequently visit Boca Grande is that of George H. W. Bush. But more on that later.

So, you may ask, what does all this have to do with fly fishing?

Well, Boca Grande is known for tarpon fishing with live bait on heavy conventional tackle in Boca Pass, but it is nevertheless where I bought my first fly rod and attempted to cast it. I bought it from local guide and good-guy Sandy Melvin, who also owns Gasparilla Outfitters, and I can remember my first fly-fishing trip with him struggling in vain to plop one of his redfish flies at least within the same zip code as some tailing redfish we were staring down in the backcountry's Whidden's Creek. I still remember what Captain Sandy said as cast after cast fell woefully short.

"It's challenging, Frank."

Man, was he right. Many years later, when my casting had improved, I was wade-fishing that same Whidden's Creek on low water and catching a few redfish out of schools on a red-and-silver-colored topwater popping bug fly. Presently, another school came along, I made the cast, hooked up, and the fish began a blistering run rather than the typical "dogging it" fight of a redfish.

Oh boy, I thought to myself, *it's a huge spawner that took a wrong turn at the channel marker out by the pass, lost its way, and ended up in the backcountry.* When I finally fought the fish close enough to get a look at it, I realized it was not a redfish. *Oh crap, it's a jack!* But as I finished the fight and was able to get my hands on the forked tail of the fish, I saw what I had caught: a permit!

It's the only permit I have ever seen or heard of on the backcountry flats of Boca Grande.

In our wonderful years at Boca Grande fishing as a family, we finally caught about as many tarpon, snook, redfish, trout, cobia, and various snappers and groupers on conventional tackle as we needed to. But the impetus for me in moving to fly fishing was watching legendary guide Phil O'Bannon casting for tarpon with his 12-weight from his Lake 'N Bay skiff off the Boca Grande beaches and sometimes in the backcountry. Phil was the captain of the hundred-and-something-foot Berger yacht *Galpo* that was owned by DuPont descendant Bayard Sharp, who also owned the Gasparilla Inn. Mr. Sharp, as Phil referred to him, kindly let Phil run his tarpon fly-fishing trips on the skiffs (also owned by Mr. Sharp) and made sure Phil took him on plenty of such trips. As Bayard Sharp aged, he would cast, hook a large tarpon, get a jump or two, and then hand the rod to Phil.

Next thing you knew, I had an array of tarpon rods, and Patti and I were spending lots of time and money with Captain Phil. Most of our fishing was up and down the beaches off Boca Grande in anywhere from five to twenty feet of water with intermediate sinking (rather than floating) fly lines.

Sometimes I got lucky. In fact, the first tarpon I ever caught on fly I hooked while I was stripping in my line to recast. But there was this one day after our casting improved: Patti and I hooked nine large tarpon and landed seven! Phil said it was easily his best day that year. Indelible in my memory is one of those fish, well over a hundred pounds, that, during the fight, tried to beach himself in little more than a foot of water in shallow, clear Johnson Shoals. But as I recall, Patti had the largest fish that day; Phil estimated it at around 140 pounds.

That wasn't the first or the last time Patti outfished me. Another trip with Phil O'Bannon took us at first light to Captiva Pass where some tarpon had convened for breakfast. There were only a few fish there, and they were surrounded by our skiff and several others, all chunking their purple flies at the occasional rolling fish. But ours was the only one carrying a female angler—Miss Patti—who, while the male anglers in the other skiffs watched slack-jawed, hooked and landed a nice eighty-pounder. We then cranked up, idled gently away from the other skiffs (as the guys in the other skiffs just stared at Patti), and made the run to the Tarpon Lodge for a celebratory breakfast.

Anglers tarpon fishing the Boca Grande beaches and backcountry find it different from fishing the Keys or even Homosassa because the water is deeper and not as clear. But this does not mean it's not sight-fishing. It's just that, except for a very few shallow, clear areas like Johnson Shoals, the bars that parallel Boca Grande Channel, the flats over by Burnt Store Marina or maybe even Captiva Shoals, it is necessary to see the fish roll to know where they are. Intermediate sink lines are standard equipment as are trolling motors on the skiffs. In fact, many skiffs have *three* trolling motors—two high-powered fixed ones on the stern and the normal direction-changing one on the bow.

In fishing with Phil O'Bannon, I have been trolled alongside a school of rolling tarpon (the depth of the water at Boca Grande allows this procedure without spooking the fish), casting in front of them continuously without a take until I was ready to give up. Then I would hear Phil say, "Keep casting!" I followed his orders, sometimes the result being an eventual hookup.

Along with Bill Horn's book *On the Bow*, the gold standard of tarpon fishing books may be Andy Mill's *A Passion for Tarpon*. Both books have helped me immensely. But if you're focused on tarpon fishing purely in Boca Grande, the bible may be my friend Bill Bishop's *High Rollers*. Bill has probably caught more Boca Grande tarpon than anyone else, and most of them have been from his skiff fishing by himself! He has some very special techniques he discusses in his book that I eagerly lapped up.

While it's a little embarrassing to share that my first tarpon eat on fly came while retrieving my line for another cast, the experience opened up for me the fascinating world of stripping techniques, or as the real pros like Bill Horn, Bill Bishop and Andy Mill would say, "feeding the fish."

My great guide and friend, Phil O'Bannon, started out by telling me to let the fly sink and to strip "long and smooth." At Boca Grande, it was effective, but after lots of tarpon fishing in other locations, I have embraced additional stripping techniques. And I learned to, when stripping long and smooth, quickly reach "up the fly rod" to grab the line to minimize the pause in the action of the swimming fly, therefore making smooth even smoother.

There are three basic methods of stripping for tarpon: long and slow, two-handed, and tick-tick-tick.

The two-handed retrieve came into vogue as more anglers began to fish with fly patterns that mimicked the Florida Keys palolo worm, regardless of whether their hatch was occurring. This method involves jamming the fly rod under an armpit so you can strip with both hands, thereby causing the fly to "swim" at a constant, fluid pace with no pauses. (Palolo worms don't pause; they swim at a consistent pace.)

In recent years, I have begun to use the two-handed strip with almost all types of fly patterns as I believe it may be more effective. And the two-handed strip has one very powerful advantage: It is impossible to "trout-set" (prematurely raising the rod) when you get a take.

ANDY SEZ...

"When you're stripping with two hands and the fish eats the fly, you won't have to worry about yanking the fly out of the fish's mouth with a trout strike—a cardinal sin in tarpon fishing. It's a common mistake we all make at times but one that particularly plagues anglers new to tarpon fishing. When you see that huge

> mouth open to bite your bug, believe me, it's hard not to lift your rod and rip the fly out of the 'poon's mouth. After twenty years, I still do it on occasion . . . a valuable phrase is DON'T STRIKE YOUR 'POON TOO SOON!"
>
> —Andy Mill, *A Passion for Tarpon*

So, there is the long and slow and two-handed strip, but I also like tick-tick-tick, particularly on daisy-chaining fish. Don't ask me why; it's just that I've gotten a lot of takes from chaining tarpon using that method. Tick-tick-tick is the same as long and slow except making very, very short strips—just a few inches at a time—in rapid succession. Andy likes the tick-tick-tick best when fishing a shrimp pattern since it may best mimic the sometime darting movement of a live shrimp.

But interestingly, Andy Mill suggests that stripping the fly at all may be overrated. He contends that most well-tied flies these days impart substantial undulating action of their own even while not being stripped and believes less may be more. Here's what he says:

ANDY ALSO SEZ...

> "I rarely give life to my flies with my stripping hand. I slide the fly forward by moving the fly line forward with a long, smooth stroke with my stripping hand. But I create the undulating movement I want my fly to make with my rod tip through my ROD HAND. This is an important distinction."
>
> —Andy Mill, *A Passion for Tarpon*

So, Andy, for lack of a better word, "wiggles" the tip of his rod while very slowly stripping to muster a little extra action on the fly. If he says it, that's good enough for me. His reputation as a legendary tarpon angler and his exemplary tournament results bear him out.

Just the Facts

Names of Lodges: Gasparilla Inn, Anchor Inn, various rental properties through Boca Grande Real Estate and others

Location: Boca Grande, southwest coast of Florida on Gasparilla Island

Nearest Airports: Tampa, Sarasota, Fort Myers

Drive from Airport: From Tampa, about two hours; from Sarasota, about one hour and fifteen minutes; from Fort Myers, about one hour and twenty minutes.

Dining: Scarpa's Coastal; The Temptation; The Pink Elephant; and many others.

Guides: Captain Cole Fairbanks: 941-258-1683; Captain Sandy Melvin: 941-628-2175; Captain Joe LeClair: 774-263-2675; Captain Phil O'Bannon: 239-229-1661

Author Comments: Since that stray fish I happened onto, I've not heard of another permit passing through Boca Grande on its way to who knows where. However, the odd single bonefish has been spotted around the Charlotte Harbour area lately and even as far north as Tampa Bay. That said, I would not go to Boca Grande looking for a flats grand slam. Now, a "Boca Grande Slam" is indeed possible. That's a tarpon, snook, redfish, and sea trout all in the same day. Very doable. The guides I've listed all specialize in fly fishing and have caught their clients—on fly—tarpon, snook, redfish, sea trout, cobia, pompano, sheepshead, triple tail, and probably some species I don't know about. It's true Boca Grande is no longer anywhere close to being a secret, which means you're likely to have company out on the water. But it retains this unique aspect: A mere thirty minutes from the interstate highway, you can be in a skiff that can take you to a vast backcountry, infiltrated with snook, redfish, et al., where you neither see nor hear anything of man's creation. Pretty special.

Sixteen
How About Leaving Me Alone

In addition to actors, actresses, football coaches, and news anchors, the Bush family continues to love visiting Boca Grande. This is no doubt owing to family tradition and their enduring friendship with DuPont descendants—the Farish family from Texas—who now own the Gasparilla Inn.

Reprinted here is my blog post from a number of years ago that describes my encounters in Boca Grande with a sitting president.

PRESIDENT BUSH WON'T LEAVE ME ALONE!
Not talking about "W" here but his dad: George Herbert Walker. Number forty-one. The guy who's now eighty-eight years old and, sadly, uses a wheelchair and a walker. I'm told he has some degenerative muscle affliction with a name I can neither pronounce nor spell.

Regardless, he was the president who wouldn't leave me alone. Let me explain.

All the Bushes were, and are, devotees of a little Southwest Florida paradise named Boca Grande where I had a second home for many years. (Which is why my first two novels, *Boca Moon* and *Boca News*, were set there.) When Bush 41 was the prez, he usually visited the island resort in the winter, the time of year I rented my house to an Ohio couple as an antidote to their bouts of January teeth-chattering.

How About Leaving Me Alone

But one time, George H. W. came to Boca Grande when my wife and I were there, and he would not leave me alone. And still won't!

It wasn't because we encouraged him. On the contrary, we decided we would do everything in our power to avoid the poor man and give him and Barbara some peace. We figured it wouldn't be too difficult, mainly owing to the army of Secret Service we expected.

We couldn't have been more wrong.

It began when we arrived "on island" (that's what the Boca Granders say) and retrieved our twenty-two-foot backcountry fishing boat from the high and dry marina. We followed our ritual: my wife drove the car to our dock and waited for me while I idled the boat down the bayou with our jet-black cockapoo perched elegantly on the bow like a Phoenician figurehead, occasionally barking at a brown pelican.

My route took me under the bridge that the famous old Gasparilla Inn uses to get to their golf course. As I drew closer to the bridge, I noticed a man in a golf cart stopped at the top of bridge watching me. I did a double take because the man looked rather like the president, but I dismissed the thought as there was absolutely no one else around (read: bruisers in dark suits wearing hearing aids).

As I crept closer to the bridge, barely moving at idle speed, I felt my throat go a little dry as I realized that, in fact, the leader of the free world and I were staring at each other. I slipped the boat into neutral, and since I was moving against the tide, came to a virtual stop, never breaking eye contact.

"That's the weirdest looking boat I've ever seen in my life," said POTUS, with a large, Dana Carvey-like grin.

Now, you may think I had just been insulted. Indeed, I had not. It was actually a high compliment from the president, who, like me, is a fanatical angler and knows a leading-edge backcountry "fishing machine" when he sees one. And that's what that boat was. One of the first of its kind, it had a mostly flat bottom, a tunnel drive, a jack plate, a center console tower, and gunwales just high enough to trip over. It was designed to run in eight-inch-deep backcountry water and sneak up on redfish and snook.

George Bush knew all that, and he knew I knew he knew it. Consequently, he also knew he was on very safe ground telling a constituent his boat was "weird."

"Thank you, Mr. President," I got out after a couple of gulps.

A brief conversation ensued, mostly about my boat, but it touched on a wonderful chap named Captain Phil O'Bannon (www.obannonscharter.com), the president's longtime local fishing guide, and the fact that I also used Phil for tarpon fishing with fly rod in the Gulf waters off the Boca Grande beaches.

"Well, gotta go," he suddenly said with another grin and a wave over his shoulder. I had read accounts of Bush's record golf rounds—not the scores, but their short duration. Maybe that's why there were no Secret Service around—who could draw a bead on this dragonfly of a man who would light here and there for moments at a time?

He never asked my name. I thought that would be that.

But once again, I was wrong because the next day on the way out fishing, I pulled into the Inn Marina for fuel and there was the throng. The hearing-aid guys were there this time, along with a small crowd of islanders. The president was boarding Captain Phil O'Bannon's flats skiff to go snook fishing. Once again, I had eye contact with POTUS.

"There's that boat again," he said with jocularity, this time even more Carvey-like.

Well, that would surely be it, I thought.

Nope.

On Sunday, my wife and I took our usual seats down front in the little Episcopal church on the island. Hadn't been sitting there two minutes when guess who sat right beside us. Yep. There was one suit wearing a hearing aid sitting right behind us. During the offering, Barbara leaned toward POTUS and, in almost a stage whisper, said, "Do you have any money?" whereupon the president began groping in each pocket, wearing a panicked expression. Finally, Barbara solved it by reaching in her purse.

After the service, he turned to me. I said, "Good morning, Mr. President."

He studied me for an instant, and I saw something register in his eyes. He stuck out his hand. I took it. He said, "You're the guy with the weird boat."

I beamed with delight and opened my mouth to say something else. I wasn't sure what, but my thoughts were yes, we were available for cocktails that evening, and yes, I could accompany him fishing the next day. But, while my mouth was still open, he uttered a quick "nice to see you again," turned on his heel, and left, shaking hands with other parishioners on the way out.

Some years later, when I became a novelist, I sent him a signed copy of my first book, *Boca Moon*, which was set in his—and my—beloved Boca Grande. In my note, I reminded him of my "weird boat" and received a lovely note of thanks—one of his trademarks.

So, why do I say he *still* won't leave me alone?

Because I gave a copy of the second book in my "Boca" series, *Boca News*, to my friend, former congressman Lou Frey (*The Frey Report*: www.loufreyinstitute.org). Lou is a good friend of H.W., and I suggested he give the former president his copy and tell him about my new book, *Catch a Falling Knife*, which is coming out any day now. I thought Bush might be particularly interested in it because it's about an attack on one of our container ship ports.

"Lou, please tell that fellow with the weird boat that I want a copy of that new book!"

According to Lou, that's what George Bush said.

I plan to send him one. Maybe then he'll leave me alone.

These days we only occasionally return to Boca Grande. But not long ago, Patti and I were there for an event and stayed at the Gasparilla Inn. During some free time, I found myself in the gift shop browsing their selection of bow ties, to which I am partial. There was one that drew my attention as it had a navy-blue field that was peppered with pink elephants. (The Gasparilla Inn owns a nearby restaurant, an island fixture called The Pink Elephant, commonly referred to as "The Pink.")

I was holding the tie in my hand in momentary deliberation over my decision when I noticed an attractive lady at my side, her pretty and smooth-complexioned face wearing a pleasant expression. Our eyes met.

It was Laura Bush.

"What do you think of this one?" I asked the first lady.

"I would definitely go with that one," she said.

"Okay, thanks, but why do you like it?"

Her face spread into one of her trademark genteel smiles.

"That's easy," she said. "It has elephants."

Seventeen

I Wonder If You'd Mind...

Any discussion of tarpon fishing on fly would be incomplete were not Homosassa included. Charming Homosassa Springs is on the west coast of Florida about seventy-five miles north of Tampa and is the stuff of angling legend.

I have had the good fortune of having been invited there to tarpon fish several times by my great friend (and lawyer until he retired) Ron Clark, who used to have a house right on the Homosassa River. We had some decent tarpon fishing on the Gulfside flats the times I was there, but from all I can determine, Ron and I missed out on Homosassa when it was in its heyday. The tarpon still come and are still fished and caught, but the numbers of fish are way down from the golden times back in the 1970s and 1980s. In its heyday, Homosassa was the site of world records up to 202 pounds by legendary anglers like Billy Pate, Tom Evans, baseball slugger Ted Williams, Stu Apte, and Lefty Kreh.

Those golden days are superbly chronicled in Monte Burke's absorbing book *Lords of the Fly*, which provides a behind-the-scenes look at competitive, world-record angling at Homosassa, both on and off the water, which at times resembled a soap opera.

Burke's book expertly chronicles how Homosassa tarpon fishing has evolved over the years. In the golden times, schools of enormous tarpon would swim around Chassahowitzka Point and onto the famous Oklahoma flat to be pursued by those anglers seeking world records.

That was a flat onto which do-it-yourself anglers ventured at their peril as Homosassa guides were not known for their social graces when they felt amateurs were encroaching where only professionals should dare to tread. This was particularly so when said amateurs ran their outboard-powered skiffs up on the "fleet" of guide skiffs. The language could get as blue as the water.

WHERE HAVE ALL THE HOMOSASSA TARPON GONE?

"Back in the day, maybe 10,000 fish used to come in every May. The times I have been there, we'd have many days of just sitting there bobbing in the water and not seeing a damn thing for the entire day, sometimes three days in a row. There are sometimes little glimpses of the old days.

"A lot of this has to do with pressure, but it wasn't just pressure that kept the fish away. It's the great freshwater springs, including these four big rivers, which all emptied into that bay. The flow of those rivers is down to 40 percent of their historical flow. This is man-made environmental degradation—a government, a state government, and a governor's office that have never done a damn thing except for encourage people to keep building and sucking up water. I think it's all coming to a head now.

"Still, all that said, if someone told me tomorrow, 'Hey, I got an opening, do you want to go down and fish?' I would jump on it. Just to spend a day in the presence of those fish is amazing. I see why Ponce de León supposedly went there looking for the Fountain of Youth. Florida is magical. It is this otherworldly place. There's no place like it in the United States. It's more Caribbean than it is American. It's a hard place to give up on."

—Monte Burke, from his book *Lords of the Fly*

Yes, Homosassa guides are not only very expert but also colorful, especially one named Captain Mike Locklear. Ron and I fished with him a few times, and he was a real character. One of my favorites was Captain John Bazo, a bear of a man who I suspect could pole a flats skiff from one end of Oklahoma flat to the other with one hand if he had to. And Captain William Toney was the guide Patti and I fished with for redfish and trout when we were fortunate enough to be invited on a couples trip for several nights to the famous Homosassa Fishing Club (mostly Atlanta members) that has been in continuous operation since 1899.

But it was Captain Jimmy Long I tarpon fished with right after the outstanding Orvis Helios rods were introduced. Captain Jimmy had a brand-new 12-weight all rigged with a beautiful Orvis reel and fly line from the Nature Coast Fly Shop. He offered it to me at what was actually a very attractive price but still a very large number. The witty Captain Jimmy is all Florida-cracker, and when I whined about the large price, he grabbed me by the shoulders, looked me in the eye, and said, "Frank. I ain't never seen a trailer hitch on the back of one of them hearses!"

I erupted in laughter. And bought the rod.

There was an unforgettable tarpon outing with Captain Bazo. As we were leaving the dock, he said, "Lemme ask you something."

"Sure," I said.

(You will see in a moment why it would be bad form for me to name the rod manufacturer he was about to mention as it is an iconic brand of the utmost quality and reputation.)

"[Brand X] has decided to get in the saltwater fly-rod business," Bazo said.

He reached under the gunwale of his skiff and produced a gleaming 12-weight tarpon rod, fully rigged with a tarpon fly tied on the end of the tippet.

"I wonder if you'd mind fishing with it today," he said. "They've asked me to see if I can get a picture of the first tarpon caught on it."

Without hesitation, I nodded my assent as I took the rod from him. It was a beautiful piece of gear. When we arrived at the flat we were going to fish, I stripped out line and made some casts. I loved the way that rod casted.

We didn't see a fish for a couple of hours but then happened on a small school of daisy-chaining tarpon circling counterclockwise. I made several casts to the left side of the chain. Nothing. They broke the chain and started stringing. Big John Bazo, huffing and puffing, gave his push pole (and himself) a brisk workout and somehow got us in front of them. My first cast found an eater, and it was game on.

It was not a particularly large fish, particularly for Homosassa, probably around eighty to ninety pounds. He jumped only twice, drawing the required "bow" from me each time, and after I went "down and dirty" on him a few times, he was at reasonably close range but not ready to land. That's when it happened.

That new rod broke like a pencil.

The break was about two or three feet above the butt. But that didn't stop us. I continued to fight the fish with only an abbreviated portion of the butt section of the rod, and we landed the fish!

"So, Cap," I said. "Ready for that picture?"

John Bazo's face broke into something halfway between a grin and a smirk. "Uh, maybe not," he said.

Just the Facts

Lodging: MacCrae's, Chassahowitzka Hotel, Seagrass Resort

Location: Near the Gulf, seventy miles north of Tampa on Florida's Nature Coast

Nearest Airport: Tampa—a one-hour drive

Dining: Crumps Landing, Nature Coast Bar and Grill, Margarita Grill

Guides: John Bazo: 352-895-7811; Jimmy Long: 352-422-1303; William Toney: 352-422-4141

Author Comments: Indeed, the tarpon do not visit Homosassa like they did in the old days. But some are still there and, given declines in fish numbers for a variety of reasons, the tarpon fishing may still be almost as good there as almost anywhere else in Florida. That is, obviously, a matter of conjecture by those far more expert than yours truly, but I surely would not turn down an invitation to tarpon fish in Homosassa. As for other species, the sea trout and redfishing is as good as ever, and more and more snook are finding their way that far north. Even without a rod in your hand, Homosassa and nearby Crystal River and their old-Florida charm are mighty pleasant places to spend time.

Eighteen
I Said Cast the Fly, Frank!

There are some people I miss and some things I miss. One of those people is a fellow named Don Causey, and one of those things is his newsletter, *The Angling Report*.

Don was an English major and an investigative journalist before he merged those with his love of the outdoors and rose to become executive editor of the magazine *Outdoor Life*. He founded *The Angling Report* in 1988, and it ran twenty-eight years before he sold it. I was a devoted subscriber and the pluperfect embodiment of the newsletter's target audience: "For the Angler Who Travels." Don wrote most of *The Angling Report*'s articles about fishing locations and lodges around the world but no small part of the content was supplied by subscribers reporting on their experiences. A highlight of the newsletter was always the subscriber-written section Don called, "The Good, the Bad and the Ugly." Often, no punches were pulled if a trip was below par. Sadly, we lost Don to pulmonary fibrosis in January 2024.

It was an article in the newsletter that caused Don and me to meet. It was about trout fishing in Italy organized by a fellow named Claudio Tagini who books fishing in the stunningly beautiful rivers of Italy's Dolomite mountains. Ultimately, Patti and I met Don and his lovely wife Maria in Italy and enjoyed several dinners with them. We became fast friends and stayed in contact until he died.

We also became friends with Claudio Tagini and his American wife Naomi and stayed with them in their home in the Marche region several nights. Claudio, of all things, was an acclaimed designer of women's fashions while living in Los Angeles where he met Naomi. He's a cognoscente who can spew intimate details of everything epicurean, including cuisine, fine wines, growing olives (which he does on his property), art, and literature. He's always the last one to leave a museum. Moreover, he is, of course, a superb angler. But beyond all that, Claudio is a delightful, gracious chap whose company we always enjoy immensely, just as we did the fishing he booked for us in the Dolomites. Our only problem was the trouble we had aiming our casts while constantly distracted by astonishing vistas.

Don Causey and *The Angling Report* make me think of another person and another thing I miss: Unlike Don, he's still with us but I miss fishing with my great friend Sidney Thomas at his Water Cay Bonefish Lodge.

Like so many of the Bahamas elite bonefish guides, Sidney worked at Deep Water Cay Club before becoming owner and head guide at his lodge on Water Cay. So, where the heck is Water Cay? It's a discrete cay off the north shore of Grand Bahama Island that can be located on any nautical chart. (Folks in McClean's Town on the east end of Grand Bahama distinguish it from Deep Water Cay by calling it NORTH Water Cay.) When Sidney lost his lease on the lodge building on Water Cay, he relocated his operation to Crown Haven on Little Abaco. I have not yet been to Sidney's new venue but plan to. In his heyday at Water Cay Bonefish Lodge, the fishery was amazing, serviced by Sidney's nice lodge and excellent skiffs. Between Sidney, his brother Ezra, and his brother-in-law Greg, there were no finer guiding skills available anywhere in the world.

Don Causey never went to Water Cay Bonefish Lodge, so he asked me to write a report about it for *The Angling Report*. I have included it here without asking anyone's permission as, to my knowledge, the publication no longer exists.

Don Causey Note: It's not often that a successful novelist agrees to send you a trip report, but that is what happened recently when

Frank Foster called with a question about fishing a particular part of the world. Obviously, you don't bury a report like that in the critique section; you handle it as a stand-alone feature and make the author an Honor Roll subscriber. Frank's Honor Roll fishing cap is already in the mail. You can read more about our Honor Roll program on page 2 of this issue. In the unlikely event you don't know Frank Foster's books, his latest, Catch a Falling Knife, *is an exciting and disturbing thriller about a terrorist plot to exploit some weaknesses in our container shipping industry. His other two books are* Boca News *and* Boca Moon. *You can get copies of all of Frank Foster's books in the usual places, including Amazon. Thanks, Frank, for sending the report!*

A Very Special Report on Water Cay Bonefish Club
by Frank Foster

The three worst words in the game of golf are, "still your turn." The three worst words in bonefishing could be, "they're gone now," and the three best words could be, "point your rod!" But for me? The three best words a bonefish guide can say are, "it's a permit!"

That's exactly what Capt. Sidney Thomas, owner and head guide of Water Cay Bonefish Club on Grand Bahama Island, said to me one April morning. I had been wiggling my bare feet on the casting platform of the Beavertail skiff, making sure I wasn't feeling my fly line with my toes. But at his words, it seemed that everything I had began to wiggle. Began to shake was probably more like it. I had trouble swallowing. I managed to squeak out, "Where?"

"Point your rod!" (Ah, those magical words.) And I did.

"More left," he said. Then, "Left, left, left—there!"

I saw the fish.

In a moment I'll get to what happened next, but first a word about this wonderful Bahamian bonefish lodge that is largely a secret. It's so sub-rosa that many regular guests of Water Cay Bonefish Club on Grand Bahama will likely see this piece in the Angling Report and groan. In fact, I admit to being reluctant to write it after just being turned down on dates for two future trips I had contemplated. The only way was to choose less-desirable dates and totally upend my schedule. I did so without hesitation.

Water Cay Bonefish Club is not to be confused with the legendary Deep Water Cay Club, which is on the same island about seventy-five miles to the southeast. If one looks at a nautical chart, Water Cay is actually identified. It's a cay off the north coast of the island due northeast of Freeport. It was a settlement and technically still is. Although only five families still live there, the Baptist church still holds services every Sunday.

The rather Spartan (but lady angler-friendly) lodge sits right on the water and is a single-story white frame building, which, charmingly, looks older than it is. In the middle is the dining room, bar, and public room, with sleeping rooms on each side—guests on one, staff on the other. The lodge accommodates six rods.

It's a Bahamian family operation through and through. Owner and head guide Sidney Thomas's brother and brother-in-law are the other two guides, and Sidney's mother-in-law and daughter expertly handle housekeeping and cooking the excellent Bahamian fare of conch, lobster, fish, and to-die-for Bahamian mac 'n' cheese. Sidney's delightful wife runs reservations and finance.

But back to that permit.

"You see him, right?" Sidney said.

"Y-y-yes," I said.

"Give me a cast. Land it on his nose."

I had never caught a permit. But, in fairness, I had never fished solely for permit. For years while bonefishing I would carry an extra rod with a permit crab but was finally persuaded that fumbling for a "permit rod" was counterproductive and that permit would eat a bonefish fly. After that I continued to cast at many a permit but never got a take. A hot bonefish fly at Water Cay is the Enrico Puglisi spawning shrimp with lead eyes. I mainly fish the tan body with orange but for some reason this day had tied on the olive-green color. I made the cast, and it was a good one. The permit, which looked as big as a nuclear submarine to me, took a close look at it and did exactly what every permit I've ever cast to has done: it turned away from it.

"*Well, that was exciting,*" *I said to Sidney, turning to face him.*

He did not answer, and he did not look at me. He was busy. He was furiously poling after the permit, which had gone upwind of us and to the right of where he had been.

"*He's still there. Cast again,*" *Sidney said. The urgency in his voice was palpable.*

The stiff breeze seemed at the same time to be both in my face and on my right ear, and the fish was seventy feet away. Besides, the permit had just refused my fly, and everybody knows they never eat anyway.

"*Aw, I don't know, Sidney,*" *I said.*

"*Cast the fly, Frank!" It wasn't a request.*

So I did. Somehow I got the green Italian fly in front of the fish. I let it sink a few seconds, began to move it very slowly and smoothly, and, unlike scores of other casts like it, this time the permit tipped up and ate the fly!

The usual fire drill ensued: making sure the line cleared to the reel, cranking up the outboard for the chase, getting the camera at the ready.

We worked the fish—close to twenty pounds—over to a shallow area, and Sidney and I exited the skiff for the landing (we were going to tackle the permit, if necessary) while my sweet wife (and best fishing buddy) manned the camera.

We got him. Everybody hugged.

And I wept.

I also told Sidney that, thanks to him, my life was now complete, that I could go ahead and die!

I also told Sidney that the Water Cay fishery was obviously the permit capital of the Bahamas. That got a chuckle from him as he informed me that it was only the fourth one ever caught there. I believe him, but I have seen permit on almost every trip to Water Cay.

The Water Cay fishery is simply marvelous. Why? It is vast, which means little pressure (just look at a nautical chart, and you'll see what I mean), and the bonefish are plentiful and big. I would describe the run-of-the-flats size as four to six pounds. A three-pound fish is uncommon, but a seven- or eight-pound fish is certainly not. The biggest one I've landed there was nine pounds, but I've seen and lost a number of double-digit fish (and I'm not over it yet). Not only are there some real monsters, but the nice thing is there are few schools, at least during the spring months I have fished there. And there is plenty of excellent wade-fishing. I recently counted the Bahamian fisheries I have experienced and came up with seventeen different lodges or fisheries on five different islands. I can tell you that I have fished with few guides as good as Sidney and his crew, and none better. And their equipment is top-notch. The Beavertail skiffs can float in a street puddle, have zero hull slap, and, in my humble opinion, take a chop as well as their look-alike cousin, the Hells Bay skiff. Perhaps the most appealing attribute of Water Cay Bonefish Club is the fishing hours. How many times have we all been surrounded by huge bonefish and see the guide look at his watch at 3:30 or four o'clock and declare the day over? Not at Water Cay. Instead, the day continues until the fishing dwindles. The work ethic, enthusiasm for the fishing, and the dedication to the client's satisfaction on the part of Sidney and his crew is in a class by itself in the Bahamas. But if you go and take advantage of this great feature, I hope your tip will reflect it. At least a hundred dollars per skiff, per day, is appropriate when you get to fish until six p.m. or later.

    Now, so you won't think I have an ownership interest in the place, I feel compelled to come up with at least something negative. Not an easy task. Sometimes there is contention with the staff for the TV remote, and although there is unlimited high-quality free phone service to the states and a huge HD satellite television, WiFi and, therefore, Internet remains on Sidney's to-do list. All that said, this is not a rum drink with a little umbrella kind of place; it's about the superb fishing.

    How to get there? Fly into Freeport. Sidney or one of his folks will pick you up and drive you about forty-five minutes to a boat ramp where you and your gear will be loaded onto one of the skiffs. Ten to fifteen minutes later you'll be at the lodge with a Kalik and some conch fritters. The next morning your walk from the dining room to the

skiffs is less than 100 feet. After boarding your skiff, you could either be casting to monsters in five minutes or run as much as forty-five minutes east, west, or north to diverse and interesting flats. But that permit was caught on a flat within sight of the lodge.
　　Perhaps you'll ask Sidney to take you there first.

— Frank Foster

Postscript: You can book a stay at Water Cay Bonefish Club through a number of booking agents. The direct e-mail contact address is turketta@hotmail.com.

　　Bonefishing with Sidney Thomas at Water Cay revealed something I had never seen before and have not seen in any other fishery.
　　Although bonefish almost always feed by grubbing on the bottom, it is sometimes possible to catch them with some kind of topwater fly or lure. With Sidney, I have seen something fascinating, not on the wide-open flats, but in narrow, mangrove-lined creeks where there is fairly strong current.
　　It's quite remarkable, really. I'm talking about floating, individual mangrove leaves carrying tiny crabs that are clinging to the tops of the leaves, zipping along in the current. I have seen bonefish come up and snarf down the whole thing to get the crab! Naturally, after seeing this, I tied on a floating fly (trout, actually), and Sidney and I would present it. We caught a few bonefish this way but, on balance, our success was limited. Sure was fun and interesting, though.

Sidney Thomas had his Water Cay fishery all to himself. Well, almost.
　　Patti and I were recent guests at North Riding Point Club (NRPC). Although the Club is located on the south shore of Grand Bahama, right on the ocean, the guides can trailer their anglers to the north shore, launch their skiff, and access the same water Sidney used to fish.
　　Our NRPC trip was a good one fishing Sidney's old water with the Club's famed guide, Bully, who was as expert at guiding as he was

excellent company on the skiff. We had some memorable catches to eight pounds and one permit shot.

One day we were fishing fairly close to Sidney's old lodge on Water Cay itself, and we asked Bully to ride us by there. What we saw broke our hearts. It made Sidney's loss of his lease a moot point as his former lodge was…well, it simply wasn't there. There was not even a sign or remnants of the lodge's foundation. I remember tracking Hurricane Dorian and remarking to Patti that it appeared the eye went right over Sidney's old lodge. What we saw—or didn't see—confirmed it.

JUST THE FACTS

Lodge Name: North Riding Point Club (NRPC)

Location: South shore of Grand Bahama Island

Nearest Airport: Grand Bahama International Airport (FPO)

Drive from Airport to Lodge: Twenty-five minutes

Getting There: Bahamasair, American Airlines, Connections from Nassau via Western Air, Charters from South Florida

Capacity: Eight guests

Fly Shop: Yes, fully stocked

Rate for Five Nights Lodging, Four Days Fishing: $6,132 (2025 rates)

Includes: Lodging, all meals, guided fishing, airport transfer, double occupancy, shared skiff, open bar

Does Not Include: VAT, tips

Website: www.nrpcbonefishing.com

Author Comments: NRPC is unique in several ways, starting with the ownership structure. Many bonefish lodges have the word "club" in their name. But North Riding Point Club really is one because it's semi-private. The ownership group (it originally included former Treasury Secretary Robert Rubin and some gentrified folks from the United Kingdom with "Sir" in their names) numbered around forty before mortality began to reduce that number. I've been told that the well-heeled group substantially subsidized the operation for many years until the current general manager, Paul Adams, took over and stopped the bleeding, bringing the operation to either break even or a tiny surplus. While Paul runs a tight ship, he totally gets the hospitality business and all the important customer service precepts—a genial host, to be sure. The partners are admirable if only for this: When Hurricane Dorian forced the place to close for a lengthy period, they not only continued the salaries of all the staff and guides but also financially helped them rebuild their homes. Our guide Bully's eyes got moist as he told us this. The physical plant, perched right on a lovely Oceanside beach framed in sea grapes, is so, so appealing. It's an unsullied expression of the understated... not so much elegance but pure classiness. It has stalwart bones with a bygone Bahamian colonial flavor that promulgates pleasurable decorum and civility. The sleeping rooms are spacious and luxurious, and the lodge itself has the look and feel of the Bahamian home of an English gentleman. NRPC has a bona fide chef, and the cuisine reflects that. The guides? We've only fished with Bully, who is outstanding. Another unique aspect of NRPC is their approach of trailering their anglers to a variety of locations within the fishery. An example? Our ability to fish Sidney Thomas' old stomping grounds from our Water Cay days.

Nineteen
"Bair's-Tagonia"

Bair's Lodge on South Andros Island was founded in 1989 by a couple from Atlanta named Andy and Stanley Bair. I never went there when they owned it and thus never met Stanley, although I recently met Andy when we were both guests at East End Lodge on Grand Bahama. I am told Stanley has courageously dealt with some health problems for many years and is a delightful lady. Andy and Stanley now own a lovely inn in historic Cedar Key, Florida. Bair's Lodge was a favorite of anglers worldwide and has remained so after Andy and Stanley sold to an Argentine company, Nervous Waters.

I have never met Fernando de las Carreras or his very accomplished right-hand man Santiago Seeber (with whom I've booked many Nervous Waters trips), but in the forty years since Fernando founded it, his Buenos Aires–based Nervous Waters has become a force in the fly-fishing industry as they are now up to about a dozen lodges in Argentina, Chile, and the Bahamas.

Under the Nervous Waters flag, I have been to Bair's Lodge multiple times both with my angler buddies and Miss Patti. It is right on the ocean in an intoxicating, tropical setting among voluptuous palm trees that can seduce guests into believing they are on a movie set. It can be mesmerizing to the extent of *almost* making one forget about hunting large bonefish and permit on the nearby flats.

Yes, Bair's is first cabin all the way. That means accommodations featuring luxuries like down pillows and comforters and cuisine at a much higher level than standard-issue Bahamian fare of cracked conch with peas 'n rice. It also means excellent guides. Two of them, Leslie and T. (short for Theophilus), have been at Bair's for almost thirty years.

The fishery is vast and productive. Deep Creek and Little Creek sit on either side of the lodge and open into a large collection of bays, bights, and other creeks, all infested with large bonefish. When the lodge's skiffs head south, there are the very fishy Grassy and Little Grassy Creeks plus a huge area of wading flats on the southern tip of Andros Island in the Jackfish Channel area. Jimmy Buffett would often land his seaplane there before disembarking to wade for bonefish.

And it is also possible, on the proper tide, to navigate a small creek and eventually emerge on the west side of Andros Island. I did that once and was rewarded with a bonefish that went just over nine pounds on the BogaGrip we were still, in our ignorance, using at the time. However, if the tide is right, an angler staying at Bair's Lodge doesn't even need a boat. Instead, a walk out the door of the lodge to the ocean flat can deliver some marvelous fishing. It's a good bet for early risers or anglers returning from the flats still looking to sate their craving for casting to a bevy of bones.

Getting to those flats on the south end of the island can be a little "sporty" in a skiff as there is some relatively deep water to be crossed when going around the old naval station. But Bair's has wisely replaced their Dolphin skiffs with more stable Maverick Mirage HPX-Vs, thereby greatly mitigating that issue.

So, if you suspect that "Bair's-Tagonia" may have something to do with Patagonia, you're right. But why is it in a book about bonefishing?

The answer: One of the times Patti and I fished at Bair's the lodge was between managers. An advantage a large operator like Nervous Waters has is the ability to temporarily plug a management hole by tapping their widespread staff and balancing the seasonality of their operations. This resulted in Nico and Cece Botting (Nicolas and Cecelia) taking charge of Bair's on one of our trips there. They are a wonderful

Argentine couple who spoke perfect English and harbor a deep understanding of how to accommodate guests.

Nico and Cece's Argentina connection intrigued Patti and me because we had never fished Patagonia and, as our stay wore on, the topic began to dominate our conversations. The next thing we knew, a trip to Patagonia was planned for us by Nico and Cece for the following winter (their summer).

And a marvelous trip it was. Like everybody, we flew to Buenos Aires, hit the museums, saw the opera house, Eva's tomb, and a leg-wrapping tango. Then it was a flight southwest to Esquel, where we stayed in a bed-and-breakfast owned and operated by—guess who? Cece's parents. They were a delight, as was their home, and we enjoyed getting to know them around the dinner table.

While in Esquel, we fished, with some success, the famous spring creek, Arroyo Pescado, and also did a little bonefishing.

What?? Bonefishing in Argentina?

Well, almost.

There was a very interesting lake that lay right up against a mountain with one shoreline featuring a crystalline flat that looked more like a bonefish flat than… a bonefish flat. It provided a memorable angling experience as we were able to sight fish with dry flies individual rainbow trout that, since there was no current, were cruising around like, well, bonefish. I have a picture of a monster rainbow I caught that came right at me providing the treasured dream shot.

Nico and Cece were our hosts at Nervous Waters' delightful Futa Lodge, and our reunion with them was just as pleasurable as the fishing was excellent.

But back to Bair's Lodge. When we were there with Nico, he would occasionally guide the guests, thankfully including us, and we found him to be very good at it. He had an amazing set of peepers, seeing bonefish from distances that seemed to me telescopic. We fished with him one day when the wind made you feel as if you were standing right behind a 747 with all four engines revved to the max for takeoff. It's days like that when things happen, and something did to me.

When the wind compromised the accuracy of my cast to a bonefish cruising against the mangroves, I snagged a leaf with my fly and, shall we say, rather aggressively yanked it back. The result was my fly coming back at me—not sure if it was at the speed of light or sound—and embedding itself in the back of my hand to the extent that the barb of the hook was buried. When I looked down at my hand, my spirits deflated with a whoosh, as I thought my fishing was over for the day and a trip to a hospital in Nassau was next. Boy, was I wrong.

It was my first initiation to "the secret method."

Nico cut a short length of monofilament leader material and tied it to the curve of the hook. I couldn't look. As I continued to divert my gaze he said, "All right, be still and on the count of three, it's coming out. Okay?"

"Okay," I said, meekly, my pulse rate elevated.

"One," he said, as I remained still.

He never said two. Not only did I never feel a thing but there was no blood, no scar, and zero pain afterwards. The whole thing took about a minute. It was amazing. When I asked, he showed me the technique for future reference.

FOOLPROOF HOOK REMOVAL TECHNIQUE BY ALEX MCCRICKARD

I have spent a considerable amount of time teaching novice fly anglers in my years as a fly fishing guide on Wyoming's Upper North Platte River. From experience, I will say that one of the less-enjoyable aspects of being a guide is getting impaled with your client's fly as they are learning how to cast for the first time. I have been accidentally hooked many times, including having flies embedded in my leg, arm, back, and even nose. I am lucky and have never had to take a trip to the emergency room with any of these injuries. The technique outlined below can help you remove an impaled hook while on the water.

"Bair's-Tagonia"

Photo by Lynda Richardson/DWR

The technique for removing an impaled hook is actually quite simple. Start by cutting off a two- to three-foot-long section of heavy monofilament, 15 or 20 lb. test line. If you're fly fishing, 0x tippet will work fine.

Next, thread the monofilament between the shank of the hook and your skin, situating the loop of monofilament at the bend of the hook. Make sure you have at least twelve inches of monofilament on either side of the hook. With your thumb, press down on the shank of the hook until the shank is parallel to your skin. Once you have pushed down, quickly jerk the monofilament with your other hand in a motion parallel to the shank to remove the embedded hook. It's a simple push-and-pull technique that is highly effective. I have performed this on myself many times, but it can certainly be beneficial to have a family member or friend assist you in the process, especially if you hooked yourself in the back or arm.

The tips below can help you in the process as well as decipher when it's essential to seek medical attention:

- **This technique will NOT work with treble hooks.** Treble hooks on lures pose an entirely different situation, and it's best to seek medical attention if deeply impaled by two out of three treble hooks.
- Consider pinching the barbs on your hooks before fishing, especially for beginners. A barbless hook is a lot easier to remove than a barbed hook.
- Trust your gut—if you think you need medical attention, then it's best to go to the emergency room. If you are hooked deeply in the neck or face, it is best to seek medical attention.
- Larger and heavier hooks, especially saltwater hooks that are deeply impaled, might also require a trip to the emergency room.
- Always wear a hat and polarized sunglasses when fishing on the water. Not only will sunglasses protect your eyes, but they also cut down against the glare and help you spot fish in the water.
- Spread out and give yourself ample casting space when fishing together with friends and family.
- Carry a first-aid kit in your car when wade-fishing or in your boat so you are ready when a situation arises.

—Alex McCrickard, Aquatic Educational Coordinator, Virginia Department of Wildlife Resources and Former Guide

It was a number of years until the next time I stopped a flying hook with my tender flesh. It was while salmon fishing in Iceland. This was all walk and wade-fishing with single-handle rods rather than Spey, and we were driven in SUVs to the fishing, often fording the rivers in the vehicle. Our first day, the wind was flag-ripping fierce, and for the second time in my angling career, I once again found my fly embedded in my hand with the barb buried. Not to worry, I thought, because my experience at Bair's Lodge with Nico had taught me that this problem was easily resolved.

Except I couldn't remember exactly how.

I showed the embedded hook to our guide and said, "You know what to do, right?"

"Sure," he said. "Let me get my pliers."

Patti and I looked at each other in horror.

"Pliers?" I said.

"Yeah. Gotta yank it out of there."

"So…you don't know the technique where you use a piece of monofilament and then…" My voice trailed off as his expression told me I may as well have been speaking Swahili.

"Let's go back to the lodge," I said.

Once there, I went to the lodge's laptop, googled the secret method, and, in minutes, the hook was out of my hand, once again with no pain or blood.

One of the guests at Bair's Lodge that time when Nico and Cece were managing it was an octogenarian widow from Orlando who had traveled the world with her husband fly fishing. She was charming and refined, was wonderful company, and fished alone. She entertained us with a little humorous thing that happened:

During cocktail hour the first night, Patti and I were browsing in the lodge fly shop and became interested in a new Orvis shirt bearing the Bair's logo. We asked our genteel fellow guest if she saw anything that appealed to her, and she gently replied, "No, I won't be buying anything. I don't like to brag about where I've been."

We nodded in understanding. But the next morning after breakfast when we were all heading to skiffs to fish, we looked at the cap she was wearing. Embroidered above the bill was: "Andros Island—Bahamas."

JUST THE FACTS
Name of Lodge: Bair's Lodge
Location: South Andros Island, Bahamas
Nearest Airport: Congo Town (MYAK)
Drive from Airport to Lodge: Twenty-seven minutes

Getting There: There are many commercial flights to Nassau where connections to Western Air to Congo Town are regularly scheduled. Watermakers flies nonstop from Fort Lauderdale to Congo Town.

Capacity: Sixteen guests

Rate for Five Nights Lodging, Four Days Fishing: $6,950 (2025 rates)

Includes: Guided fishing, lodging, all meals, transfer from airport, double occupancy, shared skiff, open bar

Does Not Include: VAT, tips, airfare

Website: www.bairslodge.com

Author Comments: As you can see, Bair's Lodge is pricier than some of its competitors. Is it worth it? Well, perhaps the fact that I've made repeat visits says something about that. The lodge itself is absolutely dreamy, from down pillows on the four-poster beds to serious cuisine, nice wines, and its setting right on the ocean. And yes, I believe I recall that guests get something like a chocolate on their pillow with the turndown service. It may go without saying that the staff at Bair's is always professional and highly attentive. To say Bair's is lady-friendly is a gross understatement. South Andros is crawling with bonefish, many of which are "hogs." It seems to me a preponderance of Bair's guests prefer the long run in the skiffs to the south, even fishing as far as Jackfish Channel. I have had some outstanding fishing there; in fact, I remember breaking my rod trying to land a double-digit fish while wading with guide Gary. We got one hand on him before he found his freedom—no opportunity for even a measurement. But my preference is fishing the nearby creeks. Deep Creek, in particular, opens up to a vast area of flats, and I have found the fish there to be every bit as large as anywhere else in the fishery. Quicker and easier to get to, therefore expanded fishing hours, fish just as big—Deep Creek is usually my request.

Twenty

Stopped for a Loss!

One of my favorite Bahamas bonefish guides is Andros Island–based Andy Smith. He comes from storied lineage as his late father was "Crazy Charlie" Smith, who enjoyed that nickname for a long time before he invented the world-famous Crazy Charlie bonefish fly. The axiom "necessity is the mother of invention" applies here. That's because many years ago the pressure was on for Charlie to produce satisfying bonefish catches as he guided two prominent visitors at his Bang Bang Club located on Pot Cay in the Andros Island archipelago. Those visitors were prime ministers of their respective countries—Pierre Trudeau of Canada and Lynden Pindling of Charlie's own Bahamas. Charlie Smith designed and tied his new fly on the spot and hit the flats with his important guests. The Crazy Charlie produced three large bonefish for the Canadian prime minister but only two for his Bahamian prime minister Pindling, whose nickname for Charlie was "Life."

Back at the Bang Bang Club, Pindling said to Charlie, "Life, that new fly of yours is no good. Only two fish for me and three for Trudeau!"

"Prime Minister," Charlie replied, smiling. "We must take care of our visitors. They might want to come back."

CRAZY CHARLIE

Crazy Charlie Smith was born in 1936 on Grand Cay, which is a piece of rocky Bahamian land tucked up against the southeast corner of the better-known Walkers Cay. His dad taught him fishing at age seven, and by the time he was eight, he became a guide, such as it was, as his father would send anglers with him because Charlie had learned where the fish were to a better extent than his dad. At age thirteen, Charlie went to Grand Bahama to work at the missile base that was there then and was transferred to Autec on Andros when he was eighteen. Later he became the chef at the Lighthouse Club in Fresh Creek and a yacht captain, jobs he did in parallel with singing in public accompanied by his own accomplished banjo and guitar playing. And, of course, he fished. In 1960, he became bonefish guide and fly-tier extraordinaire and opened his own bonefish lodge, Charlie's Haven. He lost the lodge to fire in 1983 and took over the Bang Bang Club. Charlie guided the likes of baseball's Ted Williams, writer Ernest Hemingway, the big band era's Benny Goodman, tenor and movie star Mario Lanza, and golfer Jack Nicklaus. Along the way, he became the father of fifteen sons and nine daughters. Three of those sons, Andy, Prescott, and Benry, own and operate their own bonefish lodges, all on Andros Island.

Charlie Smith's son Andy, with his football offensive guard's physique, looks nothing like his slender dad. Instead, he's a gentle giant who wears a perpetually pleasing smile and is as unflappable as anyone I know. Moreover, his talent and resourcefulness as an entrepreneur are formidable.

What do I mean by that? Well, I have found most Bahamian bonefish lodges designed and built by local Bahamians are rather basic if not spartan while those built by offshore interests are more involved, elaborate, and luxurious. This is not to be critical of the former category. On the contrary, they are all attractive, comfortable, and have a parochial, tropical charm that is inimitable. It's why I'm a frequent guest.

But Andy Smith *with his own hands* built his Broad Shad Cay Lodge (located on...yep, Broad Shad Cay in the North Bight of Andros) in a way that blends substantial luxury and comfort with the local flavor so many of us anglers treasure. Self-sufficient with its own power generation, satellite, and water system, it's a petite gem that takes only four rods in its two spacious rooms, each sporting matching luxurious four-poster queen beds. And the tasteful common room features a sitting area and library alongside the dining area. Andy, who eats fish every night of his life, always dines with his guests and is an engaging raconteur.

I've had some wonderful fishing with Andy whose guiding skills are surpassed by no one I know. And, interestingly, he has two brothers who also own bonefish lodges on Andros—Benry Smith with his Red Bay Sunset Lodge, and Prescott Smith with his Stafford Creek Lodge. I've fished with both, and their guiding skills equal Andy's (the apple didn't fall far from Crazy Charlie's tree).

THE BANG BANG CLUB

A man named Hank Thorne built the Bang Bang Club in 1936 on Pot Cay. It's in a magical, palm tree–ringed setting with coral stone cottages and private baths surrounded by lush tropical gardens. But now it's closed and crumbling in neglect. I regret never staying there, but I've ridden by it in guide skiffs many times while fishing Andros.

How did the Bang Bang Club get its name? Well, I can tell you how it did not. I was often told that since Al Capone was a guest there it became known as...well...bang bang. Not true. Instead, the name was bestowed by Mr. Thorne, the founder, because he built the club for duck and boar hunting. It was much later that fly-fishing anglers took over the place, many of whom were guided by Crazy Charlie himself. The noteworthy list of visiting anglers included Williams, Hemingway, Goodman, and Lanza along with JFK's dad Joseph Kennedy, Frank Sinatra and his "Rat Pack," and famous anglers Joe Brooks and Lee Wulff.

Of Andy's two bonefish-guide brothers, Prescott is perhaps the more interesting, as his political activism has made him somewhat controversial. In fact, one day when I fished with him, he was frequently on a cell phone with the Bahamian prime minister. His dad, Crazy Charlie Smith, often said Prescott should *run* for prime minister. I have no idea what these phone conversations were about, but I do understand that, to Prescott's credit, he was instrumental in preventing the government's approval of mining aragonite in Andros' bonefish- and birdlife-rich Joulter Cays.

It's Prescott who is famous for his demonstration of casting into a strong wind. He did it with us on the water one day by getting his skiff up on a plane running at thirty miles per hour and asking me to take the helm and run the boat in a straight line on the open water. He grabbed my 8-weight rod and stripped out *all the fly line*. He then carefully climbed up on the casting platform (the water we were running in was fairly calm) and began casting the entire fly line straight at twelve o'clock on the bow—essentially into the teeth of a thirty-mile-per-hour wind—with what appeared to be the greatest of ease. He did this right-handed after which he changed hands and cast the entire fly line into that wind with his left hand! I'm still trying to figure out if I was more impressed or humiliated.

Prescott and his sister, Stacy, who is the culinary-trained chef at his lodge, dearly loved their dad Crazy Charlie Smith. One evening, we got to talking about Crazy Charlie, who was still living at that time. The two siblings were bemoaning their dad's insistence that his doctor told him he needed to drink eight glasses of red wine each night.

"We're still trying to find that doctor," they said, in unison.

I've made a number of visits to Andy Smith's Broadshad Cay Lodge and most of the time been fortunate enough to fish with Andy himself. But that doesn't mean Andy does not use other guides who are excellent. In fact, I am in Andy's debt for introducing me to an outstanding guide named Shawn Riley, who lives about halfway between Andy's and his brother Benry's lodge and fishes for both.

My first exposure to Shawn was the year I took my entire family to Andros for the Thanksgiving holiday. Thanks to Andy Smith referring us, we hired Shawn for the entire trip for bonefishing, yellowtail fishing, and lobster diving. He was fabulous. I took my grandsons and son bonefishing on different days, and I still treasure a picture of my older grandson Matthew and me holding our double-header six-pound bonefish Shawn guided us to in Conch Sound near the northeast corner of Andros Island. I also have a picture of grandson Will with a bonefish that easily went seven pounds.

But it was the time Patti and I were fishing with Shawn out of Andy's Broadshad Cay Lodge that the craziest thing happened. We were fishing pretty close to the lodge, poling in Turtle Sound near Big Wood Cay. The bottom there is one of pristine beauty, mostly hard-packed white sand but of varying depths depending on which small cay we poled around.

As we made our way around one of those small cays, the water became too shallow to pole just when Shawn saw a school of a half dozen nice bonefish tailing about a hundred yards away from us—way out of casting range. I was on the bow at the time.

"Frank, it's too shallow for me to pole to those fish, you'd better get out. You won't need your booties on this bottom."

Following Shawn's instructions, my rod and I quickly slid over the side of the skiff to begin stealthily pursuing our very attractive prey. As bonefish often do, the small school seemed to keep the same distance between them and the angler (me) as I advanced on them. But persistence and continued stealth finally brought me within casting range and delivered me the thrill of catching and releasing a member of the school, a meritorious bonefish I judged to be between four and five pounds.

That's when it got interesting. The area in which I was wading opened up into a much larger area of the exact type of bottom and depth and, looking up into that area, I saw more fish! In fact, a lot more. I called for Shawn, and he quickly exited the skiff and, after a while, caught up to me to join my pursuit of these newly sighted fish. Again, the fish seemed to maintain a constant distance between us, which took quite a while to reduce to casting range.

When we finally got close enough, and after a few misfires, I hooked a fish in the six-pound range that made my reel scream in mechanized agony. I hung on, rod held high in case there was any rocky bottom we had not seen, and listened to the sweet sound of my whirring Orvis reel. After a rather lengthy fight and with the fish finally at our knees, Shawn grabbed the leader to release the fish.

That's when it happened.

The tippet broke just above the fly.

That left Shawn holding a limp piece of leader. And in the next instant, this horrifying realization hit me: I had exited the skiff to only— I thought at the time—fish the small school we saw. I neglected to do what I *always* do when getting out to wade: grab my box of flies!

A glance ahead of us revealed lots more fish. That made me crane my neck to look back at the skiff where we had left Miss Patti. Without realizing it, we had waded so far that Patti looked like a mere dot on the horizon. In the next instant, my eyes met Shawn's, and we simultaneously glanced down at the just broken-off six-pound bonefish, both fully understanding that the fly in his mouth was the only one this side of our very distant skiff. The fish began to slowly swim away with our solitary fly, getting farther and farther away from our reach.

While the speed and power of a hooked bonefish can almost melt a fly reel, a fish that has just been caught is tuckered out and swims away sluggishly after being released. But not that sluggishly. Shawn didn't hesitate. Not a small man, he began churning his tree-trunk legs like a paddle wheel on a river boat as he sprang into action chasing that released bonefish across our flat. The resulting disturbance in the water from a distance probably looked like fifty commodes flushing at once. After his zig-zagging, raucous pursuit of perhaps fifty yards, Shawn was close to beaching the fish on a part of the flat that had substantially shallowed up. I'll always remember what happened next:

Shawn Reilly proceeded to tackle that bonefish.

Stopped him for a loss!

Before releasing the fish, a now soaking-wet Shawn retrieved my fly. When I caught up with him, he tied it back on my tippet, and after waving to Patti, we continued fishing.

THE CRAZY CHARLIE FLY

Born of necessity when Prime Minister Trudeau visited, the Crazy Charlie was a glass minnow pattern with bead chain eyes. It was an immediate hit and is now used with continued success by anglers worldwide. But the Crazy Charlie was not its original name; instead it was a different one given to it by its creator. When he first tied the fly and began *absolutely destroying* bonefish with it, Charlie Smith remarked, "Mon, dat fly is NASTY." Consequently, as the fly began its storied history, it bore the moniker Nasty Charlie. Then along came a prominent San Francisco angler named Bob Nauheim, who founded Fishing International, a sport-fishing travel agency. He asked Charlie Smith if he could change the name from Nasty Charlie to Crazy Charlie and got agreement. He took it back to the States and showed it to Orvis owner Leigh Perkins, who put it in the Orvis catalog, after which worldwide sales of the fly soared.

JUST THE FACTS—ANDY SMITH'S LODGE

Lodge Name: Broadshad Cay Lodge

Location: On a cay in the North Bight of Andros Island, Bahamas, accessible by water

Nearest Airport: Fresh Creek Airport (MYAF)

Drive from Airport to Lodge: Twenty-six minutes to Behring Point by taxi, then about twenty-five minutes by boat to the lodge

Getting There: Numerous commercial flights to Nassau and either Le Air to Fresh Creek or charters. Watermakers Air direct from Fort Lauderdale or private charters.

Capacity: Four guests

Rate for Five Nights Lodging, Four Days Fishing: $4,571 (2025 rates)

Includes: Guided fishing, lodging, all meals, open bar, double occupancy, shared skiff, ferry from Behring Point to the lodge.

Does Not Include: Taxi from airport to Behring Point, VAT, tips

Website: www.broadshadcaylodge.com

Author Comments: Andy's lodge features a positively *superb* location. It gives anglers who may be based on the eastern shore of Andros a nice leg up on the long ride in a skiff to The Land of the Giants and to other hangouts for large fish on the west side of the island. The lodge itself is a pleasing blend of luxury and old Bahamian charm, and kudos to Andy for pulling it off. Remember, he built the place with his own hands—a very talented, resourceful man. You'll not find haute cuisine but will enjoy as good a Bahamian fare as anywhere in the islands. And there's just something deliciously elite about being on a private Bahamian island when you're the only folks in the lone structure there. Andy Smith's guiding chops are not surpassed by anyone, and his charm and graciousness as a host are a delight that is always treasured by all of us who have been his guests.

JUST THE FACTS—PRESCOTT SMITH'S LODGE

Lodge Name: Stafford Creek Lodge

Location: On Stafford Creek about halfway between Fresh Creek and Nichols Town, east side of Andros Island

Nearest Airport: Fresh Creek Airport (MYAF) or San Andros (MYAN)

Drive from Airport to Lodge: Twenty-seven minutes

Getting There: Numerous commercial flights to Nassau and either Le Air scheduled flights to Fresh Creek or charters. Watermakers Air direct from Fort Lauderdale or private charters.

Capacity: Eight guests

Rate for Five Nights Lodging, Four Days Fishing: $4,898 (2025 rates)

Includes: Lodging, guided fishing, all meals, double occupancy, shared skiff

Does Not Include: Airport transfer, VAT, tips, alcoholic beverages

Website: www.staffordcreeklodge.com

Author Comments: Prescott Smith's Stafford Creek Lodge occupies a lovely setting right on the creek on the inland side of the Queen's Highway. The physical plant is spacious and luxurious, definitely lady friendly. And Prescott's sister Stacy's culinary-school-trained cuisine is exemplary. It's a walk of but a few feet to the skiffs, which are modern, comfortable, stable, well-appointed Mavericks. The fishery is vast as anglers staying at this lodge can quickly access a range of water all the way up and down the east coast of the island where the mammoth bonefish can be found that typically hang around near the ocean. Stafford Creek opens up into its own large fishery and features—guess what?—some pretty good-sized tarpon. Patti and I each jumped one fishing them with Prescott. And there's more. Depending on weather and tides, Prescott will sometimes trailer his guests to Red Bays on the west side of Andros. He actually launches right at his brother Benry's lodge.

Just the Facts—Benry Smith's Lodge

Lodge Name: Red Bay Sunset Lodge

Location: Red Bays on northwest shore of Andros Island, Bahamas

Nearest Airport: San Andros Airport (MYAN)

Drive from Airport to Lodge: Thirty minutes

Getting There: Numerous commercial flights to Nassau, then Western Air. Watermakers Air direct from Fort Lauderdale or private charter.

Capacity: Eight guests

Rate for Five Days Lodging, Four Days Fishing: $5250 (2025 rates)

Includes: Guided fishing, lodging, all meals, house wine, double occupancy, shared skiff

Does Not Include: Airfare, airport transfers, VAT, tips

Website: www.redbaysunset.com

Author Comments: Benry Smith's lodge is unique in two ways. First, to get there from the San Andros airport, one must drive through a fascinating, still-thriving settlement of Seminole Indians. How did they get there? The settlement was founded in the early 1800s by a group of Seminoles and escaped black slaves fleeing Florida during the Seminole Wars. These migrating Seminoles were inspired by stories of a tropical island sanctuary. The black Seminoles of Red Bays are known for their unique culture that includes weaving, basketmaking, and working with wood and fabric. The other uniqueness of Benry's lodge is its strategic location. It's perched on the northwest coast of Andros Island, which offers its anglers access to a vast fishery on the west side of the island known for big fish. But the west side is also known for becoming unfishable after several days of west winds make the shorelines too milky from the resulting tumbling sandy bottom. However, if you're staying at Red Bay Sunset Lodge…no problem, Mon. Because the lodge has easy access to the marvelous fishery that is the Joulter Cays and beyond to areas like Conch Sound. While Benry's lodge is not quite as luxurious as those of his brothers, it is comfortable and very well-appointed. And wife Diane runs a tight ship that includes as tasty a Bahamian fare at the table as anywhere in the islands.

Twenty-One

Lord Jim

This has nothing to do with the protagonist of Joseph Conrad's classic novel. Nobody, including me, called my now dearly departed friend Jim Weeks by the handle "Lord Jim" (I'm just using it with great affection as a title for this chapter). Instead, his buddies often called him "Weeks"— usually "Hey, Weeks!"—followed by whatever comment or jibe was at hand. This verbal salutation often drew Jim's grinning rejoinder: "That's MISTER Weeks to you!"

Jim Weeks was the quintessential Midwesterner whose life embodied those solid values. From a little town in Ohio, he went to Ohio University, not the massive Ohio State. There he met and later married the lovely daughter of a Columbus orthodontist. She occasionally dated her high school classmate Jack Nicklaus. Her maiden name was Miller, and Jim called her "Mills."

After college and a hitch in the Army, Jim and "Mills" moved to our little Central Florida town of Lakeland to begin his job selling Brach Candy. He had only one customer. It was Publix Supermarkets, an industry giant now sporting around 1,400 stores across eight southern states. After Chicago-based Brach transferred Jim around the country a few times, he'd had enough. He resigned, moved back to his beloved Lakeland, and transitioned from candy to finance as he entered the equipment-leasing industry, eventually founding his own successful firm.

So, what does my dearly departed friend Jim Weeks have to do with fly fishing? Well, I introduced him to Marsh Harbour on Great Abaco

Island in the Bahamas, and it wasn't long before he and Mills built a lovely waterfront home that included a dock. With the abundance of nearby flats, I then convinced him to become a fly-fishing angler and taught him casting as best I could. Before long, he had cleaned out his nearest Orvis store—Allen Wyatt's Andy Thornal Company in Winter Haven, Florida. Jim and I then embarked on a multi-year sporting odyssey chasing bonefish on the flats on Abaco and other Bahamian islands. It was quite a ride.

Jim had a sign on his Marsh Harbour house with the same name as his thirty-one-foot Ocean Master center console offshore boat. That name was *LEA-SING* (in a Polynesian font), after his chosen industry, and we would always have fun with taxi drivers from the airport saying we were going to the Chinese couple's house. His wife's little Boston Whaler, on the other hand, was named *MILLS*.

Patti and I had some wonderful trips visiting Jim and his wife at the "LEA-SING" house in Marsh Harbor. And there were many gentlemen angler trips there that included David and Jay Kennedy from Tampa, Philip Vaiden from Memphis, and Ron Clark from Lakeland.

GREAT ABACO AND MARSH HARBOUR

The original inhabitants of the Abacos were the Lucayan Indians, a branch of the Tainos. But when Columbus came, he brought to the New World diseases to which the natives had never been exposed. By 1520, most had disappeared. In 1783, about 1,500 British Loyalists fled New York after the American Revolution and settled on Great Abaco at Carleton Point, which is near present-day Treasure Cay. They planted cotton in 1785, which was a good strategy for a few years until caterpillars and other pests took over. Many of these settlers moved away, but Abaco today has perhaps the largest white population of all the islands, mostly descendants of the original Loyalists. There is a good concentration of them on Man O' War Cay, where their boat building still endures and another concentration in Marsh Harbour that became the commercial center of the Abacos.

Our fishery for those trips based from Jim's Marsh Harbour house was the famous Marls of Abaco, a vast area of cays and flats due west from Marsh Harbour extending all the way to the twenty-foot depths of the Bight of Abaco. It gets its name from the nature of the bottom, which is…well, marly. Many believe that the entirety of the Marls is soft and unwadable, but there is some bottom hard enough to provide some excellent wade-fishing.

I once jumped a large tarpon in the Marls. On a bead-eye bonefish fly! The fight was over almost before it began, and I haven't seen one there since. I've seen a few permit on the outer cays but never really got a good shot. But bonefish? No shortage of those. In fact, the Marls may be the most dependable fishery in the Bahamas as the bonefish are always there, and they are always cooperative. The only downside is they are (almost) always small. The run of the Marls flats is fish in the two-to-three-pound range, but I have caught some six-pounders there and have hooked and lost larger ones on the outer cays near the Bight of Abaco, which is closer to the ocean.

GOT ANY COPPERTONE?

Over the years, I have sometimes taken friends, new to the game of fly fishing, on my trips and tried to help them learn it. One of these times I took a friend from my hometown to fish the Marls off the west side of Great Abaco in the Bahamas. I chose that fishery because of its plentiful, accommodating fish. He casted pretty well for a rookie. In fact, he put the fly in front of some number of bonefish in a row, but uncharacteristically for friendly Marls bones, they refused his fly. A couple of fly changes later, it was still happening when he remarked that he was having trouble stripping. "What do you mean?" the guide and I asked simultaneously. "Well, my hands are slippery from all the sunscreen I keep putting on; I don't want to get burned." The guide and I rolled our eyes and gave each other a look that said, "Bingo!" We then explained to my friend that, while bonefish don't see all that great, their sense of smell is acute. We made him lean over the side and use the mud of the marly bottom as soap for a sunscreen-ridding hand wash. Afterwards, he began regularly hooking fish. Some guides I've fished with even recommend rubbing your fly in the bottom—mud, sand, whatever—before making your first cast.

"The 2015 Hannan study tells us that sunscreen has deleterious effects when bonefishing in two ways. One is that, with their keen sense of smell, bonefish may refuse flies handled by anglers with excessive sunscreen on their hands. The other is that handling a landed bonefish with sunscreen-laden hands can diminish the chances of that fish surviving on its release."

–Dr. Aaron Adams, Director of Science and Conservation, Bonefish & Tarpon Trust

We always fished the Marls with the same two guides: Town Williams and Terrence Davis.

Edmund "Town" Williams was born on Abaco and, like so many Bahamians, lives off the sea. That means not only guiding bonefish anglers but also diving for lobster and fish and selling them, catching fish on hook and line and selling them, and subsistence fishing. Town always lived in Spring City, a sort of "suburb" of Marsh Harbour. At least until he became divorced and began spending lots of time in Freeport on Grand Bahama with his new lady friend.

I can't remember who referred me to Town, but I do remember having two days booked with him the first time we fished. We had a typical day of Marls bonefishing—lots of shots, lots of fish, lots of fun. When he dropped me off after that first day I said, "Well, Cap, that was a mighty fine day of fishing. See you in the morning—same time, same station?"

As I reached for the door handle on his truck, Town said, "Okay, but you gonna pay me?"

I already had the truck door open. "Of course I'm going to pay you," I said. "But we're fishing again tomorrow."

"I'd like you to pay me for today," he said.

"Okay," I said, a little irritated. "But this is like going to a restaurant and having to pay after each course."

Town just looked at me in silence, so I reached for my wallet and paid him. He showed up right on time the next morning—Town is always right on time or even a little early—and we had another fine day in the Marls.

This was the only little rough spot Town and I ever had. After that, Jim Weeks and our buddies, staying in Jim's "LEA-SING" house, fished with him for many years, and we became close friends. I often just chatted with Town on the phone even when I wasn't on island. One of Patti's paintings of certain unique rock formations near the shore of the Abaco mainland in the Marls hangs in Town's home.

Town was always short of money and did not mind telling us that, but our relationship was so close that Jim Weeks did something extraordinary. He bought Town a shiny, red Ford F-150 truck after his old one expired. It wasn't new but close to it. Jim's deal with Town was that he would be repaid for the truck by applying his guide fees to the amount until it was satisfied. I never learned if it was ever completely paid off.

I understand Town has recently acquired a new skiff. His old one needed replacing worse than his old truck because, though always clean as a whistle, it was an ancient Dolphin that would jar your fillings returning to the dock in a stiff chop.

One time Ron Clark and I were fishing with Town on the outer cays of the Marls, a very long way from the dock, when a weather system moved in between us and the mainland of Abaco Island. The day was about finished, and we had no choice but to run into the teeth of the storm. We put on all our jackets with our raingear on top of that and Ron and I sat on the cooler in front of the center console. Town turned his old Dolphin into waves that, despite our running on skinny-water flats, seemed mountainous. The rain kept visibility to near zero and our internal organs wailed in agony each jarring time the flat-bottomed Dolphin slammed into the next wave. Our rainsuits were leaking, and we were counting the minutes until it all ended. That's when I felt Ron nudge me with his elbow. I turned to him and managed to see enough of his face under his rainsuit hood to realize he was grinning.

"What?" I yelled over the noise of the engine and the storm, still looking at him.

The grin continued as he yelled back, "Frank. You know, it just doesn't get any better than this!"

We all pitched in to help Town in other ways. We considered it a privilege to be blessed enough in our own lives to be able to send Town money to help him rebuild after Hurricane Dorian.

And it was our fellow angler Philip Vaiden from Memphis that gave Town some special help. We were all staying in Jim's LEA-SING house as usual. Jim had an SUV there that got us all to the dock to fish and out to Marsh Harbour restaurants such as Mango's and Wally's for dinner. Off we went to the dock at the Marls to meet our guides, one of which was, as always, Town. Philip and I were fishing with Town that day. We boarded his skiff, got all our rods and gear situated, and shoved off from the dock.

We got about 100 feet before Town's engine quit.

Permanently.

It was a few minutes after eight, the full fishing day ahead of us, and here we were—drifting.

However, by 9:45 we were running on a plane in Town's skiff to the flats of the Marls to find that day's bonefish. How did that happen? When his outboard expired, Town poled us back to the dock, we pulled his skiff on his trailer, got in his shiny red F-150 Jim had bought him, and drove to the Yamaha outboard dealer in Marsh Harbour. A quick mount of a new engine purchased by Philip Vaiden's credit card allowed us to get in almost an entire day of fishing. As with the F-150 truck, I never learned if Philip ever recovered the total amount of the new engine by offsetting Town's guide fees. But in both cases, I feel sure it was most of the amount, if not all.

The other guide we fished with staying at Jim's house was Town's brother-in-law, Terrence Davis, whose nickname around Abaco was "See-Bo." He was a real character and, unlike the introvert Town, always jovial, but his perpetual disgorgement of technical savvy could be didactic. Terrence was a fixture in Marsh Harbour as he was known as the "Conch Salad Man." He had his own stand in downtown Marsh

Harbour where locals would scarf up all the fresh conch salad he could make for them. But the locals were not the only ones. Indeed, our crew of anglers were welcome recipients when Terrence would set up shop in Jim's kitchen and go to town making his special conch salad.

When this was followed by Ron Clark's superb cooking and some of the first and second growth red Bordeaux he brought…well, life was good at Jim Week's "LEA-SING" house in Marsh Harbour.

Terrence taught his brother-in-law Town bonefish guiding, and we considered the two of them professional equals. Once Jim and I were fishing with Terrence, and Jim hooked a bonefish that was larger than many in the Marls. After a boisterous initial run, Jim's line suddenly went limp. This was perplexing to us because the run the fish made was to an open flat with a smooth, sandy bottom—no rocks to aid the fish in breaking Jim off. I climbed up on the bow with Jim, looked down in the water, and saw what had happened. The fly line had separated from the end of the backing and was lying in the water motionless in front of us. (When bonefish believe they are "free," they usually stop running.) Jim got down on his belly, picked up the end of the fly line, and proceeded to hand line the nice Marls four-pounder to the boat.

After our high fives, I asked Jim if he was aware that Bahamians, when fishing from the shore for food, routinely use a hand line. I added that the Bahamian hand line is often called a "Cuban Yo-Yo."

Jim broke out in his usual broad grin before saying, "Well, you can just start calling me Yo-Yo Weeks!" Which we did for the rest of that trip.

Terrence was one of the most resourceful guides I've ever known. He was undaunted. Once when he was guiding us on a mothership at Moore's Island, the air-conditioning on the yacht failed. The captain found the culprit—a simple generic part. It was almost dark but Terrence got in his skiff, made the three-hour round-trip run to Marsh Harbour, and somehow returned with the part, amazing all of us.

But sometimes Terrence could get a little too resourceful. Once he had a gig to deliver a new center console offshore boat from Florida to Treasure Cay on the east side of Great Abaco, but the boat wasn't quite ready, causing a very late stateside departure. He made it in complete darkness across the Gulf Stream okay, but when he was coming around the northeast side of Abaco near Spanish Cay, he hit a bank of rocks at full speed. The new boat was destroyed, and Terrence spent months in the hospital in Nassau and more time after that getting his mouth and teeth rebuilt.

Years later, still undaunted, Terrence went with two friends yellowtail snapper fishing in the Atlantic, offshore and due east of Marsh Harbour. It was a small boat, an old twenty-two-foot Mako center console. The weather turned bad, and the boat capsized. His two friends clung to the inverted hull of the Mako, but Terrence, still too resourceful for his own good, insisted on swimming to shore for help. Tragically, our friend Terrence "See-Bo" Davis was never seen again.

I have had falls on boats, on rocky flats bottoms, and in rivers. But my injuries have never been particularly serious.

I can't say the same for my dear friend Jim Weeks. Once we were fishing the Joulter Cays on the extreme north side of Andros Island, each of us on different skiffs. The Joulters is almost purely a wade fishery featuring crystal-white flats that stretch for miles and are covered with beautiful bonefish and the occasional tarpon. Some Bahamas flats are tricky and difficult to wade with bottoms that are either "lumpy" with mounds, soft, or even rocky. Joulters flats, on the other hand, are uniformly smooth and sandy. Wading them is almost like taking a stroll on a concrete sidewalk.

Our guide's cell phone rang with a call from Jim's guide with news that surprised me. Our guide relayed that Jim had stepped in some kind of hole and was calling it a day. It never occurred to me that he was actually hurt in any way, but when we got back to our guide's rental house where we were staying, I found out differently. Jim's lower leg had almost all its skin peeled off, and he was in terrible pain. It was a grotesque sight, and it scared the hell out of me.

One of our guides made a phone call and then took Jim and me to the airport where we boarded a chartered Piper Aztec. Twenty minutes later, Jim and I had crossed the Tongue of the Ocean and arrived at the Nassau airport. Twenty more minutes and we were in the hospital emergency room where he received what appeared to me to be expert treatment for his wound administered with attentiveness and courtesy. Jim went home to Florida the next day and spent lots of time thereafter at the wound center of Lakeland, Florida's highly regarded Watson Clinic.

My dear friend—Lord Jim, I'm calling him here—was never really the same after that. Before long, his dementia and some accompanying physical problems developed and finally took him from us. He was one of those special humans who redefined the concepts of thoughtfulness of and kindness toward his fellow man. He was a giver, not a taker. I loved him dearly and miss him constantly.

If you're looking to bonefish the famous Marls of Abaco, you can't go wrong with my old friend, Town Williams (242-359-6013). But there are other independent guides that fish the Marls, like Marty Sawyer (242-366-2115), Danny Sawyer (242-367-3577), or Jody Albury (242-375-8068). Plus, there are two lodges that fish the Marls: Abaco Bonefish Lodge and The Delphi Club.

JUST THE FACTS

Name of Lodge: Abaco Bonefish Lodge (owned by Nervous Waters)

Location: Just south of Marsh Harbour on the shore of the Marls

Nearest Airport: Marsh Harbour (Leonard M. Thompson Intl.—MHH)

Drive from Airport to Lodge: Eleven minutes

Getting There: Delta flies nonstop from Atlanta and Watermakers from Fort Lauderdale. There are many commercial flights to Nassau with connections to Marsh Harbour on Western or Bahamas air.

Capacity: Twelve guests

Rate for Five Nights Lodging, Four Days Fishing: $6,950 (2025 rates)

Includes: Lodging, guided fishing, all meals, open bar, airport transfers

Does Not Include: Airfare, VAT, tips

Website: www.abacolodge.com

Author Comments: Closed for an extended time after being severely damaged by Hurricane Dorian, this Nervous Waters–owned lodge is now fully restored and once again thriving. Only eleven minutes from the Marsh Harbour airport, it's strategically located right on the shores of the Marls. A walk of less than 100 feet and anglers are in their skiffs each morning ready to roar off in the lodge's skiffs in attack mode. Like other Nervous Waters properties, the lodge is luxurious, the cuisine formidable, and the hospitality warm and attentive. Of course, the most important thing at any lodge is the guides, and Abaco Lodge's are as solid as they get. I actually stayed at Abaco Lodge and fished the Marls from there before it was Abaco Lodge. Back then, it was called The Sunset. It had sleeping rooms and a restaurant that was open to the public. Four of us fished with Town Williams and Terrence Davis. Not long after Fernando of Nervous Waters and good-guy Oliver White acquired it and turned it into Abaco Lodge, I dined there as Oliver's guest. It was the first time I met the outstanding chap (and superb angler) who is now my friend and sometimes fishing companion: Dave Perkins of the Orvis Company. Be assured, you will have a good experience at Abaco Lodge.

SOME MORE FACTS—DIFFERENT LODGE

Name of Lodge: The Delphi Club

Location: Twenty-five miles south of Marsh Harbour on the Queen's Highway

Nearest Airport: Marsh Harbour (Leonard M. Thompson Intl.—MHH)

Drive from Airport to Lodge: Thirty-three minutes

Getting There: Delta flies nonstop from Atlanta and Watermakers from Fort Lauderdale. There are many commercial flights to Nassau with connections to Marsh Harbour on Western or Bahamasair.

Capacity: Twenty guests

Rate for Five Nights Lodging, Four Days Fishing: $6,850 (2025 rates)

Includes: Lodging, guided fishing, all meals, shared room and skiff, airport transfers, VAT

Does Not Include: Airfare, alcoholic beverages, tips

Website: www.delphi-bahamas.com

Author Comments: The Delphi Club's physical plant is spectacular. It's located right on the Atlantic Ocean high on a bluff offering dazzling views of the water. A series of stairs lead guests down to a beach beautiful enough to make anybody's postcard. The sumptuousness of the lodge challenges description. This is a down-pillow, marble-bathroom affair with large public spaces that are easily reminiscent of a fine private club with all the accompanying appointments, including important artwork. It doesn't stop there as there is an infinity pool, and spa services are available. Naturally, the cuisine and hospitality of the staff are exemplary. When I've been a guest, Delphi took the occasional transient diners when the lodge was not full, and I assume they are continuing that practice. But the pricing of the dinners did a fine job of keeping that clientele polished and congenial. To fish the Marls, Delphi trailers guests a very short distance to a ramp at a place called "Nettie's Cut" (named after a lady who used to have a nearby lodge). But they also trailer to fish a variety of other places, such as Sandy Point, Cherokee Sound, and Crossing Rocks, all excellent. Delphi's guides are as good as you'll find, as is the experience if you go there.

TWENTY-TWO

Now You Tell Us!

When Jim Weeks and I, along with Philip Vaiden and Ed Richmond from Memphis, were planning a saltwater fly-fishing trip, somebody suggested a change of venue followed by the idea: "Why not Mexico?"

Humble Servant (me) did some research and recommended a place called Isla Holbox. We quickly learned that the phonetic pronunciation "ISS-LA HOLE-BOX" got us nowhere. Instead, it's pronounced "EES-LA OLE-BOSHE," so we all became temporarily bilingual and said it that way. "Isla," of course, means "island," and Holbox is, indeed, an island just off the north shore of the Yucatán.

It was advertised as a combination of two fisheries. One was a vast backcountry offering bonefish, juvenile tarpon, and snook. The other was fishing for large tarpon in the open ocean just off the Yucatán where the Gulf of Mexico and the Caribbean merge. Sounded good to us, so off we went.

We flew to Cancún, were picked up in a somewhat dilapidated vehicle, and driven north over roads featuring a preponderance of teeth-rattling potholes. It's only forty miles from Cancún to Isla Holbox, but it took almost three hours just to reach the little village of Chiquila, where we commenced a twenty-minute ferry ride to the island.

Holbox (remember, now...it's OLE-BOSHE) has no cars, only golf carts and some dune buggies. We arrived on the island and were greeted by Alejandro Vega Cruz (whose nickname is "Sandflea"), the head guide and owner of The Tarpon Club. We knew our lodging was not at The Tarpon Club because there is no such facility; rather it is a name for Alejandro's guide service. Instead, we stayed at a lovely hotel named HM Paraiso del Mar that was right on the beach with a stunning view overlooking the confluence of the Gulf of Mexico and the Caribbean Sea.

We began with a review of our fishing program by Alejandro. We had four days of fishing, and it was decided that we'd start with the "ocean" tarpon for two days and finish with two days in the backcountry.

Since we were experienced in ocean tarpon fishing on the outside flats of the Florida Keys, we had our floating lines with us and also the intermediate sink lines we have used tarpon fishing in the slightly deeper Gulf water along the beaches of Boca Grande. But, boy, were we in for a surprise. It turned out that the ocean tarpon fishing at Holbox was unlike anything with which we were familiar.

It was indeed ocean fishing but was the "deep blue sea" kind of ocean. We learned we would be fishing in Panga boats (long, narrow-beamed skiffs with an upswept bow named after the panga fish) in twenty to thirty feet of water as much as five to six miles offshore, and while it would be possible to occasionally see a school of tarpon roll at the surface, most of our fishing would be blind casting. Moreover, we learned that the fly lines we brought would be useless. Instead, we would need 450-grain sinking lines, which are very "heavy" and more difficult to cast, particularly when faced with hours of blind casting.

We all looked at each other and, I am certain, shared the same thought: "*Now* you tell us!"

The next morning, we were on the beach boarding the Panga boats at six. Alejandro had fortunately equipped us with the 450-grain sinking fly lines. That first day was slow, with each boat raising only one fish.

The second day, however, was different. I was fishing with Ed Richmond, and we landed five large tarpon between us, ranging from around eighty to nicely over 100 pounds, according to one of Alejandro's guides we were fishing with. Despite the depth of the water, we were rewarded with some spectacular jumps. But after heaving those sinking lines with one blind cast after another, we got a little lazy. We'd take breaks from the blind casting and wait for schools to roll. When the fish did show, it was momentary, so we learned to anticipate their direction and resume our repeated blind casting.

Ed and I wrapped up our day about a quarter to four and repaired to the hotel for cold cervezas—Dos Equis, I believe—as we waited for Jim Weeks and Philip Vaiden, who were fishing with Alejandro. When they didn't show, we ordered another round along with some nachos, which were quite tasty.

Five o'clock came, and there was no sign of the other boat. We had a clear view of the water from where we were having our cold ones, and our vigilance heightened. At five-thirty, we began to become mildly worried. Six o'clock came, and our worry escalated. By six-thirty, I think it was safe to say we were pretty much frantic.

We decided we must do something. But what?

I previously said the Tarpon Club did not have a facility, but that's not exactly true. While they do not have lodging, dining, or a clubhouse of any kind, they do have on the beach a little shack that provides for some storage and a very small fly shop (without which we would not have had the sinking fly lines). So, Ed and I went to the Tarpon Club, and the place was closed and shuttered.

Next, we tried the hotel front desk—still plenty of daylight, but it was almost seven by now—and we were met with blank looks and shrugs.

"Do you have a cell phone number for Alejandro?" we asked.

More blank looks and shrugs.

"We'd like to see the manager," I said. I knew there was now an edge in my voice.

Presently, a man in a business suit came out and, in excellent English, asked how he could help us. When we explained our situation, he excused himself and was gone almost ten minutes. When he returned, he said, "I found Alejandro's cell phone number, but he did not answer. I am very sorry."

Now we were nearing hysteria.

"Do you have something like the coast guard here?" I asked. "This is an emergency! Please call the authorities!"

He held up his hand and said, "Just a moment." He held his now-vibrating cell phone to his ear. He said nothing but just nodded repeatedly at what was being said on the other end. The call concluded, he said, "Go to the Tarpon Club and wait."

"Wait for what?" my voice was getting shrill now.

The manager displayed a thin smile. "Wait for your friends," he said. "They are on the way in."

Ed and I looked straight at each other and almost lost it. But we quickly gathered ourselves and hustled down to the beach to the little structure that was the Tarpon Club and trained our eyes on the water. In a little over five minutes, Alejandro's Panga boat became visible, up on a plane, and heading right for us.

A casual bystander on the beach looking back and forth between Ed and me and the three occupants of the Panga boat would have been struck by the stark contrast in countenances. Ed and I were on the verge of becoming emotional with relief. But the Panga boat being beached on the sand in front of us was occupied by three grinning, high-five-ing guys—one guide and two anglers—the latter pulling on their bottles of ice-cold Corona that Alejandro had packed in his cooler.

"Man, what a day!" they said almost in unison.

"Where in the hell have y'all been? You scared the crap out of us!" Our question was delivered in a tone that was anything but collegial.

Some more back and forth finally got Ed and me our explanation. It made our testiness dissolve and quickly become jubilation. Like us, they had caught and landed several large tarpon. But around three o'clock, the Memphis Flash—Philip Vaiden—hooked a monster tarpon that only jumped once (and therefore did not tire quickly), and he fought it until right before they came in. Alejandro thought the fish went at least 180 pounds. Philip was using his 11-weight Orvis T-3, and his rod snapped in two at the same moment Alejandro touched the leader and the fish finally jumped, boatside, and drenched the three of them. Completely and classically thrilling.

Philip said he slept like a hibernating grizzly that night. Once back home, he said talking to the Orvis repair department was a blast because, even though it was their company's rod that broke, the guys he talked to were going nuts with excitement hearing Philip's fish story.

The next day, we switched to the backcountry, specifically the Yalahau Lagoon, a gorgeous expanse of mangrove cays and flats filled with a fascinating variety of birdlife. We were thrilled to see flamingos and one small crocodile but did not see any of the jaguars that are purported to be there. While the water on the flats was very clear and beautiful, it was an unusual dark color. Alejandro told us it's how Holbox was named because in English it means "black hole."

As for the fishing, we caught a moderate number of juvenile tarpon and one decent snook that we took to a restaurant and had them cook. But in two days of fishing, we only saw one bonefish and a small one at that.

With the trip over and settling our tips with Alejandro, we asked why there were no bonefish. He hesitated, looked at the sand in front of the Tarpon Club shack as he pawed it with his bare foot, and finally said, "Well...the truth is, two years ago the government started to allow netting of the fish in the backcountry."

The four of us did the same thing as when we found out about the deep-water tarpon fishing—just looked at each other and thought: "*Now you tell us!*"

But make no mistake. Isla Holbox is a stunningly beautiful place. And it is culturally rich with interesting murals on many of the village walls. And, in addition to the birdlife, it's a destination for observing bioluminescence. We were lucky enough to have the right moon phase to see it each night. It's caused by plankton microorganisms that live in the water and create a spectacular neon light show. Isla Holbox. But don't forget how to say it..."EES-LAH OLE-BOSHE."

Just the Facts

The Tarpon Club (remember, it's not a "club"; in fact, it is little more than a tackle shop) has a website (www.tarponclubislaholbox.com), but you could contact any of the top outfitters to get current information on Alejandro (the Sandflea) and his operation. Outfitters like Yellow Dog, Orvis, Frontiers, The Fly Shop, and the like. We booked through The Fly Shop in Reading, California, but there is nothing on their site now about Holbox. Good luck!

Twenty-Three

Pittypat's Pursuit of Piscatorial Pleasure

I have already talked about my best fishing buddy, also my roommate, my sweet wife Patti. Although she bears no resemblance to Laura Hope Crews who played Aunty Pittypat in the classic movie *Gone with the Wind*, and although she has nothing to do with the Atlanta restaurant Pittypat's Porch, her grandchildren have always called her Pittypat. Indeed, the porch at our North Carolina mountain house is dubbed Pittypat's Porch in honor of our family's beloved matriarch.

She may be beloved, but sometimes, I get so mad at her! She never practices her casting, has no clue about fly selection or how or why they are tied, and doesn't know a 5-weight from a 12-weight. But when I hand her a fly rod, she somehow throws this beautiful tight loop, makes precise, delicate presentations, and—dammit—outfishes me more often than I care to admit.

Of course, I secretly love it.

She is a little eccentric about her fishing. Her preferred method to fish the flats is to wade rather than pole. That's because she likes to get *way* off by herself, find her own fish, cast to them, and catch them. Why does she like that over poling the flats? Because when poling she must take her turn on the bow and, when presented with a casting opportunity to a sighted fish, perform under the keen, watchful eyes of both me and our guide. She prefers wading off by herself, free from any self-imposed pressure. I guess it's one of those woman things.

She won't carry a fly box, which means we have to wade all the way to where she is to replace her fly, if necessary. But to her credit, she releases her own fish. But there are exceptions to that. It's when she catches a *really* big one that she calls for help. I suspect it may simply be because she wants us to witness her accomplishment, and I certainly can't fault her for that. On the contrary, it's thrilling to share her joy.

I'll never forget one of her solitary wades at Gorda Cay when she and I were fishing with Ricardo Burrows. She wanted to get way up by the mangrove shoreline and wade in water that was barely mud-puddle depth. Ricardo told her, "You probably won't find anything in there. Too shallow." She ignored that advice, and about twenty minutes later, we heard her whistle. (My wife somehow can whistle as loud as a train approaching a crossing.) Her rod was heavily bowed. Rambunctious splashing told us she was enjoying the thrill of fighting a very large fish in something less than a foot of water. When we finally got to her, we had to wait for the long fight to end and her enormous bonefish to surrender. Ricardo landed that one for her and held it in the water while she graced us with the details.

"He was way up by the mangroves," she said, breathless from the combination of the long fight and her joy. "The water was a little deeper there, and he was tucked up under the branches, so I didn't feel like I could get off a proper cast. So I waited and watched, and sure enough, he started very slowly swimming away from the mangroves right toward me! He was in almost NO water, and I knew he was big because his back was out of the water!"

Ricardo and I looked at each other knowingly. We were trying to maintain a semblance of professional calm but the almost-ignited joy in our guts was just before detonating.

"I made the cast," Patti continued. "I thought I'd over-casted because the fly landed right on his nose. But he ate it before I could even strip. My first strip was the hookup! He went into the backing three times, and I thought I was going to lose him. He only went back toward the mangroves once, and I somehow managed to steer him out. I'm SO happy!"

I weighed her fish in my sling and then released it in excellent shape. It came in at nine and a quarter pounds!

There have been times when Pittypat's desire to be a loner has backfired on her. On one of our Sandy Point trips, we were wade-fishing on the outside of Blackwood Creek near Top Cay Point with Perry Adderley as our guide. Patti, as usual, was off by herself. She had hooked a medium-sized bonefish and, when she got it at close quarters, noticed that she and her fish had some company—a lemon shark, about a four-footer.

No stranger to sharks, Patti horsed her fish in as quickly as possible and de-hooked it. But she had two concerns. One was her reluctance to provide a free lunch to the nearby shark. But another was her desire to create some distance between the angler (Miss Patti) and the shark.

So, with the de-hooked bonefish in her left hand and the shark in front of her, she *flung* the fish with all her might behind her and, therefore, in the opposite direction from the shark. In the process, she strained her shoulder and had to gobble ibuprofen for the rest of the trip. Thankfully, it was not her casting shoulder.

A similar thing happened once at Chub Cay when she was wading a gorgeous, almost-always-productive flat by herself called the Sand Bank. But this time, she had hooked a very large bonefish that drew the attention of a much larger shark, about a six-footer. But she was lucky. Guide David Lightbourne and I had been heading her way anyway in the skiff as it was time for lunch. We arrived just in time for David to give the shark a "graphite sandwich" (poked it hard in the gills with the end of his twenty-foot push pole). The shark fled, and Patti landed her fish, a solid eight-pounder.

Without committing the cardinal sin of revealing a lady's age, I will just say that Pittypat recently determined there were three sporting endeavors she had not yet attempted.

One was to, instead of either the guide or yours truly doing it for her, get out of the skiff herself to wade up into the mangroves following a hooked bonefish that had wound its way around the branches trying to break her off. At Thrift Harbour on Grand Bahama, she pulled that one off with great aplomb. Our guide, Simeon, and I stayed in the skiff, and she was *way* back in the mangroves tediously unwinding fly line and backing from each and every branch.

Eventually, we heard one of her loud whistles. We looked, and she was triumphantly holding her now-landed fish over her head wearing an ear-to-ear grin.

Another thing Patti wanted to accomplish was to take up golf so she could get in on the fun she saw her friends having both on and off the course. The matriarch of our family declared she was going to tackle this frustrating sport "while she was still young." On her own, she called our club pro, took lessons, bought clubs, and is now an enthusiastic player. Is she any good? Well, in her first scramble with the "nine-holers," her tee shot was used on the first par-three hole as it came to rest about eight feet below the hole. Her playing partners suggested she try the first putt, and she drained it for a natural birdie on her own ball!

The third sporting accomplishment Pittypat has her eye on is catching her first permit. Like so many anglers, she's had some shots, had some looks, and...yep, had refusals. That one is still in her future.

Patti is a formidable lady sportsman who, when she hits either the flats or the river, is clad in the latest breathable garb and looks like she just walked out of an Orvis store. But when the sun sets, she is still the consummate, refined lady. She always dresses for cocktails and dinner in flowing, feminine things that, after all these years, keep me very, very interested.

Our beloved matriarch angler has other talents and interests. While she loves our fly-fishing trips, she is often the last one to leave a museum or lovely gardens. To her delight, on one of our trips to Patagonia, she got lucky by ending up with a twofer.

The first was: One of the lodges we visited on this trip was Chile's El Saltamontes Lodge ("The Grasshopper" in English) on 5,000 acres owned by the interesting Gorrono family. The head guide there, whose first language was obviously Spanish, almost every evening dazzled us with his other talent: playing his guitar and singing—guess what?—Beatles songs! He knew every one of them and was fabulous.

The second one was: El Saltamontes had an amazing china collection! It was salvaged from ships sunk in the South China Sea in the

1700s, was mostly blue and white, and very heavy. Lodge guests dined each night on museum-quality artifacts and could admire more of these amazing works of art in elegant display cases, some encrusted with barnacles from centuries under the sea. There's a book about the collection: *The Legacy of the Tek Sing* by Nigel Pickford and Michael Hatcher.

TIME'S UP!

Another reason Miss Patti prefers to wade a bonefish flat rather than be poled is that, instead of alternating on the bow, both anglers can fish!

But when alternating on the bow, how to divvy up the fishing time?

A technique I use will initially draw a smirk or even a good-naturedly derisive comment when I introduce it to a new angling partner. An effective system for sharing the bow is to get on the casting platform for thirty minutes or a caught fish, whichever comes first, whereupon the other angler assumes the bow. (A hookup that results in a reasonably long "run" is equal to a caught fish.)

This system works very well, but the tricky part is the timekeeping. Using one's wristwatch can be problematic because it's not so easy to remember what the wristwatch displayed when the guide issued the order to reel up to move to the next fishing spot.

My technique is simple: a stopwatch. The non-fishing angler simply clicks the watch on when his partner is on the bow, stripped out with fly in hand. If, after some number of minutes of poling, the guide says, "Reel it up, we're moving," another click of the stopwatch obviates the need to remember what the wristwatch read. After arriving at the new flat to be poled, another click easily resumes the remainder of the bow angler's thirty minutes.

After my new angling partners get their snarky comments out of the way and see how efficient the stopwatch is, they have always embraced its use and complimented me on the idea.

Twenty-Four

Ray Charles

"Humble Servant Bonefishing—est. 1986" described the first bonefish I ever caught and how, when I began organizing trips for my angling buddies, I started signing my emailed trip memos, "Your Humble Servant."

I recently had tee shirts made and sent them with compliments to my angling colleagues. On the front of the shirts was an outline of a bonefish along with "Humble Servant Bonefishing—est. 1986." On the back of the shirts were printed phrases frequently spoken by a bonefish guide poling a skiff and his anglers across a flat and here's what it says:

Point your rod—More left, more left—Your other left—Strip, strip, stop—long strip!—Pick it up and go again—They didn't see it—Check that fly—Change that fly—No problem, Mon!—Gimme a backcast, 3 o'clock—3 o'clock, not 9 o'clock!—You're standing on your fly line—No trout set!—Tip down—Long, slow strip—40 feet, 10 o'clock—Drop it!—Leave it—Hand me a Kalik—De-barb your hook—They're coming at you—They turned—Bring it in, we're moving—Don't forget your passport!—That's a 'cuda—That's a shark—It's not the fly—Don't guide the guide—Mon, even Ray Charles could see those fish!—Put your booties on, we're wading—They're going away—Wait on your backcast—The little one ate it—Pick it up and drop it, one cast—Gimme some more distance—They're gone now

I'm the last person on earth with any proclivity to make fun of folks with infirmities like blindness. So, let me stipulate that "Mon, even Ray Charles could see those fish!" did not come from me. Like every other phrase listed, it was spoken to me by a bonefish guide. Early in my bonefishing "career," Chub Cay's David Lightbourne was poling Miss Patti and me in the large area of mangroves just off of Frazier's Hog Cay and I was on the bow. There was a school of fish just hanging right in front of us, begging for a cast. My yet-to-be-sharp-for-flats-fishing eyes couldn't see them to save my life, but David told me how far to cast and in what direction (resulting in no hookup). This was after David, never known for being diplomatic with his anglers but nonetheless one of my favorite guides, uttered the Ray Charles quip. For the very competitive and often testy David, believe me, it was no quip.

THE EYES (OR NOT) HAVE IT!

David Lightbourne showed me something that I've not seen used by any other guides or anglers. It happened when I was wading for bonefish in very skinny water and experiencing two problems. One was spooking the fish on the very shallow flat and other was, when I did get a follow, my fly snagging in the grass, also spooking the fish.

One answer to these problems is a classic fly pattern with no eyes like the Bonefish Special, usually in the orange-and-black color. But here's something even better:

A popular and effective bonefish fly throughout the Bahamas is the Enrico Puglisi spawning shrimp pattern. It's available from most fly catalogs and shops in bead- and lead-eye versions, but the lead eyes make it easier to do what David does and that is break the eyes off with a pair of pliers. David showed me how to take my fishing pliers and twist off the dumbbell-shaped lead eyes on the Puglisi shrimp fly thereby making it a fly with no eyes! The reason this works better than the Bonefish Special is that the Puglisi fly has a fluffy body. That, together with the absence of eyes, makes this large, bushy fly land like a butterfly after it is cast. It can be deadly.

Twenty-Five

Where's the Fire?

The question, "Where's the fire?" always reminds me of a movie, the title of which I cannot recall. It was set in France with an American main character who spoke little or no French. In the movie, he was driving in the French countryside and was stopped for speeding by two local gendarmes who did not speak English. But they did know one English phrase, no doubt acquired by watching an American movie, and when they realized the driver was American, they began salivating over their opportunity to use it. Grinning with delight, their heavy, Inspector Closeau-esque French accents in unison, the two French cops loudly asked the American character: "So, Boody. Waar's the far?" And then they laughed uproariously before saying it again.

This, however, is about a real fire, and it happened in the Joulter Cays.

THE AMAZING JOULTERS

The 92,000-acre Joulter Cays lay just off the north coast of Andros Island, and The Bahamas National Trust has now designated it as a national park.

The Joulters are nature's magnum opus with what seem like thousands of small and large mangrove cays interlaced with broad flats and deep channels that allow bonefish skiffs to access the entire archipelago. A unique feature of Joulters flats is its sand, which, technically speaking, is not really sand. Instead, it's something called oolite. The oolite "grains" are more like tiny, round pellets (think, miniature fish roe) that range in diameter from one-half to one millimeter. The nucleus of these pellets could be a tiny grain of shrimp feces, a grain of conventional sand, or a shell fragment. Oolites are popularly used in aquariums.

The tropical grandeur of the Joulters mesmerizes. Its mangrove islands are home to exotic flora, including lots of stately palm trees. The bird life is an Audubon Society member's dream as the cays are a sanctuary for flamingos and endangered species like the piping plover.

The Joulter Cays abound with large schools of bonefish that cruise and tail on the vast, smooth, oolite flats, and the ivory bottom yields outstanding visibility on sunny days and good viz even on cloudy days.

To explain how remarkable that visibility is, I can remember a trip with David and Jay Kennedy and Jim Weeks fishing my favorite of the Joulters—Josie Cay—under socked-in clouds that produced a gentle, all-day rain. That alabaster bottom allowed us to easily see the constant strings of cruising bonefish, and we stood in our rain gear and wading booties and caught them all day long.

Joulters bonefish are not known for their size, but the outer cays (closer to the Tongue of the Ocean) hold some big boys, along with large permit. As for tarpon, a few reside in the finger channels that wind their way through the Joulters. Intermediate sinking lines are best.

I first fished the Joulters with the guide who was known as "The King of the Joulters"—Philip Rolle, along with his sidekick, the great Elias Griffin. On my initial trip with Philip, we pulled up to our first Joulters flat and, with his usual sparkling grin, he said, "Okay, let's see if we can find some flashing diamonds!'

"Some what?" I asked, perplexed.

"Look over there at nine o'clock, about eighty yards," he said, pointing.

I then understood what "flashing diamonds" were. The angle of the morning sun reflected off the tails of a school of about a dozen bonefish and made them look exactly like that.

My friend Philip's guiding skills were as good as anyone on the planet, and he was the consummate gentleman. It is with great sadness that I use the past tense. You see, Philip and his wife Betsy contracted the coronavirus in 2020, and neither survived. I miss him greatly.

Philip was quite the entrepreneur. He had his own little three-bedroom house for lodging his anglers and would hire a local cook to provide delicious Bahamian fare each evening. And he had street smarts. He was one of just a handful of locals wise enough to move his vehicles to the high ground of Morgan's Bluff (which forms the extreme northeast corner of Andros Island) during vicious Hurricane Matthew.

That storm hit the Nicholls Town/Lowe Sound area of north Andros on October 6, 2016, packing 140-mile-per-hour winds. We arrived there for bonefishing the Joulters in mid-November. The first thing that greeted us as we arrived in Nicholls Town from the airport was the cell phone tower. Or what was left of it. It had snapped exactly in half, leaving its top half barely attached and sagging toward the ground, inverted. To say the sight of it was awesome would be understating the optics. To me, it conjured a vision of the aftermath of a scene in one of the old King Kong movies.

When it was time to fish, we drove as usual to the boat ramp at Lowe Sound to launch the skiffs. For years there was a little store there of perhaps 800 square feet. It no longer existed. I took a photo of the remaining slab along with a nearby hulk of mutilated metal that, at one time before the hurricane-agitated water tumbled it to its resting place, was an automobile. That riveting sight taught me that the power of rushing water is easily as violent as pure wind.

More than eighty residents of Lowe Sound lost their homes to Matthew. One of these was a man who almost lost his life by staying in his home less than a block off the water until the water rose to within a few feet of the ceiling before his roof disappeared.

We know that man. He's a bonefish guide (also a plumber) named Louvan Seymour, but nobody calls him that. Instead, to everybody, he's

"Skeemer." We fished with Skeemer many times and never did learn how he got that name. After Matthew, we anglers came up with some money to help Skeemer rebuild. And Fred and Penny Wheeler, who used to own *The Outpost* mothership, worked with us to bring some relief supplies over to the folks in Nicholls Town and Lowe Sound.

So, you may ask, where is this fire I mentioned?

After we lost Philip Rolle, and after Hurricane Matthew, we continued fishing the Joulters with our friend and wonderful guide Elias Griffin. Another guide we fished with was Keith Russell, who is also a certified outboard motor mechanic. On one trip, we were fishing with Elias and Keith while staying at Robby's Place, a very nice three-bedroom, three-bath home right on the water that accesses the Joulters. It's owned by a dentist in Nassau who provides an excellent private chef for his rental guests.

The anglers on this trip were yours truly along with David and Jay Kennedy and our great friend Rich Fulton. On this trip, we unleashed all our fly-fishing armaments in mounting a frontal assault on the Joulter Cays bonefish. To our delight, we victoriously overwhelmed them.

One day Rich and I were fishing with Keith (remember, he's also a certified outboard mechanic), and by lunchtime, we ended up way out near the Tongue of the Ocean at Josie Cay. We'd had a good morning that included a couple of six-pounders. Our smoked turkey sandwiches from Honey Baked Ham safely in our bellies, it was time to crank up and head to the next flat to fish. No problem, Mon. Right?

Wrong.

Keith turned the switch to crank the engine, and his ninety-horsepower Yamaha outboard promptly burst into raging flames.

Rich and I promptly jumped overboard into the two-foot-deep water.

I have never been more impressed with anyone's reaction to a crisis than our guide. His motions were almost a blur as, in a split second, he released the engine cowling clips on either side of the engine and yanked the cowling off. He then used it as a bucket and repeatedly dipped copious amounts of water from the flat we were anchored on and dowsed the flaming outboard until the fire was out.

It's funny the thoughts that enter one's head during times of crisis. All I could think of as I saw Keith drowning the innards of his engine in salt water was whether he was ruining it.

The fire out, mechanic Keith reached for his toolbox. Fifteen minutes later, the cowling was back on the engine, and we were up on a plane, racing across the flats to the next group of unsuspecting bonefish. I will tell you that, as we ran, Rich and I kept sneaking glances back at that outboard.

Two days later, with the trip over and time for farewells, Keith and I hugged, and I said, "Hey, Cap, I just want you to know I can't think of anybody I'd rather be in a fire with than you!"

Many anglers fish the Joulter Cays while based from Prescott Smith's Stafford Creek Lodge (see earlier chapter). Others fish the Joulters based from the very ritzy Kamalame Cay Resort (www.kamalame.com). But both of those involve a drive of forty-five minutes to an hour. Let me tell you about options that are much closer.

One is the late Philip Rolle's operation, which, after his surviving brother took it over, is still called North Andros Bonefishing. The other is Robby's Place, the rental house located right on the shore of the Joulter Cays.

JUST THE FACTS—NORTH ANDROS BONEFISHING
Name of Lodge: North Andros Bonefishing
Location: Nicholls Town, North Andros, Bahamas
Nearest Airport: San Andros (MYAN)
Drive from Airport to Lodge: Fifteen minutes
Getting There: Numerous commercial flights to Nassau, then Western Air. Watermakers Air direct from Fort Lauderdale or private charter.
Capacity: Four guests
Rate for Five Nights Lodging, Four Days Fishing: $2,800
Includes: Lodging, guided fishing, dinners, airport transfers, double occupancy, shared skiff

Does Not Include: VAT, airfare, tips, beverages

Website: www.northandrosflyfishing.com

Author Comments: Philip Rolle's brother, Mark, has taken over the operation, but I have not been a guest since Philip passed away. From the website's pictures, I recognized the "lodge," which is a very comfortable three-bedroom, two-bath house in a Nicholls Town neighborhood. Four anglers are normally accommodated, two of which share a bedroom with en suite bath, and the other two are in their own room sharing a hall bath. We always prepared our own breakfasts and lunches, and a cook came each evening bearing a delicious Bahamian supper. Anglers are picked up by their guide each morning and trailered to the ramp at Lowe Sound, a drive of fifteen minutes or so, for the day's fishing. I am not sure which guides Philip's brother Mark is using. Neither am I sure if Mark is a guide. But most of the guides in the area are quite good. Over the years, we had some marvelous trips staying at this place. It will not likely escape your notice that the rates are, in some cases, less than half of the more swishy Bahamian lodges reviewed thus far.

JUST THE FACTS—ROBBY'S PLACE

Name of Lodge: Robby's Place

Location: Nicholls Town, North Andros, Bahamas

Nearest Airport: San Andros (MYAN)

Drive From Airport to Lodge: Fifteen minutes

Getting There: Numerous commercial flights to Nassau, then Western Air. Watermakers Air direct from Fort Lauderdale or private charter.

Capacity: Four guests

Rate: $450 per night

Includes: Lodging

Does Not Include: VAT, airfare, tips, beverages

Website: www.robbysplaceandros.com

Author Comments: Bonefishing based at Robby's Place is, unlike at most Bahamian lodges, taking an "unbundled" or à la carte approach. By that I mean you rent Robby's Place, you get a taxi from the airport, you hire your own guide, you fix your own breakfast and lunch, and you bring your own beverages. However, Robby (he's a dentist in Nassau and owns several of these houses on Andros) offers a neat service for an additional fee—a bona fide chef who comes in and prepares delicious dinners. Robby's Place is a very well-appointed private home located right on the shore of the vast Joulter Cays fishery. No trailering necessary, as the guides pick up their anglers right on the beach in front of the house. The place has a spacious living and kitchen area, a lovely porch with killer views of the water, and three bedrooms, each with en suite baths. That means two anglers get their own sleeping room while the other two share the largest bedroom. What about guides? We have always hired Elias Griffin (242-471-5299), Shawn Riley (242-471-6830), or Keith Russell (242-471-1535), all outstanding professional independent guides. Their rates vary, but the total trip cost will compare quite favorably with bundled rates from Bahamian bonefish lodges. Yes, Robby's Place is a winner.

Twenty-Six

I Want My Mommy!

Please kindly change "Mommy" to "Mother." As in "mothership," which is a marvelous way to access remote areas to fish the flats for bonefish, tarpon, or permit. Here's how I got started fishing from motherships.

On a trip to Andros Island Bonefish Club (AIBC) with my son, I met a man at the Nassau airport who was to become my great friend and angling colleague—Philip Vaiden from Memphis. On this trip, AIBC owner and guide Rupert Leadon could not stop talking about how phenomenal the bonefishing was at Williams and Billy Islands on the west side of Andros Island north of the big bay called the Wide Opening.

"Mon," Rupert kept insisting. "You can go there and only have to pole a hundred yards all day!"

To put it delicately, our dear Rupert was known for his hyperbole. But he was one of the top guides in the Bahamas and, so long as he was taken with a shaker of salt, was not to be ignored. So, I couldn't get out of my head his insistence about Williams Island as I wrestled with the conundrum of how to fish there.

You see, from Rupert's lodge to Williams Island is a three-hour ride in a skiff.

One-way.

When I saw Philip Vaiden again at the airport on our way home, we had a lengthy discussion of how to fish Williams without spending six hours each day beating our brains out in a skiff. We both had some ideas.

My idea involved a dear friend from Bradenton who married a gal from my hometown. Dick Turner was a very successful banker and rancher and a wonderful friend. And guess what? He owned a luxurious sixty-three-foot Hatteras motor yacht named *Hi Hatter*. When I got back to Florida, I somehow talked Dick into graciously furnishing his yacht as a mothership to fish Williams Island. Dick, despite living right on the Manatee River in Bradenton, was not a fly-fishing angler. So, on the trip, he served as our captain and brought along his mate, Glen, who was top-notch.

Philip Vaiden was in charge of the other piece of the puzzle—our guides. He had fished for years with an entertaining Andros guide named Simon Bain. He convinced Simon to bring another guide and make the three-hour ride in their skiffs from Cargill Creek to Williams Island where they would stay on the yacht and guide us for five days of fishing.

Philip loved fishing with Simon, a superb guide. And why wouldn't he? Because Philip told me he'd caught dozens of double-digit bonefish with Simon. Although this statistic didn't come even close to passing my sniff test, I said nothing. But the first time Philip and I fished together with Simon, I resolved how this rather fantastic stat came to be. You see, the first fish Philip caught was, at best, in the six-pound range, whereupon Simon said, "Congratulations, Mon, that's a ten-pound bonefish!"

That first mothership trip was in the early 2000s before anyone I knew about was offering something like that commercially. I should have exhumed Eisenhower to help with the planning—it approached the scale of D-Day. We had to account for everything that a mothership outfitter normally handles—provisioning, fuel for the yacht, fuel for the skiffs, and a lot more.

Just the fuel was a daunting task. We had to be self-sufficient because the nearest marina to our anchoring location was the better part of a day's journey in the motor yacht. To solve this, we purchased a large quantity of plastic fuel containers, filled them to the brim, and stowed them on the extensive bow area of the yacht, lashing them with heavy wire to the bow rail. As we took off across the Gulfstream to Andros with the prow of the yacht crashing into the waves, we all realized that we were a floating, undetonated bomb!

Philip and I decided we would each bring an angling friend. His was a childhood friend from Memphis, a wonderful fellow named Ed Richmond, and I brought my dear friend from my hometown, Tom Bayless. The four of us went together on many ensuing trips.

Dick Turner and his mate Glen sailed south on the *Hi Hatter* from her home base in Bradenton to Fort Myers, where they turned east. Then it was across Florida via the Caloosahatchee River and Lake Okeechobee, arriving at the intracoastal waterway for the turn south to Miami. Tom, Philip, Ed, and I met them at the marina of The Grove Isle Club in Coconut Grove and immediately embarked on a trip to the nearest Publix supermarket for provisioning. It took hours.

After a luscious dinner at the Grove Isle Club, it was off to bed (on the yacht) in preparation for crossing the Gulfstream early the next morning to the Great Bahama Bank. The crossing in a docile sea of two to three feet on a clear day was delightful, with our first stop being Cat Cay (near Bimini) to clear Bahamian Customs. Then it was on to the west side of Andros Island. It was mid-afternoon before one of us exclaimed, "Land, ho!" as the long, low outline of some kind of terra firma began to replace the empty horizon.

But now came the tricky part. Philip Vaiden, who had arranged for our guides, broke out in a cold sweat, and his pulse became elevated. He had a death grip on the yacht's strong binoculars as he swept the horizon back and forth, looking for our guides. Our plan was to anchor the ship right between Williams and Billy Islands, and as we continued running east, we got close enough to easily see the western-most of the two: Billy Island. I joined Philip with another pair of binoculars and began scouring the horizon. Nothing.

Philip and I lowered our binoculars and looked at each other for about two beats. His expression was one of utter despair. Back to the binocs for both of us.

"I can't believe this," Philip said, becoming more distraught as, binoculars welded to his eyes, he peered at the water. "Simon has never let me down."

In a few moments, I was somehow the first to see it, and without the binoculars. It looked like some whitecaps on the horizon, which didn't make sense to me as we were on the Bahama Bank in barely ten feet of smooth water. I raised my binoculars and rotated the focus to get the sharpest image. It told me what I was looking at: the wakes left by two flats skiffs running in circles near Billy Island.

I nudged Philip.

"Look," I said, pointing to what I had just seen.

His shoulders had slumped in pessimism, but they came erect as he alertly raised his binoculars again. He looked hard for several long moments before dropping the glasses and looking straight at me. His countenance displayed a radiant joy reminiscent of a baby about to come in contact with his favorite pacifier. A tear may have appeared; I'm not sure. Our trip was on!

And what a trip it was. After long, hard days of fishing, we returned to the ship in the skiffs knowing that the edge of our pleasant weariness would soon be smoothed by the luxurious comfort of the yacht and a cold, delicious Kalik. Our anchorage between the two islands placed us in magical, tropical serenity resplendent with daily sunsets that occupied our senses in an ethereal way.

As for the fishing, Rupert Leadon was correct as the bonefish were abundant, large, and cooperative. Tom Bayless and I fished together the first day, and suddenly around three o'clock, he turned to me and did something I'd never seen him do: He high-fived me. The fishing was that good. And Tom and I were gratified to collect high fives from our companions after teaming up to produce the evening's grub each night.

SMUGGLER'S BLUES

In the 1980s, Andros was mired in a rampant drug trade until the Bahamian government invited the United States to help them clean it up. On remote cays and flats it is not unusual to see, even today, wrecks of crashed drug planes. The vast, desolate, uninhabited west side of Andros Island was like a cross-dock warehouse for illegal drug distribution except there were no loading docks, only marshy, mangrove-dotted cays. But the smugglers actually fashioned a makeshift runway on a section of Williams Island that was barren of mangroves to the extent it made it possible to do so. On that spot today there are still three crashed planes, one a Piper Navajo Chieftain. Approaching it, one can see that it is riddled with bullet holes.

When we were anchored between Williams and Billy Island in the early 2000s, at least some traffickers were still operating. In the wee hours one night, Philip, up top on the flybridge battling insomnia, witnessed our yacht being buzzed several times by a strange-looking small private plane. Scared the you-know-what out of him. We speculated the plane mistook us for the rendezvous for their "drop" before finally deciding otherwise and moving on.

Other highlights of that first mothership trip? Simon Bain gave us a few casting lessons standing on the swim platform of the yacht during cocktail hour. Like many Bahamian guides he proceeded to shame us anglers by casting the entire fly line and some of the backing *with either hand*. And we saw an enormous sawfish just sitting on a flat by Billy Island in inches of water. It looked as long as an alligator. A thrilling sight.

I still remember narrowly missing a flats grand slam. By afternoon one day we had already caught a bevy of bonefish and were poling on the east side of Billy Island when along came three tarpon. I was on the bow fishing with Tom, and there was plenty of time for him to retrieve my rigged tarpon rod from beneath the gunwale. Top-notch Andros guide Andy Smith has always said the tarpon on the west side of his island are suicidal, his metaphor for the fact that, if you get a fly anywhere near them, they will inhale it. Well, I put the fly pretty much in front of these tarpon and the lead fish promptly...yep, inhaled it. In the process of the hookup, I repeatedly drove the hook into the fish's mouth, allowing us to, after a fight of little more than fifteen minutes, get a nice seventy-pound Andros tarpon to the boat.

Years later, I am still furious about what happened next. I will not name the guide Simon brought with him, but he was fishing Tom and me that day and, to our horror, he pulled out a long-handled gaff.

Before we could stop him, he gaffed that beautiful tarpon in the gut with which we had just been interacting as sportsmen. There was no saving the fish from death. I will not say Tom had to restrain me, but it was close to that. We later learned that the guide in question was a rank rookie and has since distinguished himself professionally. I'm still not naming him.

It was at least thirty minutes before I had any interest in holding a fly rod, during which time Tom landed another bonefish. Somewhat calmed, I finally took the bow again. Almost immediately, a small school of fish appeared. Permit! And they were big ones. At that time, I was still carrying a separate rod with a permit fly tied on and Tom scrambled and got it in my hand. I furiously stripped out line just in time to make a cast in front of the lead fish in about two and a half feet of water, and I let the Merkin Crab fly sink.

The lead permit tipped up on the fly! "Grand slam," I said to myself!

Well, you know what happened. A whiff, swing and a miss, air ball…pick your favorite sports metaphor. But, suffice it to say, that permit did what most of them do. All I've got to show for it is that I *casted* for a grand slam.

DON'T FORGET TO CALL ME

Anglers planning a private mothership trip to a remote area in the Bahamas like the desolate, uninhabited west side of Andros or the Marquesas Keys—places far from the nearest cell phone service—should strongly consider taking a satellite phone. It is important to have a way to communicate for an emergency or other purposes, and a satellite phone is easier and more practical than a yacht's single-side band radio.

The devices have become, smaller, cheaper, and more efficient over the years and the satellites more reliable. They can be either be purchased or, for incidental use, simply rented. A look at the Internet will reveal many options.

I Want My Mommy!

We rented a satellite phone for our mothership trip to Williams and Billy Island as our anchorage was nowhere close to a cell tower. We thankfully did not have an emergency or, God forbid, a real estate deal to try to close, but most of us did call home several times. But it should be noted that this was in the early days of satellite phones, and there were still issues.

An example:

When Tom Bayless got home from that first trip his lovely, charming wife Bena was giving him the deep freeze. It took until dinner time that night before she even spoke to him.

"All right," he finally said. "What have I done now? It's not like you didn't know I'd be gone for six nights."

Continued silence.

"So, are you ever going to say anything?"

Finally, she opened up. "Yes, I'm going to say something. I knew you'd be gone six nights, but I thought you were going fishing. I didn't know you'd be drunk every night!"

Tom answered. "Well, if that's not the pot calling the kettle black. You were drunk every night, too. What were you doing, making all the bars?"

Here's what happened. In the early 2000s when we took that trip, satellite phone operation was not only a little flaky in terms of making connections with the satellite but there was one other problem: voice quality. Listening to someone on the other end of a satellite phone conversation often reminded one of those television documentaries where a witness or undercover agent is interviewed with their face covered and voice disguised. It sounded as if the person you were speaking with either had a mouthful or marbles or was...yes, drunk.

Tom and Bena quickly figured this out and made up. Satellite phones are much better now, and I recommend them.

TWENTY-SEVEN

More Magnificent Mothers

That first crossing from Miami to the Bahamas on the *Hi Hatter* was in friendly seas. The next one was not. While Tom and I did not get seasick, I remember poor Philip and Ed lying prostrate on the aft deck. The smoothest ride on any boat is as far aft as possible, but I suspect they had another reason for choosing that location. You see, it was the closest proximity to the yacht's scuppers, which became a conduit overboard to the sea for their reappearing breakfasts.

That second mothership trip was to Moore's Island, a series of cays and flats due west of Great Abaco known for very large bonefish, given its location adjacent to the ocean. It's not a tarpon destination but a juicy spot for permit, large mutton snappers, and large barracudas on the flats.

A mothership is the ideal way to access Moore's as it is otherwise a forty-five minute skiff ride across the twenty-foot-deep Bight of Abaco from Sandy Point at the extreme southern end of Abaco. That's when the seas in the Bight of Abaco are docile. When the sea in the Bight is, shall we say, too sporty, Moore's is simply unavailable to Abaco-based anglers going there in their flats skiffs. Moreover, it's not uncommon to make the run in a skiff from Sandy Point to Moore's in relatively smooth conditions only to find a freshened breeze in the afternoon requiring rain gear for the ride home to deal with the spray from a heavy chop.

This second mothership trip proved productive with guides Town Williams and Terrence Davis, who ran to Moore's all the way from

Marsh Harbour and stayed on the ship with us. I still have a picture of a 'cuda I caught on the flats with Town using a streamer fly that we weighed on the BogaGrip at a formidable twenty-two pounds.

After Moore's Island, there were two more trips on the *Hi Hatter*. Both ended up diverted to an alternate location because of lousy weather. One of those was the time we ended up at Great Harbour Cay fishing with Percy D'Arville and learned the duck walk. The other was when we ended up at the Boat Harbor Marina in Marsh Harbour fishing with Town and Terrence. This rendered impotent the mothership advantage because the guides picked us up at the marina each day in their vehicles and drove to the ramp at the Marls.

It was after that trip that something happened to end my great friend Dick Turner's graciousness in running our mothership trips: He sold the *Hi Hatter* (Damn!).

I'm not sure he really wanted to sell her, but his sons kept after him to replace the motor yacht with a sportfish boat until he granted their wishes. The result was a fifty-four-foot sportfish boat that was lovely but lacked the capacity for all of us anglers plus two guides, Captain Dick and a mate. A wonderful chapter closed.

That was when I discovered *The Outpost*.

Fred and Penny Wheeler were an interesting couple living in Summerland Key, Florida, where their *Outpost* was docked. Fred was a veteran boat captain who at one time ran the ferry from Key West to the Dry Tortugas, and Penny was an accomplished swimming instructor. They both loved to dive and fish. They operated their *Outpost* mothership charter business as a team—Fred was the captain, and Penny was first mate and chef.

The Outpost is a sixty-one-foot Hatteras motor yacht that Fred and Penny took down to the gunwales and rebuilt as a flats-fishing mothership. The result was a tall, boxy affair that would win no beauty contests but was ideal for the purpose. Fred and Penny's design yielded four comfortable staterooms for as many anglers—two below deck and one above—a shared head for the anglers on each deck, quarters for two guides with their own head, crew quarters, and a very nice galley and dining area. It was perfect. I loved it.

After my discovery of *The Outpost*, I took many trips on her between the Bahamas for bonefish and the Marquesas for tarpon. Our Bahamian destinations were the west side of Andros, Moore's Island and the Berry Islands. And we took one trip to Great Sale Cay between Little Abaco and Walkers Cay. We fished Great Sale Cay, Carters Cays, Strangers Cay, and Grand Cay (where "Crazy" Charlie Smith was born).

I usually arranged the guides for our *Outpost* trips, but for that Great Sale Cay adventure, it was a challenge. I contacted my great friend Sidney Thomas, owner of Water Cay Bonefish Lodge, and tried unsuccessfully to convince him to guide us. The best Sidney could do was suggest a Grand Cay guide named Prince, whom he knew personally but not professionally. I engaged Prince, who brought another guide whose name escapes me.

The guide Prince brought fished my dear friend Bumpy Hughes and me one day. *The Outpost* was anchored on the southeast side of Carters Cays, but this guide wanted to run northwest for about ten miles to fish Strangers Cay. We arrived at Strangers, and the water was nice and low, so it was on with the booties and over the side to wade. Bumpy and I had waded about 200 feet from the skiff when we looked over our shoulders and noticed our guide back in the skiff cranking the engine.

"Forgot my push pole, Mon. I'll be bock in a few minutes," he yelled. (Bahamians pronounce "back" as "bock.")

Bumpy and I helplessly watched our skiff, up on a plane, become smaller and smaller and eventually become a dot on the horizon, after which it disappeared altogether. We then turned to each other in a long, silent look. And believe me, it was silent. Because Strangers Cay is a remote cay many miles from any civilization. It was an eerie feeling standing there in the water very much alone except for the sea birds. Bumpy still talks about it.

There was nothing to do but wade and fish and, despite always cutting our eyes toward the horizon checking for the hoped-for return of our skiff, we each landed a couple of nice six-pound bonefish and had a shot at big mutton snapper. In about forty-five minutes, our guide returned, push pole in its rack, whereupon Bumpy and I exchanged another long look, this time of relief.

Some of my best mothership trips were to the Marquesas Keys. The Marquesas are the only natural atoll in the Western Hemisphere and were formed thousands of years ago by a meteor. They are located twenty-five miles due west of Key West, and it is another thirty-six miles west to the Dry Tortugas where John Wilkes Booth's physician, Dr. Mudd (as in "your name is Mudd"), was imprisoned in Fort Jefferson.

The Marquesas hold tarpon. *Lots* of tarpon. And fishing there from a mothership gives anglers a huge edge. Here's why.

First, it's a twenty-five-mile run in a skiff from Key West that requires crossing Boca Grande Channel, a wide one that separates the Marquesas from Boca Grande Key. Trust me, when it's windy, Boca Grande Channel can get very, very sloppy, sometimes impassable, particularly if the wind and tide are in opposite directions. But if you're already parked at the Marquesas on a mothership...no problem, Mon.

Next, if you are indeed parked at the Marquesas on that mothership, it's a ride in the skiff of five minutes or so just before first light to the tarpon hotspot just outside of Mooney Harbor. On many occasions we have been on that hotspot at first light casting to tarpon. Then off to the east toward Key West we hear the hum of the skiffs' outboards getting closer until the occupants of the boats can pick up the silhouettes of our skiffs sitting on the hotspot. Their engines stop, and in the ensuing early dawn stillness, we can hear across the water the stream of expletives.

When the Marquesas are "on," it is fabulous tarpon fishing with shots at permit as well. But the skunk can be out, too, making some trips great and some the opposite. We've had outstanding guides at the Marquesas, my favorite being Jacksonville-native Grif Helwig who has become a Marquesas regular for many anglers. The Marquesas' tarpon fishing is marvelous, but so is the beauty of its keys and the wonder of its wildlife.

One day we were fishing with Grif on the north side and witnessed a twelve-foot bull shark pushing an enormous wake chasing a large, free-swimming tarpon for a good hundred yards before beaching him and then having his way with him. The spectacular optics of this natural phenomenon included a chase-induced wake equaling that of a sportfish boat and, at the beaching and conquest, the beautiful blue-green water becoming bright, foamy red. I've seen Grif, as competitive a guide as there is, roundly curse any shark eating his client's hooked tarpon. But, observing such a primal event of predation as this, his reaction was the opposite. I honestly thought he might wet himself in excitement as he whooped and hollered at this dramatic spectacle of unfettered nature.

One year, some of my buddies and I had a trip scheduled on *The Outpost* for bonefishing the west side of Andros. But before we could take the trip, Fred and Penny accomplished something they had been trying to do for several years—they sold the boat! The buyer was a company named Eleven Experience, founded by a chap named Chad Pike, a fanatical angler who had become a billionaire in real estate as a Blackstone partner. Eleven owns one other mothership, a seventy-four-foot Hatteras motor yacht, and land-based lodges all over the world, both fishing and skiing.

Chad Pike was recently the honoree at Bonefish & Tarpon Trust's annual dinner in New York City, and while I have yet to meet him personally, I have respect for his company because they honored our reservation for the Andros trip we had with Fred and Penny and, moreover, upgraded us to their larger mothership.

On that trip, we anchored in Millers Creek on the west side of Andros in a place called the Tarpon Hole. And that's what it was. Eleven eventually kindly stopped anchoring there when the locals so suggested.

On that trip while anchored in the Tarpon Hole, one night after dinner Jay Kennedy decided to see if the spot deserved its name, and on his third cast of a black-and-purple fly, he hooked a sixty-pounder that refused to jump. That is until Jay had him right at the boat, whereupon that 'poon finally jumped onto the aft deck of the yacht where Jay was standing and ricocheted off his shins! If he'd been sitting while fighting the fish, the tarpon would have landed in his lap. But Jay was okay, and after he removed his fly from the tarpon's mouth, we all pitched in and sent his fish back from whence it came.

We then celebrated with a glass of tawny port from the yacht's bar.

Just the Facts
Very few facts here because, as I write this, Eleven Experience has retired the seventy-four-foot Hatteras ship and is currently not operating *The Outpost*, the sixty-one-foot Hatteras. I'm hoping that will change, and soon. But, for now, all I can provide is Eleven's website, which is www.elevenexperience.com.

TWENTY-EIGHT

Mutton Mutterings

Moore's Island is one of my favorite fisheries. It sits smack-dab next to the deep blue sea, which is why the bonefish are so mammoth. A prime example is my bonefish that was eaten by a shark after which we weighed the remaining head at seven pounds.

In addition to shots at large bonefish, permit, and big 'cudas, Moore's is home to some massive, munificent muttons.

The muttons starring in this chapter are not white in color, do not yield wool, and do not bleat. They most definitely do not respond to any initiative to be herded. Instead, they are magnificent snappers that are sought-after prey for flats anglers.

Mutton snappers are handsome, elusive critters that will wage war with an angler at a level of ferocity approaching that of the prized permit. They are generally grey in color, which lends them camouflage against their preferred grassy bottom. But they are easily distinguished by their tails, which, in a quirk of God's creation, are, of all things, red. On top of all that, if an angler is so inclined to take one, they are excellent table fare.

On one trip to Moore's with David and Jay Kennedy and Randy Ashcraft, we began our fishing on arrival one afternoon by wading our favorite hotspot on the north side of Mangrove Cay.

On that afternoon, the hotspot was indeed hot. David landed a gorgeous bonefish that was in the seven- to eight-pound range. Soon after that, my vigilant scanning of the water picked up something causing a substantial, moving bulge in the skinny water. It progressed at a steady, deliberate pace, meandering in a zig-zag pattern. Presently, its trajectory straightened, and it came right toward me. My senses quickened as I prepared to false cast. Even my occasional bumbling could not screw this one up as I got an immediate take. Almost fifteen minutes later, I had my hands on the most fetching mutton snapper I'd ever seen, his characteristic red tail in picturesque contrast to his grey body. I didn't weigh this trophy, but Ricardo put him somewhere around fifteen pounds.

Now, when I snook-fished a lot at Boca Grande, I would, on rare occasions, keep a yummy linesider to eat but that slowly faded away. However, on this Moore's trip, we were doing our own cooking, and my fellow anglers erupted in a chorus of insistence that we all dine on that mutton that evening. My protestations finally overcome, I reluctantly agreed to kill that fish for our supper.

So, with that decision painfully made, what to do with this large fish? We were all standing in the water on the flat we had been wading and the skiff was by then hundreds of yards away. It was then I noticed that fellow angler Randy Ashcraft was wearing a large backpack that looked sort of lumpy in a way that suggested that it was not nearly full.

I looked at Randy and his backpack.

He looked at me.

"Oh, no you don't," he said, taking a few steps in the water in the opposite direction.

"Come on, Randy, do you want fresh mutton snapper for dinner or not?"

After I unleashed more of my persuasive skills, the fish finally ended up jammed into his backpack. We supped as if we were royalty that night, but unfortunately, Randy had to destroy that backpack, which, after carrying that now-dead mutton snapper for the rest of our afternoon of fishing, had become, shall we say...a bit ripe.

All told, I've had some good mutton snapper fishing on Bahamian flats. But, make no mistake, while they are not as difficult as permit, they may be a close second. In the first place, you see relatively few of them on the flats. And when you do, they are spooky and rival permit for playing hard to get.

But it is possible to, on rare occasion, stumble onto a nest of them on the flats. That happened once to Patti and me at East End Lodge fishing with Simeon, and we landed four or five from that one spot. On our mothership trip fishing Carters Cays, one of our anglers, Cary Kresge, landed three nice big muttons from one spot in the space of thirty minutes.

But I have lost some beauties. One was in Grassy Creek on South Andros when the hook on my fly straightened. I'm pretty much over that one. But not the one I will tell you about now.

Bumpy Hughes and I were fishing with Ricardo Burrows at the airport flat at Moore's Island, and I was on the bow being poled across one of the loveliest flats in the Bahamas as we scoured the bottom with all eyes looking for bonefish. I was fishing with an orange-and-tan Enrico Puglise spawning shrimp pattern. We poled a good distance down that flat seeing nothing when Ricardo broke the silence.

"Frank!" he said. The urgency in his voice was palpable.

"What?" I said, my anxiety level soaring.

"You see that big stingray coming right at us, about 200 feet?"

I peered at the water.

"Yeah. Yeah, I see it."

"Okay, listen to me," Ricardo said, not at all calmly. "When he gets closer, I want you to land the fly right on the nose of that ray. Right between his eyeballs."

"Okay," I said. "But why?"

"Because there's a mutton snapper following him that looks like at least twenty-five pounds!"

When Ricardo said that I suddenly couldn't swallow, wasn't even sure I was breathing. When the ray got within about 100 feet of us, I began my false casting. Incredibly, I did precisely what Ricardo had asked—my fly landed squarely on the ray's nose. That mutton tipped up, pounced on my fly, and then slurped it. I strip-struck him, came tight, and raised the rod. It was a solid hookup followed by a blistering initial run.

It's painful for me to describe what happened next.

In my early days of fly fishing, I made many stupid mistakes but, over time, gradually eliminated them from my repertoire. However, on this sad occasion, one of my long-lost rookie miscues somehow resurfaced and caused me to lose that fish. Yes, sadly, in clearing my line after the hookup, the flyline got caught on the butt of my rod. It was the first time that had happened to me in at least ten years, maybe more.

Did I say I'm over it? What do you think?

Twenty-Nine

Conched Out? Not Yet!

I have a friend from Orlando who had a house in the Bahamas he cleverly named "Conched Out." And there is a house on the Eastern Shore at Marsh Harbour on Abaco named "Done Reach." Bahamians use that phrase to announce that they have arrived at their destination.

For some of this to mean anything, one must understand that conch is pronounced as though it were spelled "conk." It's the visually artistic and tasty shellfish found on grassy bottoms in the Bahamas and the Florida Keys. It's still commercially harvested in the former but not the latter. Conch salad, cracked conch (deep fried), and grilled conch are delicacies any visitor to the Bahamas keenly anticipates.

But conch is also a term affectionately used to refer to someone from Key West, Florida, and is part of an alternate name for Key West itself, namely, The Conch Republic.

In 1982 when drug trafficking drew heavy attention from the US government, a blockade was erected at the beginning of the overseas highway to inspect all vehicles travelling to and from the Florida Keys. Key West Mayor Jeff Wardlow and his constituents were furious over this bureaucratic insolence that severely damaged tourism. They sought an injunction from the courts, and when it was denied, they decided to really get serious: Key West seceded from the union and became The Conch Republic.

Following the secession, in Key West Harbor, The Conch Republic schooner *Western Union* launched an attack on the US Coast Guard cutter *Diligence* with water balloons, conch fritters, and stale Cuban bread. *Diligence* returned fire with water hoses. It was later called "The Great Battle of The Conch Republic." "Prime Minister" Wardlow surrendered and asked for foreign aid from the United States, for which The Conch Republic is still waiting. But the road blockade was quietly removed, and The Conch Republic was born.

Some folks believe whacky, fun Key West is too touristy, and I get that. But Patti and I have always enjoyed it—the lodging, the restaurants, and, in particular, the fishing. In fact, we once took our entire family there and did all the tourist stuff, including the neat floatplane ride to the Dry Tortugas, along with plenty of fishing. One of my grandsons had worked hard on his casting and was double-hauling to beat the band. He landed his first tarpon on fly, which made me very, very happy.

One Key West trip Patti and I made was during the height of the COVID-19 pandemic. All the hotels were closed, but our favorite guide, Grif Helwig, arranged for us to stay at his girlfriend Noelle's house since she was away.

After fishing, I would ride Noelle's bike around town. It was eerie. Almost zero traffic or pedestrians on the normally clogged streets of Key West. The closest thing I saw to a person was Marilyn Monroe. Well, it wasn't really Marilyn but instead a life-sized statue of her in front of the theater made from some kind of composite material and painted to achieve amazing realism. It replicated the famous photo of her with her skirt blown up and panties showing as she stood over the NYC subway grating.

It was a perfect representation of the legendary star—the image only sullied by the fact that she was wearing a mask to protect her from the virus!

It was on that trip that Grif picked us up just before first light at Noelle's house for our first day of fishing. As we slid our tarpon rods into his SUV he said, "Gonna try something different this morning. Instead of heading straight to the Lakes, we'll stop at a place just off the ship channel near Sunset Key. Good show of fish there the other day."

Well, guess what? Because of the pandemic, ours was the only boat, and those tarpon were still there! Big time. The water was so calm and slick that, against a still-cloudy sky, it almost looked like Saran Wrap. Those 'poons were showing beautifully as they rolled to gulp oxygen. After the trip, Grif sent us videos of our *two* double-headers! One of them was a bit of a fire drill as our respective hooked fish insisted on running in different directions. Patti came within a hair of getting spooled.

All of my mothership trips to the Marquesas on *The Outpost* were stag. But on one of those, I went down early to Key West with Miss Patti so just the two of us could chase some tarpon. Grif was unavailable, but we found a marvelous guide named Lenny Leonard. The afternoon before our first day with Lenny, I dropped by the Saltwater Angler fly shop for something I needed and was asked who my guide was for the next day's fishing.

"Lenny Leonard," I said.

"Oh, you'll like him. He's so nice they named him twice!"

Well, Lenny was indeed nice and a marvelous guide to boot. We caught a *lot* of tarpon with him, including one we hooked on the ocean side of Shark Key bridge that was a behemoth. That fish drug us all the way to the ocean, and when we finally had him at close quarters, the two tip sections of my rod separated from the ferrule and dangled in midair. After fighting that fish for a while with a disassembled fly rod, somehow Lenny managed to reinsert the sections, and we landed the fish that Lenny estimated at 130 pounds.

It's very difficult to get on Lenny's book, so I haven't fished with him in quite a while. But I heard something about him that was very upsetting, if true. Apparently, one of his clients inadvertently hooked a small shark while tarpon fishing, and poor Lenny, while releasing the shark, lost a couple of fingers. Hearing that made me sad, but knowing Lenny, it won't keep him down!

Thirty

Miss Liz

Although the Bahamas were granted their independence from the British Commonwealth in 1973, there are traditions held over from the Crown. For example, many Bahamian things have "Royal" in the name, the national anthem is still *God Save the King*, cars drive on the left side of the road, and school children wear uniforms.

Another is that Queen Elizabeth II is still on Bahamian stamps. She visited the Bahamas several times, the last being in 1994, on the royal yacht, *Brittania*.

Patti and I have had two encounters with *Brittania*. The first was when the ship visited Boca Grande in 1991. The Queen and her yacht had made port in Miami and stopped to check out the Dry Tortugas on the way up the southwest coast of Florida toward Tampa, where she was to bestow knighthood on General Norman Schwarzkopf.

Imagine our surprise when we looked out on the Gulf of Mexico from our porch to see *Brittania* anchored only a hundred yards off the beach from our Boca Grande home! Along with many of our Boca Grande neighbors, we immediately drove to our dock on the bayside, jumped in our fishing skiff, and roared through Boca Grande Pass to the Gulf. When we reached the 412-foot *Brittania*, we circled her in our little fishing boat, coming to within perhaps fifty feet of her substantial hull. These were the days before terrorism changed our lives, so we exchanged cordial waves and verbal greetings with the crew. We did notice, however, that they kept a keen eye on all of us locals. We later learned that the Queen was indeed aboard. She had been scheduled to visit a British subject who lived on Cayo Costa Island for some shelling, but the weather was not quite up to royal standards.

On another occasion, we boarded and explored *Brittania*. This, too, was thrilling but I must quickly add that it occurred after her 1997 decommissioning when she became permanently docked at Edinburgh, Scotland's Ocean Terminal. I will further confess that our "exclusive" visit aboard was shared with around 300,000 fellow tourists that year.

Touring the royal yacht and some of the royal castles (again, with other tourists) was as close as Patti and I ever got to royalty.

With one rather dramatic exception.

Once, while accompanying me on a business trip to London, Patti was in a cashmere shop in the Burlington Arcade and ended up shopping with Princess Diana! Other than Diana's sole, rather-laconic bodyguard, she and Patti were the only two in the shop and exchanged pleasant conversation. In fact, Princess Di asked Patti's opinion on a sweater she was considering for Charles. Sadly, no invitation to tea ensued.

But this chapter is not about Elizabeth Alexandra Mary of the House of Windsor who became Queen Elizabeth II. Instead, it's about another Elizabeth, a classy lady who is like royalty to Patti and me. As does the staff at her Mangrove Cay Club on Andros, we call her "Miss Liz."

Elizabeth Bain is a Canadian gal who, through a family connection, had met and subsequently married a delightful Bahamian chap named Alton Bain. They came to Andros Island in the Bahamas from Toronto in 1990, and Liz Bain applied her professional background in accounting and customer service to expertly managing the Cargill Creek Bonefish Lodge.

A group of investors from the Western United States became interested in acquiring Cargill Creek Lodge, but the deal fizzled after the lodges' owner, Stanley Bain (Alton Bain's first cousin), mysteriously—and permanently—disappeared on a lobster fishing trip. Meanwhile, Liz Bain had carefully and strategically selected the site on which Mangrove Cay Club now stands. She formed a partnership with the potential buyers of Cargill Creek Lodge and provided hands-on supervision of the construction of the Club. It opened in 2000 with Liz Bain—"Miss Liz"—as part owner and general manager.

ANDROS

At 114 miles long and forty miles wide, Andros is easily the largest Bahamian island and has borne several names. The Lucayans called it Habacoa, and the Spanish called it Espiritu Santos. But during British Colonial rule it became Andros after Sir Edmund Andros, who was once governor of New York. At 140 miles in length, Andros' barrier reef that separates it from the Tongue of the Ocean is the sixth longest in the world and a destination for divers worldwide. Along with the Bahamian government, the largest employer is the Atlantic Undersea Evaluation and Test Center (AUTEC), which is operated by the US Navy. Andros has 8,000 inhabitants, who live mostly along the island's east coast.

Liz Bain's wisdom in selecting the location of Mangrove Cay Club is evident. It's ideally positioned right on the south shore of the middle bight of Andros with ready access to the North and South Bights, as well. Anglers who visit the Club enjoy proximity to all the good flats, including the Land of the Giants and Spanish Wells on the west side of Andros, nearby Moxey Creek, and lots of others. The physical plant is a gem, with eight luxurious sleeping rooms, a lovely waterfront swimming pool, and a clubhouse and dining area that is beautifully appointed and inviting. Not surprisingly, the cuisine is several steps above standard Bahamian fare of cracked conch and peas 'n rice (although Mangrove Cay Club's is superb).

Liz Bain's Mangrove Cay Club has a special attribute I can explain with this quick story:

To put it delicately, sometimes things in the Bahamas are not quite like the United States. Once I took my entire family to Marsh Harbour and rented a lovely house with a swimming pool and an outdoor shower on the pool deck. When we arrived, we couldn't get that shower to work, so I called the owner's maintenance man. He said he'd be right over and, while waiting, I began looking at the non-functioning shower a little closer. It was rusted, corroded, and deteriorated to an extent consistent with a long-abandoned house.

When the maintenance guy arrived, I directed his attention to the defunct shower. His response?

"Oh, yeah, that. Yeah...uh...it's not working right now."

What a classic that was! It was obvious that shower had not worked since Moby Dick was a minnow. That fellow's phrase—"It's not working right now"—has, for Patti and me, become a running joke about our beloved Bahamas. It's part of the islands' endearing charm ("Welcome to the Bahamas, Mon," some say).

Which brings me back to Liz Bain's Mangrove Cay Club. It may be the most immaculately maintained hospitality property I know of in any country or on any continent. The lawns are precisely manicured (thanks to Alton and his crew), the rooms and lodge sparkle, *everything* works, and there is not so much as small scrap of paper left anywhere. Being there is a joy.

Mangrove Cay Club's guides are all superbly professional and accomplished from head guide Kiki Adderley on down. If you go, make sure you ask Kiki to show you his hat trick. It's a unique way to position the bill of your cap while looking for fish that provides an advantage. It's difficult for me to describe, but it makes sense when he explains it.

Yes, Liz Bain is our special "Miss Liz." She has a profound discernment of all the concepts of customer service and goes out of her way to be accommodating. This is particularly appreciated by yours truly, who, at times, can become, shall we say...needy. (Liz may read this and translate "needy" to "picky"...we'll see).

Liz has vision and creativity. A prime example is that hers is the only Bahamian bonefish lodge, to my knowledge, offering kayak and paddle board fishing along with two micro skiffs. Patti and I are huge fans of the micro skiffs. Let me explain how they work.

Micro skiff anglers leave the Club's dock in a regular skiff. But instead of running to a flat to either pole or wade they run to a bank that is sand rather than mangroves so the guide can anchor the skiff to the land. Anglers and guides exit the skiff, taking rods, cooler, push pole and flies, and walk about a quarter mile to a bay. It's land-locked but has ingress and egress large enough for tides and bonefish, but not skiffs.

On arriving at the bay…behold!…there, beached on the bank, is the micro skiff. It's an ingenious fiberglass craft that is only slightly wider than a canoe, has a flat bottom providing excellent stability, a proper poling platform and a leaning post. There is one bench amidships.

The micro skiff uses "armstrong" power—there is not even an electric trolling motor. It's just the guide poling around a vast, flats-depth bay that provides a full day's fishing. What Patti and I like about this fishing is that we have yet to do it without consistently seeing bonefish throughout the day in a lovely place with mostly nice, white bottoms. And the fish are plenty big; we have caught them up to seven pounds.

A particularly delightful aspect of going to Mangrove Cay Club is the likelihood of enjoying the company of one of Liz's regulars, Bill Horn, and his lovely, charming wife Jeannette. Interestingly, the couple became engaged to be married at Mangrove Cay Club on a romantic evening down at the Club's waterfront swimming pool.

Bill was undersecretary of the interior under Reagan and is the consummate conservationist, having served many years on the board of Bonefish & Tarpon Trust. In fact, he remains vice-chairman emeritus. He is also a superb author of books about fly fishing (*Seasons on the Flats*, *On the Bow*, and others).

But perhaps above all is that Bill is a ferocious and successful angler, usually being the high rod in any camp (certainly when I'm at the same lodge!). In fact, on our last trip to Mangrove Cay Club when he was there, I fished a flat near the famous Land of the Giants and scratched only to learn at dinner that night that Bill arrived at the same flat twenty minutes after I left and landed a double digit bonefish.

Arrgh!

But good for Bill as that sort of thing could not happen to a nicer guy.

Being at Mangrove Cay Club with Bill Horn is a treat for another reason. After dinner, he frequently organizes among the guests a little impromptu shark-fishing tournament off the Club's dock. Liz thoughtfully equips the dock with stout spinning rods and fish scraps for shark bait. It's really a blast as Bill's prey, mostly lemon and black tip sharks, always put on a show after they're hooked, all accompanied by Bill Horn's infectious whooping and hollering.

One particular angler was a frequent guest at Mangrove Cay Club, but I never have seen him there. That's because he always bought out the entire lodge and brought his buddies. Liz had great affection for him, saying he was the nicest guy around.

His name was Jimmy Buffet.

I'll bet he was equally smitten with our "Miss Liz."

JUST THE FACTS

Name of Lodge: Mangrove Cay Club

Location: South shore of the Middle Bight, Andros Island, Bahamas

Nearest Airport: Congo Town (MYAK) or Mangrove Cay Airport (MYAB)

Drive from Airport to Lodge: Ten minutes from Mangrove Cay airport

Getting There: There are many commercial flights to Nassau where connections to Le Air to Mangrove Cay are Watermakers flies nonstop from Fort Lauderdale to Congo Town

Capacity: Sixteen guests

Rate for Five Nights Lodging, Four Days Fishing: $6,200 (2024–2025 rates)

Includes: Guided fishing, lodging, all meals, transfer from Mangrove Cay airport, double occupancy, shared skiff, open bar

Does Not Include: VAT, tips, airfare

Website: www.mangrovecayclub.com

Author Comments: If shopping is not that important, Mangrove Cay Club is quite lady-friendly as the physical plant is luxurious with engrossing water views from the porch of the lodge and a lovely pool with all the accoutrements. Of course, the rooms are a delight—four duplexes right on the water, each with its own private porch. And while perhaps not haute cuisine, the dining is way above the standard Bahamian fare at many lodges. But we mainly go for the fishing, right? The Club is very strategically located on the south shore of the middle bight of Andros, which puts so much attractive fishing water within reach. The east side of the island is very close but favorites like The Land of the Giants, Spanish Wells and Little Miller's Creek—all on the west side where tarpon roam—are regularly fished. There's a reason why Mangrove Cay Club gets so many repeat guests. If you haven't been yet, you'll find out when you go. And don't forget to try that micro skiff.

THIRTY-ONE

Cuba Without a Yo-Yo

As the birthplace of the Cuban Yo-Yo, the island nation beckoned to me, not to fish with a hand line as I did once on Andros but to deploy my arsenal of fly rods and flies in a frontal assault on Cuba's surfeit of bonefish, tarpon, and permit. I have scratched this itch twice and have a third trip planned.

The first was a cultural exchange trip with some fishing added on. It resulted from meeting a fellow member of a fishing club in New York who had fallen in love with Cuba to the extent that he went there one week a month. I'm not sure how he pulled that off legally, but he was a high-powered lawyer, and when he said he could legally host Patti and me on a visit to Cuba, with some trepidation, I chose to believe him. Thankfully, we did not end up in some Havana dungeon!

We flew with our new friend commercially from Miami to Havana and stayed in a boutique hotel with which he was somehow involved. This hotel was technically a *casa particulare*, which is the term for bed-and-breakfasts in Cuba. The "*particulare*" means it is private while if something is "*d'estato*" it is owned by the Cuban government, which is the case with most hotels and restaurants in the country.

Patti and I embarked on a guided tour of Havana, and I otherwise used our visit to do research for one of my novels—*A Lady in Havana*—that I wrote under the pseudonym Ashley Morgan. In the public room of the *casa particulare*, with our friend and other guests, we engaged in the quaint custom of playing dominoes every evening before dinner.

Our friend had arranged two fly-fishing days for us (still not sure how he dealt with the legality of it) with outstanding guides who spoke plenty of English, so off we went to the southern coast of the island. Our first day was on the Hatiquanico River with Felipe for tarpon. We landed some nice jumping-jack juveniles along the banks and then fished the middle of the river for larger tarpon. Patti landed one that went slightly over a hundred pounds. But just running the sometimes-narrow river in our guide's boat in the midst of the pristine, refulgent beauty would have come close to satisfying us had we caught nothing at all.

For our next day of fishing, we checked in to a *casa particulare* right on the beach of the Bay of Pigs. It was native and charming with a neat little bar and delicious Cuban food. We were the only Americans staying there along with a few European couples. It was eerie staying on the beach at a place of such historical significance. Being there made the choice of the Bay of Pigs for the invasion perplexing to us as there is only one road to it from the north, an impassable jungle on one side and exposure to the water on the other. Even to a non-military strategist like me, it seems obvious that it was a terrible decision that doomed the campaign before it began.

Our guide Lazaro picked us up for our second day of fishing, and what happened next was purely enthralling.

We drove on a dirt road through a swampy area with five-foot-high termite mounds and tropical trees with hanging vines. We came upon a small lagoon that served as a boat basin. It had a modest dock from which we stepped onto our skiff. I have never seen a skiff like this one before or since. It was a single-file craft! I wish I had thought to measure its beam but unfortunately went brain dead. While most flats skiffs are somewhere between six and seven feet wide, this skiff had a beam that could not have been more than four feet, probably less. I further guess the overall length at around fifteen feet, and it was equipped with a forty-horse, tiller-operated outboard, seats for the anglers in single file, a proper poling platform, and a leaning post. Amazing.

So, you ask, why such a narrow boat? We would soon find out.

After boarding and stowing our rods (yes, there were rod racks), we idled to the far side of the lagoon to what initially appeared to be a creek. It was not. Instead, it was the opening to a long, man-made brackish canal in which we spent thirty minutes running wide open to get to the Las Salinas flats. This canal was unwaveringly linear and, I swear, there was a matter of *inches* of clearance between the gunwales of the skiff and the bank of the canal while we were running on a plane wide open. It caused Patti and me to exchange tenuous glances of terror, our icy-white knuckles in a death grip clutching our seat bottoms.

Just as amazing as the configuration of the skiffs and the narrowness of the canal was this: We had to stop periodically at a series of locks. They were necessary to maintain an adequate water depth in the face of ebbing and flowing tides in the narrow canal. The locks were strange affairs that were essentially guillotines. When we came to one, the guide and I exited the skiff to operate the lock with a rope that pulled the guillotine lock up so the skiff could pass. It was a first for Patti and me, and we're not aware of anything else like it anywhere.

Once we cleared the last lock, we entered the Las Salinas fishery, a vast expanse of luminous flats occupied by bonefish, juvenile tarpon, and the occasional permit. We casted at all three, and Patti had a nice permit tip up on her fly before her potential trophy did what almost all of them do—yep, another swing and a miss—and Patti's grand slam eluded her.

That memorable trip made me want to return to fish Cuba. But that required some legal issues to become resolved.

AVALON

Some number of years ago, an Italian company named Avalon negotiated an arrangement with the Cuban government (possibly Fidel himself) that gave them the exclusive franchise for fishing the island's extensive, beautiful, productive saltwater flats. However, it was illegal for Americans to go to Cuba for recreational purposes like fishing, surfing, or vacationing by the pool of a hotel. But that didn't stop many of them. Toting their fly rods, they would fly to Cuba through

Canada, Mexico, or the Bahamas and ask Cuban customs officers to please not stamp their passport.

The more law-abiding Americans (like yours truly) eschewed this approach and waited for something to change, which it did. A native Cuban, former Wall Streeter Luis Menocal, when on the board of Bonefish & Tarpon Trust, masterminded a scientific program that made it legal for American anglers to visit the Cuban flats to fish as a part of a people-to-people cultural exchange program that provided for promulgating the scientific research activities of Bonefish & Tarpon Trust, including fish tagging and recordkeeping. Voila! It became legal for Americans to go on the Avalon trips to Cuba.

Thanks to Luis Menocal, with five other anglers, I went with Avalon to *Las Jardines de la Reina* (The Gardens of the Queen), an area of flats and mangrove islands off the southeast coast of Cuba more vast than all the Florida Keys. We flew on an American Airlines Boeing 737 to a Cuban city named Camagüey, whereupon we boarded a bus for the three-hour ride to the coast to meet our mothership. We arrived at dusk, boarded our ship, and dined on very good Cuban fare as we sailed to the fishing grounds. Waking to a hearty breakfast the next morning, our neurons and synapses were crackling with the electric anticipation of boarding our skiffs for the first day of fishing.

We had three Cuban guides for the six of us. You may have heard the expression, "kitchen Spanish," which refers to someone whose first language is English being able to speak enough Spanish to get by. Well, our excellent, hard-working guides spoke "fishing English," so communicating was never a problem. Actually, that's not quite fair as their English was a cut above that and, moreover, they were congenial chaps whose company we all thoroughly enjoyed.

But I will admit that some of us had a bit of the devil in us as (only in private) our twisted humor made us refer to our guide Bimba as "Bimbo," our guide Raundell as "Raw Deal," and our guide Ney as "Aye." Actually, instead of the devil, it may have been too many mojitos in us, no doubt grievously overserved to us by an apprentice Cuban bartender.

So, how was the fishing? In a word, superb. One of our anglers, Jay Kennedy, experienced the nirvana of a grand slam, and almost everyone on the trip casted for one. That included yours truly, who, after landing plenty of bonefish and tarpon, which was never a problem any of the days, had a permit in the twenty-pound class tip up on the fly *three times in succession* and whiff each time! Arrgh!

Despite research that suggests otherwise, we learned that our Cuban guides were acutely sensitive to what they perceive to be the excellent hearing of flats fish, particularly bonefish. On multiple occasions when poling up on a sighted fish that presented a particularly interesting angling opportunity, the guide would interrupt our conversation by sharply saying, "No speaking, please!"

It was never a request but rather a command that we always followed with dispatch and a cooperative spirit.

Avalon did a marvelous job, as they provided comfortable accommodations on the ship, plenty of good Cuban grub, ample Latin hospitality, and good humor.

Evenings after dinner were interesting. One of us was always ready to grab a 9- or 10-weight rod and head for the stern of the ship where spotlights shone on the water. That always attracts fish of varying species, and most nights, our visitors were juvenile tarpon that could be readily hooked. But tarpon were not the only critters back there under those lights. I have a photo of one of our hooked baby tarpon being chased by a saltwater crocodile that was twelve feet long if it was an inch! Fortunately, it was not quick enough to capture its midnight snack.

JUST THE FACTS
We booked our trip to Cuba through The Fly Shop of Miami (395-762-2476; www.flyshopofmiami.com).

Our next trip was not to the Gardens of the Queen but to Cayo Romano on the north coast of Cuba. On those trips, anglers arrive on a Saturday and leave the following Saturday. The lodging and meals are land-based in a nice hotel near the water and skiffs.

Getting there is accomplished by flying on American Airlines from Miami to the Cuban city of Camagüey followed by a bus ride of an hour or so to the hotel.

The cost of the trip, excluding airfare and tips, is $7,590.

THIRTY-TWO

Whither the Weather and When

I guess I'm a slow learner because it took me many years of going to the Bahamas chasing bonefish to finally learn when to go and during what weather. When I started, and for years thereafter, I followed the advice of the original books on bonefishing that maintained that May and November are the best months to go, so that's what I did for a long time. I still go in November but never in May any longer, and now, I much prefer February, March, and April over any other months. Here's why.

First, what's wrong with May? What took me so long to realize is that you can almost count on a high-pressure system being parked in the Atlantic over Bermuda (the weather guys call it a Bermuda high) causing brisk to stiff wind patterns to funnel off of it and pound the tropics daily from an east-southeastern direction. It has, for me, relegated some May mothership trips to the refuge of marinas.

The other thing about May is that it has begun to get hot. I like to say "too hot for the anglers and too hot for the fish." Well, it's not too hot for this native Floridian angler, but as the water temperature rises, the bonefish that come on the flats are not as large as during months when the water temperature is lower. Months like February, March, and April.

What else is wrong with May? Well, it's a prime month for tarpon fishing.

Living in Central Florida where we get the occasional frost and even some transitory freezes, I always thought February, March, and April would be too cold to fish the flats for bonefish. While I had heard and read that February was the time to chase the biggest bones on Andros, I had visions of going there bundled up as if ice fishing. Boy, was I wrong and for much too long. In the many trips I have now taken to the Bahamas in the winter months, I cannot recall even one where cold was an issue. But I can tell you what I do recall: The fish on the flats are definitely bigger.

It is indeed true that the winter allows cold fronts to push much further south, certainly through the Bahamas. And if you are there when this happens, a day or two of fishing can be materially affected. But between the fronts when the wind has laid and the sky has become bright...well, it can be gangbusters. Some years ago, I discovered a government website that is helpful in forecasting frontal passages. It's NOAA's Weather Prediction Center: https://www.wpc.ncep.noaa.gov/#page=ovw.

And speaking of weather forecasting, it can be tricky when it comes to the Bahamas. Over the years, I have settled on two websites that seem to provide the most accuracy and can be location specific. One is Windfinder, and the other is Sailflow. The former provides wind, sky, and temperature forecasting five days out, and the latter provides very-detailed hourly wind speed and direction forecasts for specific locations.

But if you want to know my favorite forecasting tool, it would have to be the weather forecasting station at Chub Cay in the Bahamas' Berry Islands. This "weather station" is a sign with a coconut hanging from it. Here is a photograph:

Thirty-Three
It's Only Three Inches

One day, Patti and I decided we should go on an African photo safari. So, we did.

We chose to fly from Atlanta to Johannesburg and briefly check out that city. Then it was on to our safari in Zimbabwe because it was one of the few countries that allowed visitors on game drives to exit the vehicle. In fact, one day we crawled with our guide underneath a large baobab tree alongside a giant bull elephant and sat a few feet from this tolerant monster while he feasted on the tree. Another day, we left our camp on foot and several miles later scooched up on our bums to within 100 feet of a pride of lions. It's true our guide was toting major heat on his shoulder. But I'm not sure we would try that again as we got to thinking later about how many of those lions he could have dropped had they all charged at once.

But our safari was not *all* safari. One day while canoeing the Zambezi River, we broke out our fly rods and caught tiger fish, which was fascinating. Their teeth would even frighten a barracuda!

So, you may ask, what were we doing taking fly rods on an African photo safari?

Well, in planning this trip, we got to looking at a map of Africa and made a discovery: the Seychelle Islands, located in the Indian Ocean, were only three inches east of Africa!

We had always read about the marvelous flats fishing there for bonefish, Indo-Pacific permit, giant trevally, triggerfish, and the fascinating milkfish. So, since it was only three inches, Patti said, "Sign us up!"

Well, that three inches was actually 2,300 miles and required an overnight flight from Johannesburg to the Seychelles capital of Victoria on Mahé. We only spent one night on Mahé, a few hours really, and that was on our way home. We wish it had been more.

After arriving on Mahé from Johannesburg, we boarded a nineteen-passenger Beechcraft turbo prop for the one-hour flight to our final Seychelles destination—Alphonse Island and its lovely lodge. It was so interesting coming in for our landing on Alphonse Island. It was formerly a coconut plantation and is still covered with stately trees. Except, that is, for the landing strip, which, from the air, gave the appearance of a handsome man's full head of hair with a large part cut right down the middle of his head. It's where we landed. Smoothly.

BONJOUR, MONSIEUR ALPHONSE

Alphonse Island was first charted by a Portuguese navigator in 1562 who named it San Francisco. But, in 1730, a French ship's captain came upon the island and renamed it for himself. Positioned seven degrees south of the equator, Alphonse Island and its adjacent St. François Atoll present visitors with luminous tropical splendor of an intensity that mutes the optics seen almost anywhere else, perhaps even the Bahamas.

Alphonse has a staggering 132 recorded bird species, including red-footed boobies and Madagascar cuckoos. Perhaps the most interesting critters on the land may be the Aldabra giant tortoises. The "giant" part was apt as they weigh as much as 800 pounds. They roam the resort and appear very friendly to the guests.

Our A-frame accommodations may not sound like much, but in addition to its welcome privacy, it was somewhere between comfortable and luxurious and quite satisfactory. And I can say the same about the dining and the congeniality of the other guests who were from Spain, the United Kingdom, South Africa, Hong Kong, and Singapore.

Alphonse manages the fly fishing expertly, allowing only twelve rods and making sure you rarely see another angler. Each morning, we boarded a twin-outboard powered catamaran for the forty-minute ride to visually stunning St. François Atoll, where we boarded flats skiffs for the day's fishing with top-notch guides.

We had never experienced such a variety of fishing. We began by wading for bonefish on a white sand flat so vast and uniform we could see neither its beginning nor its end. Now get this: We waded into a school of bonefish that easily numbered 1,000! And they were mostly stationary. In fact, we could slowly wade into the school and, instead of spooking, they would politely part for us so we didn't step on them. So, what did we do? Well, there is no doubt we could have stood there and caught 100 bonefish that day. But, instead, we waded the perimeter of the school, picking out larger fish to which to cast.

After doing that for a while each day and landing bonefish to eight pounds, we moved on to the other species. Patti and I each caught a nice giant trevally (GTs, they are called) in the thirty-pound range. While many anglers relish GT fishing and travel great distances to fish for them, Patti and I have too many memories of large jacks interfering with our intense snook fishing in Southwest Florida. Consequently, one GT each sated us.

We never saw an Indo-Pacific permit, but we found the triggerfish and emperor fishing on skinny, rocky flats fascinating and challenging. For some reason, we had considerable success with the triggerfish, catching two or three each time we fished for them. The reason I deem this a success is that fellow Alphonse guests from South Africa were furious with me (good naturedly so) over our triggerfish catches as they claimed it was their third trip to Alphonse and they had yet to catch one.

While bonefish, permit, GTs, and triggerfish are available lots of places in the world, the Seychelles are milkfish central. Milkfish intrigued us. They rarely go over three feet in length, and they almost never weigh as much as fifty pounds. But their exaggerated fork tails translate into awesome swimming power, making it necessary to fish them with a tarpon rod if there is any hope of landing one. Moreover, they are vegetarians, feeding on algae. It took many years for fly tiers to develop an algae imitation they would eat.

So, did we catch a milkfish? Well, I hooked one on my 11-weight rod with an algae fly I purchased from the Alphonse Fishing Company for a handsome sum. I fought the milkfish for a little over thirty minutes before—I confess—it came unbuttoned. But I can tell you those thirty minutes were some of the most memorable in my angling life as that fish could not have weighed more than twenty pounds.

JUST THE FACTS

Name of Lodge: Alphonse Island Lodge, Seychelle Islands

Location: 250 miles southwest of Mahé

Nearest Airport: Seychelles International Airport

Flight from Mahé Airport to Lodge: One hour

Getting There: There are flights from all over to world to Mahé.

Capacity: Fifty-four guests

Rate for the Required Seven Nights Lodging, Six Days Fishing: $13,656

Includes: Guided fishing, lodging, all meals, charter flight to and from Mahé, double occupancy, shared skiff, open bar

Does Not Include: Taxes, tips, international airfare, required medical evacuation insurance

Website: www.alphonse-island.com

Author Comments: It was a few years ago, but I do not recall paying 13.5 thousand bucks per angler for our trip. I believe it was less than half that; however, we did not stay nearly as long as a week, as it was not required then. What I do recall is that we booked through Frontiers and, even though we had already paid, they kindly notified us of a reduction in our rate because Alphonse ran a special after we booked. I believe Alphonse is under new ownership, and they may be spiffing things up a bit and trying to charge more in concert with that. But I must say, when we were there, it did not need any spiffing up as the place was perfectly lovely.

THIRTY-FOUR

I'm a Little Flighty!

Thanks to God's grace I have been able to travel the world fly fishing with my wonderful wife and my treasured friends, including going somewhere in the Bahamas bonefishing four to five times per year.

My good fortune does not extend to having my own "aviation department," either individual or corporate, but I nevertheless often experience the wonderful convenience of flying private to the Bahamas and the Florida Keys. Some of this has been done with dear and generous angler friends with their own lovely airplanes. But most of it has been via charters of small, twin-engine propeller aircraft like the Cessna 421, a TBM, or the Beechcraft Baron, mostly with my angler buddies.

I have never driven an airplane and do not plan to learn. But if you go to the Bahamas a lot, or plan to start, I recommend checking out charters of some of these small but dependable airplanes. I have found that good charter companies have well-trained pilots and rigid maintenance procedures. But the best part is that if, say, four anglers split the cost, it comes to an amount per angler that is very competitive when compared to going commercial, and it is far more convenient.

All these Bahamas and Keys flights I've taken have been remarkably satisfactory in that mechanical or weather delays have been almost nonexistent. The only real problems I've had have been my own damn fault!

For example, I once left my fly rods on the plane in Key West but fortunately caught the pilot having lunch before he took off again. An

Uber driver brought them to Big Pine Key where Patti and I were about to begin tarpon fishing.

The worst was when I left my treasured orange boat bag on the plane when Patti and I were dropped off at Chub Cay. In that bag were all my fly reels and all my flies! Frantic phone calls to the Fort Pierce tower (where the plane was going to clear customs on the way home) ensued and, miraculously, they were able to radio the plane and get it turned around with my gear.

Since that episode, I have made it a point to count noses when the plane is unloaded to make sure all my stuff is there.

Speaking of clearing customs, while most of that has been at either Fort Pierce, Orlando, or Lakeland, a lot has been at Palm Beach International Airport (PBI). On the side of that airport where the customs building is located is also where we have seen some interesting airplanes.

Once we cleared at PBI and exited our little plane to see we were less than 100 yards from Air Force One. Another time, China president Xi Jinping's jumbo jet was parked almost right next to us. And once, we cleared customs at PBI on the same day Donald Trump was flying to New York for one of his legal arraignments. There were hundreds of demonstrators by the perimeter road right next to the customs building, and Trump's 757 jet was parked almost within casting range of us. We did not see Trump board his plane, but after we cleared customs, we ended up taxiing right behind his plane and took off right after he did.

While it's hard to top Air Force One, possibly the most interesting airplane we saw at the PBI customs building was a 1954 Grumman HU-16 Albatross, a rather large, amphibious plane. She had taxied and parked at the customs building just before us. We were in my dear friend Jim Weeks' twin-engine Piper Navajo Chieftain. As we deplaned, we saw a bunch of characters with guitar cases slung over their backs entering the customs building from the Albatross.

US Customs at PBI or any other airport get their hair on fire about turning your cell phone on prior to clearing customs—there are signs everywhere, and they will dress you down for noncompliance. We always carefully observe this regulation.

We entered the customs building behind the guys from the incredibly beautiful Grumman Albatross vintage airplane and I found myself standing right behind the plane's owner. If you hadn't already guessed, it was Jimmy Buffet. And what was he doing? Yep, he was literally going to town on his cell phone!

None of the customs officers uttered a peep. But…he was Jimmy Buffet.

JUST THE FACTS

Here are some Florida-based air charter companies that fly to the Bahamas and the Florida Keys. The list is surely nowhere near complete. By the way, it's worth mentioning that Delta has regular nonstop flights from Atlanta to Key West.

Tropic Ocean Airways—www.flytropic.com
Aztec Airways—www.aztecairways.com
Airflight Charters—www.airflightcharters.com
Tryp Air Charters—www.flytryp.com
KW Executive Air Charters—www.KWEAC.com

THIRTY-FIVE
A Potpourri of Piscatorial Prattle

MY GOD, WHERE'S BILL?
Patti and I had the high privilege of fishing a few times with guiding legend Bill Curtis. He lived on Key Biscayne and fished the flats from Biscayne Bay proper all the way down to Key Largo.

Bill was a force. He was the antithesis of a clock watcher. In fact, I can remember coming back to Miami in his yellow skiff, *The Grasshopper*, after wrapping up our fishing way down around Soldier Key.

It was dark.

In fact, as my mother would have said, it was "boo" dark.

Bill was running that skiff wide open using no lights and there was little moonlight. On top of that, and not everyone knows this, Bill only had one eye. After somehow making it to the dock without hitting a channel marker, Patti and I had an extra glass of wine that night!

Captain Bill lived a long, full life that involved hard running both on and off the water. Nobody was better at what he did. He died at the age of ninety-one, was cremated, and that's where his story takes on added fascination.

Bill's ashes were stolen.

It happened at Flanigan's Restaurant in Coconut Grove. A very close family friend named Dennis Dora, who was assisting with estate matters, had the box with Bill's ashes on the front seat of his Chevy Silverado pickup truck while he dined at the restaurant. The plan was to scatter them at Rhodes Key (some called it "Curtis Point") the next day. Also in Mr. Dora's truck were several items of considerable value that were untouched by the thief who destroyed the right front window of the vehicle to gain access.

The crime remains unsolved, but acclaimed writer, angler, and Bill Curtis friend Thomas McGuane was quoted as espousing this theory: "I figure the thief was a lousy angler who plans to sprinkle Bill's ashes on his Wheaties in the morning and suddenly start catching fish."

ANOTHER LEGEND

My friend Rick Bannerot, who is a fellow member of a fishing club I belong to, urged me to head to Long Island and try fishing for striped bass on fly in September when the fish come up on the clear flats and can be sight-fished like bonefish.

Things came together when Patti and I realized we would be attending a wedding in East Hampton. I am still in Rick's debt, because he very kindly arranged our day's fishing, which occurred on Shinnecock Bay.

We had never been striper fishing, but we did well. That's not surprising because, thanks to Rick Bannerot, we fished with a legend, Paul Dixon.

Paul is way more than a day-in-day-out fishing guide running charters. He ran Orvis' fishing department for a number of years and began the first Orvis fly-fishing school. He's nationally known, having appeared on *The Charlie Rose Show*, NBC, ABC's Prime Time Special on The Hamptons, and on almost every nationally viewed TV fishing show. And he's a member of the Bonefish & Tarpon Trust Advisory Council.

But what attracted Patti and me to Paul were two things: Paul was as good a guide as we've ever fished with, and he was a prince of guy—a perfect gentlemen and excellent company. To say Paul is well connected is a gross understatement. Indeed (and except for Patti and me), he's the "fishing guide to the stars" in the angling world. It's not surprising he's a legend.

A Potpourri of Piscatorial Prattle

Do You Remember Where You Were?

Patti and I have made a number of trips to England to fish the renowned chalk streams west of London with the great William Daniel of Famous Fishing as our outfitter. One of those trips was memorable in a way that was anything but pleasant.

We were fishing in the River Avon one day guided by William. It was shortly after two on a September afternoon, and something happened that was a first: the owner of the beat came out and approached us. That *never* happens. It was the lady of the house that was on the bank right where we were fishing.

"Good afternoon," she said. "I hope your fishing is going well but I was watching the news and just thought you might like to know a small plane hit a tall building in New York."

"Hmmm," I said, assuming some student pilot in a Piper Cub had drifted off course. "That's interesting. Thank you for telling us." We resumed fishing.

A few minutes later, she returned. This time something about her bearing was different. As she got closer, we saw that she was in tears. We spent the rest of the afternoon in our muddy waders in this nice lady's solarium watching the horrors of 9/11 on television with her.

As we all remember, air travel ceased for a time after this, so we were in the United Kingdom for a while. Patti and I will never forget the reaction to 9/11 on the part of the British people. We went to church the Sunday after it happened, and the liturgy and sermon were all about offering prayers for America. When it became apparent that we were Americans, the outpouring of sympathy was overwhelming. I will never forget fueling our rental car at the petrol station where another customer, a British fellow, figured out I was American and approached me. This man was a total stranger, but he came up and embraced me for a long moment before looking at me and saying, "I'm so sorry. We're all the same people, you know." His eyes were moist. When he turned away, mine became more than that.

The Guest Register

As a writer, I always pay attention to the guest register at fishing lodges and try to put at least a little thought into my comments. If I'm stricken with "guest register block," I'll usually write: "Frank and Patti Foster were delighted here!"

But I remember one entry from a bonefish lodge guest register on Abaco inscribed by a group of gentlemen anglers. It was a variation on *Veni, vidi, vici.* They wrote: "We came, we saw, we got refusals!"

The Rocket's Red Glare

Once when Patti and were fishing in Iceland, one of our fellow lodge guests was a local angler from Reykjavík. You'll never guess what his job was: He was first chair trumpet player in the Iceland National Symphony. On top of that, he was an engaging chap whose company we thoroughly enjoyed.

Our trip concluded, it was time for the van to collect us at the lodge for our very early flight. No one else seemed to be stirring on a crisp, clear July morning that, for Iceland, was positively balmy. But I could see my breath and, Floridian that I am, was bundled up. There was a circular driveway in front of the lodge, and between that driveway and the road was a distinctive rock that rose perhaps twenty feet in the air but was gently shaped like a large mound, allowing a person to easily walk to the top.

The moment we emerged from the lodge our vision picked up a man who had indeed climbed that rock and was standing at the top, waiting. He had something shiny in his hand that caused the just-rising sun to glint and reflect against our still-sleepy eyes.

The man standing at the top of the rock was the angling guest from Reykjavík. And the shiny thing is his hand was his trumpet.

While our van waited, Patti and I stood in arrested anticipation as our new friend raised the gleaming instrument to his lips and began playing. In the stillness of the morning, the piercing notes froze us in trance-like attention as they reverberated from the nearby hills—stalwart, pure, and in perfect pitch. It was the most stirring rendition of *The Star*

Spangled Banner of our lives that resulted in a tearful, hugging farewell with our new friend. Every time Patti and I think about that moment, we "get something in our eye."

I Don't Doubt Thomas

Fishing while based on a mothership or running there from Sandy Point in skiffs is not the only way to access and fish Moore's Island. Indeed, several times, Ricardo and Perry have run their skiffs over and met my anglers and me there after we flew into Moore's Island's small but good landing strip. We stayed at a place called the Moore's Island Bonefish Lodge owned and operated by a local named Thomas Hield. Tom is a very nice man but his Bahamian English is very difficult to understand. Even Ricardo has trouble but does an admirable job of translating for us.

To say Tom's place is Spartan might be an understatement. It's nothing more than a basic motel but the air conditioners work great. Anglers bring their own groceries, and Tom's daughter cooks. Every morning, we pile in Tom's truck for the ride to the graveyard where the skiffs are anchored and off we go to the flats. It's a true native experience that has produced some superb bonefishing.

Ducking Duke

One day Patti and I decided we would leave our mountain house, take a short drive, and do a little trout fishing on the Tuckasegee River near Sylva, North Carolina. It's a tail water fishery making it necessary for one to call Duke Power to learn of their plans to release water from the dam on the day one fishes. We called before we left that morning and were assured that no water would be released that day.

Wrong!

The "Tuck," as the Tuckasegee River is called, is very wide where we entered it close to Western Carolina University. We had no sooner negotiated the bottom's slippery rocks and reached the middle when the water began rising.

Rapidly.

In fact, *very* rapidly.

Patti and I were hyperventilating in terror as we struggled toward the bank, which we just barely made before the Tuck became a bold, whitewater slew.

MITCH MAKES A SWITCH

When an entire crew of rock star bonefish guides—the legendary Pinder brothers—had a fuss with Deep Water Cay Club and resigned, a chap from Ohio whose name escapes me organized the brothers with new skiffs and a guiding arrangement at Pelican Bay Hotel in Freeport (Pelican Bay is now also the home of the very good H2O Bonefishing).

Patti and I fished with the Pinders a few times. Anglers would stay at Pelican Bay, have breakfast at the hotel, and get picked up by whichever Pinder brother they were fishing with that day. After a ten-minute ride to the ramp and launching the skiff, it was on to the productive bonefish flats near Freeport on the north shore of Grand Bahama.

On a trip there in October 1998, I learned something I believe was later confirmed by news stories about animals fleeing coastal areas a day or two in advance of an approaching tsunami. Somehow critters know about impending weather before any *Homo sapiens*.

On this trip, I became convinced that phenomenon includes bonefish. How? We had five days of bonefishing with the Pinder Brothers, split between David Jr., William, and Joseph. We were vaguely aware of a hurricane named Mitch that was terrorizing folks in Central America but paid little attention.

Our first day's fishing was outstanding with multiple bonefish to seven pounds and a nice mutton snapper. The second day we seemed to see fewer fish but still caught some. The third day we poled and poled flat after flat and casted a paltry four times. The fourth day, we did not see a single fish.

It was on our return to the Pelican Bay Hotel after that fourth day that we learned that, during our first days of fishing, Hurricane Mitch had taken a turn to the northeast and pummeled the Yucatán Peninsula. But, to our horror, we further learned that Mitch had emerged in the Gulf of Mexico and, while we were futilely searching the flats for bonefish that day, became the race car of hurricanes, streaking toward South Florida and then to the Bahamas at a previously unheard of speed.

We were stuck and had to ride it out at the hotel. It wasn't terrible—the winds probably topped out at seventy-five miles per hour—but we were late getting home. It was a fascinating lesson to me as I am convinced those bonefish knew *way* before the meteorologists that Mitch was making a switch.

HOME WATERS

One of the best fishing trips of my life was to a private trout-fishing club in Pennsylvania near College Station named Home Waters Club. The trip was organized by a fishing club in New York to which I belong. It was what they call a "small outing" as there were about a dozen of us anglers there for two days of fishing with superb guides while we enjoyed comfortable lodging and yummy vittles in the evening.

We floated the Little Juniata one day and waded Spruce Creek the next, each with outstanding results.

Why do I say this was one of the best fishing trips I've ever been on? Because my angling partner was my grandson—and formidable angler—Matthew Foster.

Thirty-Six

Piscatorial Prattle Perpetuated

The Dumpster

You may recall my mentioning a chap named Gil Drake Jr. who helped his dad build the original bonefish lodge, Deep Water Cay Club. Gil became a famed fly-fishing guide in the Florida Keys, but when I snook fished with him in the Everglades, he gave me a fly I still have. It was the strangest little floating concoction that was made from a piece of white plastic tubing that was somehow square, not round. A glass minnow imitation, it was *devoured* by the snook, but I wondered where Gil got that piece of tubing. I thought to myself perhaps the dumpster, and that's what I named the fly—The Dumpster.

Congratulations!

Once when Patti and I fished in Slovenia, a weather event blew out the famed Soca River for days. We retreated to another river that was fishable—I believe it was the Sava. We had some dry fly fishing on that river, but most of the fish were tiny. Our guide, Miha, assigned us a colleague for that river, a pleasant chap whose English was limited to a precious few words.

The English word he seemed to be the most comfortable with was one he used after every single fish we landed. And it caused Patti and me to exchange a smirk each time, hoping our guide took it for an expression of pleasure at landing a fish. Even when one of our eight-inch trout found its way to our guide's landing net, he would beam with delight, turn to us, and boom, "Congratulations!"

FROM CONNEMARA TO CROSSING ROCKS

Anglers interested in Bahamas fly-fishing destinations should know about Crossing Rocks. It's on Great Abaco about halfway from Marsh Harbour to Sandy Point and is home to two notable upscale bonefish lodges.

Through a local Bahamian, we were introduced to an Irish chap named Peter Mantle, who owned the renowned Delphi Lodge in Connemara and was building what is now The Delphi Club, a bonefishing lodge right on the ocean at Crossing Rocks. When the lodge was in the final stages of construction, Peter hosted several of us for a cocktail tour with—typical of Peter—the finest wines and nibbles. Patti and I have been guests at Delphi numerous times and, as my very-Southern mother would have said, it is *divine*.

Peter sold Delphi several years ago to a group that includes a friend of mine. It's still going strong and merits your attention if you're thinking of a trip. Perhaps particularly if you are, say, a gentleman angler whose wife does not fish. I assure you she would be very comfortable and pleasantly occupied at The Delphi Club.

PASS THE RIOJA, POR FAVOR

One day Patti and I had seen one too many emails about trout fishing in the Pyrenees Mountains of Spain. Humble Servant sprang into action and planned our trip!

We were hosted by an outfit named Salvelinus that provided lovely accommodations and delicious Spanish cuisine accompanied by equally delicious Rioja. I have always been partial to Spanish wines from regions such as Rioja, Ribera del Duero, and Priorat and have some in my cellar. But, damn, it sure seems to taste better over there.

The optics of our fishing environs were stunning. One day we fished on a vast, high mountain plateau at dizzying elevations and worked a meandering stream that held fish. But we learned we were not alone. Our mountain meadow was home to wild horses that would come bounding up to us, perhaps somehow divining the fact that we had some yummy apples in our lunch basket. With some fear and trepidation, we shared.

But fear and trepidation? There were some cattle, including several large, snorting bulls, that on two different occasions mounted a mock charge on us. Did it scare us? Nah, of course not. Yeah, right!

I'LL HAVE AN ANEJO, PLEASE

I'm not much of a rum drinker but Bacardi's Anejo is supposed to be top shelf. Patti and I were fortunate to become friends with some of the Bacardi family, Eusebio and Hilda Delfin, as they were frequent visitors to our hometown to visit their cousins, Andy and Rosa Hernandez.

One year our dear friends Tom and Bena Bayless co-chaired a charity event with Patti and me, and we talked the Delfin's into contributing an auction item—a trip to Bacardi's Big Game Club on Bimini to bonefish. Well, you probably know what happened. The Baylesses and Fosters bought the trip.

We drove to Miami and did something we'd both always wanted to do and that is fly to Bimini on a Chalks Airlines seaplane, the famous (or infamous) Grumman G-73T Mallard. It was an unforgettable experience as, on takeoff, you felt as if you were drowning.

But that experience is gone forever. In 2005, a Chalks flight from Miami to Bimini crashed shortly after takeoff, killing all twenty aboard. The right wing separated from the plane due to metal fatigue. Shortly after that the National Transportation Safety Board issued their report and Chalks permanently ceased operations.

Bimini's flats are anything but vast but, since it's adjacent to the ocean, the bonefish are enormous, and we had our way with at least some of them. This trip was a number of years ago, and I'm not sure what's going on with The Big Game Club these days. But we thoroughly enjoyed it while there.

YOU'RE UNDER ARREST!

Recently, Patti and I trout fished in lovely Ireland with Andrew Ryan of Clonanav Fly Fishing, and it was superb. Probably because almost all of his fishing is on private water! What's fascinating is the length to which

Andrew goes to keep it that way. He has deployed an elaborate network of cameras hidden in trees all over the place. He backs that up with drones! They all communicate with his central computer, which then communicates with his cell phone. So, wherever Andrew may be, he gets notified when a two-legged intruder is on a bank of his private water. He told me that when he gets such a message, he immediately gets in his SUV and races to confront the interloper. Andrew is a large, muscular, and relatively young man. Without sharing some of his enforcement tales, let's just say Andrew is a perfect gentleman and always begins his confrontations (which apparently are not that infrequent) with the iron-fist-in-the-velvet-glove approach. If that doesn't work...well, I won't go into that. But Andrew works very closely with the police to keep his private water private.

IN THE BLACK

A fellow I call "Mr. Black Fly" is a chap named Vaughn Cochran who has been a flats guide in the Florida Keys, a fly shop owner in Jacksonville, a restaurateur in St. Augustine, and is a renowned wildlife artist. But along the way, it is my understanding that, while he does not own it, he started Black Fly Lodge, which, like The Delphi Club, is in Crossing Rocks.

I took a group to Black Fly when they were operating from a temporary lodge, which was a large, comfortable residence. Good-guy Clint Kemp was our host and, last I heard, is still managing Black Fly Lodge in their new facility, which rivals nearby Delphi Club in luxury. Clint has graciously hosted Patti and me for dinner at the new lodge even when we were staying elsewhere and fishing with an independent guide. While Black Fly has an executive chef in a tall hat who comes from the kitchen to announce and explain each course, I still remember Clint's minced lobster at the temporary place. He's as good a chef as you'll find.

WHO'S WHO?

On our fly-fishing trips, Patti loves the lodge experience that allows us to meet folks from all over the place. Accordingly, at lodges around the world, we have dined with what some folks would call big shots. But, like almost everybody at those venues, we never, ever ask people we meet the crass question: "What do you do?" Our preference is to simply enjoy the company of new and interesting fellow guests, apart from any particular interest in, or knowledge of, their pedigree or lack thereof. Perhaps not surprisingly, the preponderance of the conversation at these lodges is about...yep, the fishing.

Despite this, the backgrounds of fellow guests can become revealed. So, in our years of visiting lodges, we have come to know several former chairmen of the world's largest corporations, a former US ambassador to a European country, a four-star admiral, a secretary of state for an Asian country, professional golfers, Roosevelt's grandson, and even an Australian lady who was a Master of Wine (there are only 416 in the entire world). Without exception, these folks are as regular as can be and just fun to be with.

At one lodge, however, there was a guest we thought a little too forward as he did pose to other guests the question Patti and I always avoid: "So, what do you do?"

He asked that question of a fellow gentleman guest one evening, a solo angler.

That guest's answer was, "I'm retired, but I worked for the Coca Cola Company."

Undaunted, the next evening, this too-curious guest would not relent. He asked the same gentleman, "So, I believe you said last night you worked for the Coca Cola Company. What did you do at Coke?"

His answer: "I was Chairman of the Board."

Don't Forget These!

There are some excellent Bahamian bonefish lodges I have fished from that are not included in this book, and I list them and their websites here:

Swain's Cay Lodge—Mangrove Cay, Andros—www.swainscaylodge.com

Caerula Mar Club—South Andros—www.caerulamar.com

Mars Bay Bonefish Lodge—South Andros—www.androsbonefish.com

H2O Bonefishing—Freeport—www.H2Obonefishing.com

Thirty-Seven

I Love You, Too, Frank!

Miss Patti and I have made seven trips to New Zealand bonefishing.

Hold on, you say. This book is about bonefishing and other saltwater flats fishing but—are you kidding me?—there's no *bonefishing* in New Zealand! You'd better explain!

Well, I explain it this way: There may not be any bonefish in New Zealand—good old *Albula vulpes*—but there is definitely bonefishing!

I say that because, first, like a bonefish flat, the water in New Zealand rivers is as clear as denatured alcohol. Next, there is virtually no blind casting as it's stalking and hunting fish followed by strategically sight-fishing them. Sound familiar? I know, I know, the target is trout but, I swear, it's almost more like bonefishing than bonefishing.

Here's how it works:

Float boats are not used; it's all walk and wade. After arriving at your river either by SUV or helicopter, you and your guide walk slowly along the bank, looking, looking, and looking at the water. The guide leads the way with the anglers following. There's a cardinal rule: An angler never gets in front of the guide. Because there might be a yet undiscovered fish and, with the water clarity and peripheral vision of trout, venturing too far might betray the presence of the team of guide and anglers.

What often happens is that three people—a guide followed by two anglers—creep slowly along the bank staring at the water and suddenly the lead angler's nose gets planted between the shoulder blades of the guide because the guide has abruptly stopped his creeping. The guide raises his hand and points to the water and says something like, "Do you see that large, tan-colored rock there about three feet upstream from the small darker one?"

The angler right behind the guide stares at the water, summoning all available powers of concentration. Finally, he or she says, "Yes, I see that."

"Okay, now come just toward the middle of the river and another two feet upstream and tell me what you see."

It takes a minute or two for the angler, eyes possibly straining a bit, to say, "Oh, my God, he's huge!"

"Yes, he is," the guide might say. "A very nice brown. Now, here's what I want you to do."

A discussion ensues reviewing the strategy for making the optimum presentation of the fly to that fish. This considers where in the water column the fish is holding and feeding—up near the surface or down lower. If the former, a single dry fly (one that floats) is dictated. If the latter, the guide will likely choose a dry fly with a dropper (a second fly tied on below the floating one that tumbles with the current down the river closer to the bottom). This strategy session will also include where the angler stands to make the cast, taking into account trees that may hinder the backcast and the movement of the current.

It's time to make the presentation, which means it's also time for the angler's throat to become a little dry and butterflies to assume residence in the angler's abdomen. That's owing to the percentages. Most New Zealand guides will say a near-perfect first cast should give the angler close to a 100 percent chance of a take. They add that if a second cast is necessary that percentage goes down to 75 percent, a third cast to 25 percent, and a fourth cast…well, let's move on to the next fish.

This phenomenon calls to mind our first trip. We were veterans of some trout fishing out west where it's possible to float a river and catch upwards of forty trout in a day's fishing. So, one of our first days in New Zealand, our guide, on the way to our river, said, "On the beat we'll be fishing today, I predict you will see eleven fish."

Patti and I looked at each other.

I Love You, Too, Frank!

"That's all?" I said.

"Yes," he said. "And if you catch four or five of them you will have had a splendid day."

Well, damned if we didn't see exactly eleven fish, and we managed to catch four of them. The smallest was twenty-one inches, and one went twenty-six inches! We quickly learned how a four-fish day in New Zealand, which is all about sight-fishing, technical presentations, and enormous fish, can be far more satisfying than forty smaller fish floating and blind casting.

So, in New Zealand you get "bonefishing" in a magical place full of natural wonders inhabited by happy, congenial people called Kiwis. We love everything about it, especially considering the trout fishing is easily the best on the planet.

Why is New Zealand trout fishing THE best?

First, the wild trout—browns and rainbows introduced in 1867—are all monsters as there are no predators to speak of. Most New Zealand birds eat other birds or land mammals like hares. And the longfin eels that inhabit the rivers, pesky night feeders with lousy eyesight that rely on their sense of smell to target trout, are not in large enough numbers to make an impact.

However, the numbers of those sometimes five-foot-long eels in New Zealand rivers are too great for Miss Patti. We have pictures of one that, while we were fishing one day, wanted to be our friend as it kept nudging our wading boots. This eel was no dummy. Like sharks hanging around a bonefish skiff waiting for something nice to happen, Mr. Eel was hoping for one of our released trout to be tuckered out enough to become vulnerable. What was Miss Patti's assessment of that eel and all the others she's seen in New Zealand? As I recall, it was somewhere between "creepy" and "icky."

Patti and I went to both the North and South Islands and to five different fly-fishing lodges before settling on one to which we most often returned. Many anglers go to New Zealand and engage independent guides while staying in small motels near their fishing and dining at local restaurants. But Patti prefers the full-service lodge experience primarily because of all the interesting people from all over the place we dine with each night at a communal table.

On that first New Zealand trip, we split our time equally between fishing and touring and went only to the South Island, starting in Christ Church and ending up in Queenstown. Probably the most thrilling tourist thing we've ever done was a James Bond type of experience we had with the Over the Top Helicopter Company in Queenstown touring the Fiordland's Milford Sound.

We started by landing at the top of a multi-hundred-foot-high waterfall and getting out for a glass of wine. Then it was all the way down to the sea where we landed on a beach and disembarked to interact with the seals. Next was all the way to one of the highest peaks where we landed on a glacier. We were going to get out of the chopper but that got scratched when our pilot jumped out in the snow and went in up to his chest! Over the Top Helicopters was aptly named—quite an experience.

On our way from Queenstown to a fishing area called The Southland, we stopped at fly shop called The Brown Trout in a little place called Athol. I bought the neatest hunter-green fishing cap with a tan bill and the shop's name on it that surrounded a beautifully embroidered brown trout. I dearly loved that cap and enjoyed wearing it for the many years that elapsed before we made our next trip to fish the Southland. On that later trip, I looked for The Brown Trout shop, but it was no longer there. However, by chance, one day our guide was driving us back to our lodge and stopped to chat with a friend of his. It was the man, now elderly and a bit decrepit, who had owned The Brown Trout fly shop for many years before retiring and closing it. When we learned that, we got out of the vehicle and joined the conversation because, guess what?—I was wearing the hat I bought from him years earlier.

I didn't have to draw his attention to it. He saw immediately and, staring at it, told me it had been his favorite, and he regretted not saving one from his shop inventory for himself. Well, I couldn't stand it. I removed my cherished fishing chapeau and handed it to him. I saw his eyes become moist before he hugged me, a total stranger, in gratitude.

One of the lodges we visited on that first trip was in the Southland and is no longer operating as a fishing lodge. It was the Riverview Farm Lodge and was an operating sheep farm as well.

We had some amazing "bonefishing."

Our guide was a chap named Paul Pinder (same name as an excellent Abaco Bahamas bonefish guide with whom I've fished), and he showed us some superb fishing. I still remember his taking us to Gibraltar. It was a place on a bend in the river with a gargantuan rock perhaps fifty feet tall. I remember Paul telling us to wait while he climbed Gibraltar. He reached the top and stayed there several minutes as he stared at the river intently.

When he came down, he said to us, "Follow me, please."

"Did you see anything?" I asked.

He looked at me with a smirk.

"As I said, follow me, please."

We did. To a place downstream from the big rock and on the bend. Once there, he took my rod from me and pointed it at the river.

"See that?" he asked.

I peered down the length of the nine-foot, 5-weight fly rod he was using as a pointer and saw a brown trout that, in the water, looked more like a long Yule log that was somehow almost floating. This prodigious fish was holding in his feeding station lazily rising to the surface to gently sip flies floating his way. My pulse rose, and my hands went clammy.

"What do I do?" I managed to squeak.

Paul broke out in a grin. "Catch the bloody fish, Mate!" he said.

From his fly box, Paul selected a rather small cicada pattern and tied it on for me. I made a cast just above the fish but too wide of the mark for the fish to see it. Remembering that having to make the second cast takes one's percentage down elevated the clammy state of my palms to something near sopping. I tried again, and this time the fly was floating, drag-free, right over the fish. He ate it!

That's the good news. The other good news is, as we got closer to my hooked fish while fighting it, Paul estimated this colossal critter exceeded a whopping thirty inches in length. Alas, the bad news was that, after a long chase of this hooked trophy down the rocky river, with yours truly falling on his face several times in the process, he eventually broke me off.

Our favorite New Zealand lodge is the Poronui on the North Island. It's a lovely establishment with plush accommodations and cuisine to match. But the best part is that Poronui Lodge has twenty-five miles of private water to fish via a special arrangement with the Māori tribes. All of that, together with their superb guides, has drawn us back there again and again.

To be sure, bonefishing...ah, excuse me...trout fishing in New Zealand is physically demanding. There are no float boats; it's all walk and wade. At Poronui, we mostly heli-fish.

The helicopter lands right on the lawn of the lodge to pick us up for a flight of anywhere from five to fifteen minutes. The chopper winds its way through and around mountains, sometimes coming so close it feels like it's possible to see the dendritic patterns on the tree leaves. The vistas are riveting, capturing one's attention, admiration, and awe. Nearing the destination river, the machine seems to corkscrew its way from altitude down between gorge-like cliffs to a landing spot such as a gravel bar on the river. Beginning our descent, the targeted gravel bar appears as the size of one of our wading boots. But as we continue to drop, it gets larger until, often just a few yards from nearby trees, we gently land.

The first few times the entire process gets your attention!

We all exit the chopper, and Patti and I go to a "neutral corner" while the guide unloads his enormous backpack (our lunches, drinks, satellite phone, etc.) and our rods. The helicopter lifts off. There we are for the day—a guide, two anglers, the river, and its wonderful large trout. It's fabulous.

The physical demands I mentioned are due to the need to hike along the riverbank with terrain that is often uneven, rocky, or thick with vegetation. When it becomes impassible, you must cross the river to the opposite bank for easier walking. Depending on the water depth, the speed of the current, and how slippery are the river's rocks, such crossings can be, shall we say, sporty.

The difficult crossings are done one angler at a time, hanging onto the suspenders of the guides' waders. Patti always goes first, and I remember crossing a river with notoriously slippery rocks.

"They're like deer guts on a bowling ball," was the description of our wonderful guide Kunio.

When Patti and Kunio reached the middle of the river, I looked up from rearranging my fishing vest to see her body completely horizontal.

She had lost her footing, and the only thing keeping her from being swept downriver was her death grip on the guide's suspender. They made it across but...whew!

Another time the bank we were walking on became impassable, and the opposite bank was worse. It was necessary to do some rock climbing until we reached a bit of a peak where the lodge had left a rope for rappelling down to a small landing. Yes, we did it, but neither of us are anxious for a repeat.

Our favorite guide at Poronui Lodge was a former Brit named Sean Andrews who became a dear friend for whom Patti and I have great affection. But we have also fished with other Poronui guides, all outstanding.

One of those was the ebullient Dave Wood, with whom, over all our stays, we only fished one day. But what a day. We helicoptered to a beat on the Mohaka, and Dave put me on a marvelous rising brown trout that was consistently sipping cicadas on top. A truly memorable fish, he took my fly and (sometimes uncharacteristically for brown trout) began jumping all over the place. The beat we were fishing had an unusually tall far side dirt bank with no vegetation, and on the fish's last jump, he ricocheted off that bank, almost beaching himself. Dave had one of those landing nets with a built-in scale, and that fish weighed nine and a quarter pounds!

There was another Poronui guide we fished with only once—Derrick—and that was on the only water that does not have a Māori name: Mystery River. I have a video of him with his hand stuck down the back of Patti's waders so he could prevent her from falling as he followed her and her enormous, hooked rainbow trout down the middle of rocky-bottomed Mystery River. Quite a sight!

But back to our favorite Poronui guide and great friend, Sean Andrews, with whom we've experienced some wonderful fishing and many congenial hours. Sean shares our irrepressible sense of humor, and that came into play one fishing day.

I have a little thing I do when I land a particularly large fish, be it trout, bonefish, or other species. I will very briefly hold the fish to admire it and then bring its mouth within an inch of mine while I purse my lips for an air kiss. As I release the fish, filled with gratitude, I will often say, "I love you!"

Once when Patti and I were fishing with Sean Andrews, I caught and released a very large brown trout on the Mohaka River, administered my air kiss, and, once again, signed off with, "I love you!"

From behind me, I heard our witty, favorite guide Sean say, "I love you too, Frank!"

WHY NOT TRY IT?

Here are some thoughts that might be helpful to those thinking of going to New Zealand for the first time for some of that "bonefishing!" First, even if you are just touring and not fishing, there are some formidable visa requirements that require compliance. Next, if you are fishing, you must also obtain the proper fishing license. You can check all this out on the Internet or through your outfitter.

Speaking of outfitters, if you're an angler, you are likely already familiar with prominent ones like Yellow Dog Fly Fishing and Frontiers. While they can all take excellent care of you, Patti and I have booked all our trips with Mike McClelland of Best of New Zealand Fly Fishing in Los Angeles, who has done a marvelous job. If you're also a golfer, Mike's son-in-law runs Best of New Zealand Golf and can arrange for you to stay and play at the hotsy-totsy courses like Cape Kidnappers and Kauri Cliffs. And a well-known company called Kaylos also books wonderful New Zealand golf trips combined with cruises. Definitely recommend using an outfitter for a New Zealand trip.

If there is a single New Zealand tip to share, it is this: Avoid taking your own boots and waders. That's because New Zealand is very prissy about allowing foreign substances into their country. If you take your own boots and waders, you must disinfect them before you go and provide documentation (a veterinarian can do this for you). You must then declare on your passenger arrival card that you have brought waders and boots, whereupon you will be escorted to a Quarantine Officer who will then turn you over to Biosecurity for testing. If they are not satisfied, they may disinfect your stuff all over again to make certain they kill any invasive pests, such as something called didymo. And don't even think about taking felt-soled boots—strictly prohibited.

So, what's the easiest way to deal with this? Simply leave your waders and boots at home. Most New Zealand lodges furnish their guests with waders and boots at no charge, and I believe many independent guides do the same. Poronui Lodge has a room full of waders and boots that looks as large as an Orvis store.

This brings up a related topic: Waders or wet-wade. Wet-wading is very popular in New Zealand. It usually means wearing capilene long underwear with a pair of flats-fishing shorts on top along with a pair of wool socks beneath neoprene socks and wading boots. Patti will sometimes choose wet-wading on warm days, although the water in the rivers is quite cold. As for me, I am very cold-natured. I tried wet-wading once on a warm day and froze my tutu, whereupon it was permanently back to waders for me. Call me a wimp, I guess.

If you take your own flies to New Zealand, make sure you include plenty of cicada patterns as, in the summer fishing season (our winter), these fat, juicy blobs of protein are irresistible to the trout. Before my first New Zealand trip, I also acquired several mouse flies that look very much like…yes, mice. But I have never been there when the mice were swimming across the rivers getting annihilated by the gorging trout. Maybe one day.

If you haven't been there, I hope you will consider a trip to New Zealand. And please don't be put off by the distance. "Oh, it's just too far—too long a flight," some folks say. But I respectfully suggest saving that opinion for after you try it, as I have found flying to New Zealand easier than Europe. Here's why:

First, at our age, we go flat-bed business class on flights over oceans or we simply do not take the trip. Most flights to Europe are around eight hours in duration and depart the United States in the early evening, arriving at "zero dark thirty" the next morning. The first two hours of those flights are filled with loud conversation by the passengers and clinking glasses and dinner dishes by the crew. The last hour is more clinking and clattering associated with breakfast. So, that leaves only five hours for sleep and, moreover, your body time is something like three in the morning when you arrive. Can you spell "zombie"?

Sure, flying to New Zealand is a lot longer (fifteen hours from Houston to Auckland on Air New Zealand) but is leisurely and relaxing. The flights leave around eight in the evening and cocktails and dinner are at a civilized pace before your bed is made by the crew. You cross the international date line and therefore lose a day, which means you arrive around six in the morning New Zealand time with a refreshing full night's sleep and zero jet lag. As I say, why not try it?

JUST THE FACTS
Name of Lodge: Poronui Lodge
Location: New Zealand North Island near Lake Taupo
Nearest Airport: Lake Taupo (TUO)
Drive from Airport to Lodge: Thirty-eight minutes
Getting There: There are many commercial flights from the United States to Auckland, followed by connections to Lake Taupo on Air New Zealand.
Capacity: Sixteen guests
Rate for Seven Nights Lodging, Six Days Fishing: $14,572NZ (2025 rates)
Includes: Guided fishing, lodging, all meals, double occupancy, house wine
Does Not Include: Tips, airfare, airport transfer, helicopter fees
Website: www.poronui.com

Author Comments: This may be our favorite lodge in the world. It's remote and rustic yet luxurious. The cuisine, the wines, the staff, and, of course, the "bonefishing" are incomparable. On average over the years, the rate shown here translates into perhaps around $9,500 USD. Multiply that times two if you're a couple and add tips, helicopter fees, and airfare, and, well, it's pricey but, again, that "bonefishing" is hard to beat!

Thirty-Eight

'Cuda, Wuda, Shuda

I love catching large barracudas on the flats. But let me be more specific: I'm not wild about a popular technique of "meat-fishing," which is catching them on a tube lure casted by a spinning rod. Instead, I like the far less automatic but more sporting method of catching them on fly.

I call 'cudas the "poor man's tarpon." It's because they jump like crazy but, interestingly, they often jump in a greyhounding sort of way. By that I mean more horizontal than vertical like a tarpon. Another fascinating thing about 'cudas is their swimming speed of thirty-six miles per hour. But their top-end speed is only part of that fascination. That's because 'cudas tend to simply hang in the water column, motionless, until they sense nearby prey to attack. When that attack occurs, I maintain that the naked eye cannot discern when they have gone from motionless to that thirty-six-mile-per-hour speed. It's that quick. And, as an angler, it's completely exhilarating to watch.

A barracuda has to be at least three feet long for me to cast to it, and I use a 9-weight rod with 20-pound-test leader. But, as many of you know, a six to eight inch section of wire tippet must go between the leader and the fly as 'cudas have teeth reminiscent of a horror movie monster. So, fishing with 20-pound monofilament leader alone would mean losing both fish and fly. Rather than dealing with wire, I go with the much-easier-to-rig "knottable wire tippet." It's like working with monofilament leader material—ties easily and gives you the break-off protection of wire. Mainly because it is wire underneath that material that makes it so easy to work with.

The most popular fly for barracuda is a long, predominantly green-colored streamer pattern. My pal Allen Wyatt of Andy Thornal & Co. in Winter Haven, Florida ties them for me with two hooks that are about three inches apart. Allen's double-hook fly is a big help because a barracuda take is the polar opposite of a large river trout lazily sipping a surface fly. Indeed, a 'cuda will execute the aforementioned rapid acceleration from being stationary and approach its prey in a violent, slashing attack. While a 'cuda's aggressiveness is awesome, its accuracy is, well, not so much. This often means a swing and a miss if fishing with a single-hook fly, but the angler's odds nicely improve with Allen Wyatt's double-hook fly. Now, all this said, I have also had good barracuda fishing with a red and silver top-water popping bug.

So, how to fish barracuda on fly? The preferred method is to cast the fly at least fifteen feet away from the usually mostly stationary fish and another fifteen feet past him. This allows the angler to begin furiously stripping the fly in the 'cuda's field of vision in the hope he finds it appealing. But the stripping technique is of paramount importance as it must be fast, fast, fast! And when you think you're stripping fast...strip faster! A good technique for achieving top stripping speed is to strip two-handed after jamming your fly rod under one armpit. This is the same way many anglers strip for tarpon except that, for tarpon, the objective is to make the fly swim smoothly while for barracuda its simply to make it swim at the speed of a major leaguer's fast ball.

On a recent trip to Cuba, a guide there taught me a new and different stripping technique for 'cuda that was immediately effective as it resulted in a hookup each time I tried it. I'll try to describe it.

It's a conventional single-handed strip, but it's accompanied by simultaneously and aggressively separating the rod hand from the stripping hand as you strip, which results in substantially more action on the fly. That's the best I can do at describing it with words, but I can tell you that I never had seen it anywhere and, man, did it work!

While fishing for bonefish in the Bahamas, barracuda shots always draw plenty of attention from the guide because they will always accept the invitation to keep your landed 'cuda and, as big as they are, one fish can feed their family for multiple days.

So, are barracuda good to eat? Frankly, they are delicious, but there is always the little matter of whether you will die from eating one. Many who read this will know exactly what I'm talking about. It's a toxin called ciguatera. Death is actually rare, but you can be very, very sick for a very long time.

Ciguatera is mostly found in various reef fish, so Bahamians regularly eat barracuda taken from the flats in belief that flats 'cudas are safe. But I have heard of exceptions to this along with one fascinating revelation by a Bahamian bonefish guide:

"Yeah, Mon, I always eat 'cuda caught on the flats, but I wait until the second day."

"The second day?" I repeated.

"Yeah, Mon. The first day, I give some to my cat. If he be alive the second day, I figure I'm good."

I rolled my eyes at that one and did not comment. I have no idea if he was pulling my leg or not. I will tell you that Patti and I did eat a barracuda we caught at Flamingo Cay Club once. It was delicious, and we did not get sick.

One last thing about fighting a jumpy barracuda: Just like a tarpon, don't forget to bow!

THIRTY-NINE

On Vacation??

One of the most captivating lodge situations in the Bahamas is more than just a bonefish destination. It has a storied history.

Flamingo Cay Rod & Gun Club, on the barren, desolate, uninhabited west side of Andros Island, is inaccessible by roads. There is no airport, marina, or power plant and certainly no cable television. Everything runs off generators and satellite. The nearest jump-off point to get there in a fast skiff is Cargill Creek on the east side of Andros, and you're looking at a full-throttle boat ride of two hours in decent conditions.

But that's not how Flamingo Cay Club's guests arrive. Instead, they fly to Nassau and take a taxi to the owner and host's house on a lake in Nassau and board his enormous turbine-powered Otter floatplane. An amphibian, the craft seems so roomy that it could fly a football team to the lodge. The plane lands guests on a large bay called the Wide Opening and taxis to the lodge, whereupon it crawls onto the land to find its berth in a canvass-covered hanger.

So, who is this owner and host? A Bahamian from Nassau named Charles B. M. Bethel III, a descendant of a family that, among their other enterprises, controlled the distribution of liquor for all the Bahamas. In 1926, the British Crown deeded the Bethel family thirty-two square miles on the west side of Andros Island (the largest island in the Bahamas), after which the family would often host the likes of the Duke of Windsor and the Prince of Wales for shooting teal.

Charlie Bethel, by the way, is the pilot for his Otter and the rest of his fleet that includes a smaller floatplane and a helicopter. Moreover, he recently bought a small freighter that he remodeled as a mothership to base some of his anglers at Williams and Billy Islands. Oh, and he has a large airboat for fishing some landlocked bights and for teal hunting.

Charlie, in addition to flying his own fleet of airplanes, is the consummate outdoorsman and occasionally guides his guests on the flats himself. But he has another side: He is a consummate gentleman and is knowledgeable about fine wines and cuisine.

Charlie is one of those guys who can fix *anything*. In fact, on one of my stays there, we had a major overnight rain event that overwhelmed the automatic bilge pumps in his brand-new, state-of-the-art Hells Bay skiffs, and the next morning, he found them sunk at the dock. By around eleven o'clock, with his own hands, he had them all ready to rumble, and everybody went fishing. Amazing.

Charlie Bethel is a fierce conservationist and has pioneered techniques for releasing landed bonefish without the angler touching the fish. This is important because, as we know from the science provided by Dr. Aaron Adams of Bonefish & Tarpon Trust, touching the body of a bonefish disturbs its protective slime. Charlie was also among the first to campaign against using a BogaGrip to hang bonefish by their jaws. Bonefish & Tarpon Trust has sided with Charlie and strongly discourages this practice.

I'm not sure if it's true, but I heard that long ago Charlie outlawed BogaGrips at Flamingo Cay Club. I was also told that one guest insisted on bringing his and using it. My further understanding is the guest was allowed to have dinner that night but the next morning was on Charlie's Otter back to Nassau!

Charlie and his sweetheart Cindy are the consummate hosts at a lodge that cleverly provides supreme luxury and comfort while preserving the pure tropical wilderness setting and its ambiance. There are luxurious sleeping rooms and among some little thatched-roof out buildings are the "Duck Down Bar" (you must stoop to walk in) and the dining room. One of the times I was there, Charlie had a French chef who spoke limited English but produced superb cuisine. Charlie has a wine

ON VACATION??

cellar to go with that cuisine. To top everything off, there is also a spa with a masseuse.

So, what about the fishing? Almost all you have to know is that from Flamingo Cay Club (and yes, there is an excellent chance of seeing flamingos) it is but a five-minute ride in a skiff to Rupert Leadon's famous Land of the Giants and its trophy bonefish. That said, my favorite (or maybe not) Flamingo Cay fish story occurred while tarpon fishing between Williams and Billy Island, about a forty-minute boat ride from the lodge.

Patti and I had the good fortune that day to be guided by the boss, Charlie Bethel. But not all fish stories have fortuitous outcomes. Patti was the angler and hooked a perfectly lovely tarpon that easily went sixty pounds. What was the problem? Well, it was blowing twenty to twenty-five, and yours truly was the designated "line manager" for Patti's stripped out fly line that seemed to insist upon whipping around all over the boat and sometimes overboard in that wind. Yep, you guessed it. The line manager became preoccupied with watching Patti's jumping tarpon and, shall we say, took his eye off the ball. You know the ending—the line became wrapped on something on the deck, she broke off her tarpon, and began glaring at her so-called line manager who shrank away in humiliation and remorse.

But later, the disgraced line manager buoyed his crushed spirits by landing a barracuda on a red and silver popping bug that Charlie estimated went close to twenty pounds.

Sadly, the line manager wasn't out of the doghouse yet. At dinner that night, Charlie, at the line manager's expense, shared the whole story in detail with all the other guests. I couldn't get mad at Charlie—I had it coming.

Speaking of our dinners, one time Patti and I were there and all the other anglers at the lodge were couples. Charlie and Cindy always dine with their guests, and the first night, Charlie raised his glass in welcome and announced, "I just want to thank you all for choosing Flamingo Cay Rod & Gun Club for your vacation."

A gentleman guest at the far end of the table, glass still raised, replied with a grin, "Vacation? Charlie, we're not on vacation. This is what we do!"

223

Just the Facts

Name of Lodge: Flamingo Cay Rod & Gun Club

Location: Western shore of Andros Island, Bahamas on "The Wide Opening"

Nearest Airport: Nassau (NAS)

From Airport to Lodge: Float plane ride from lake by owner's home to lodge is about thirty minutes.

Getting There: Numerous commercial flights to Nassau

Capacity: Eight guests

Rate for Five Nights Lodging, Four Days Fishing: See author comments

Includes: Guided fishing, lodging, all meals, beverages, double occupancy, shared skiff, open bar

Does Not Include: VAT, tips, airfare to Nassau, charge for float plane to lodge

Website: See author comments

Author Comments: Like Abaco's Black Fly Lodge, which accepts guests only "by appointment," Flamingo Cay no longer has a website. And since it's been a while since I've been there, I have no idea what the current rates are. But I can tell you that the last time I went they were substantially higher than other lodges. I have an idea that quite a few of their guests arrive on their own aircraft. If you're interested in going, you might try one of the big outfitters like Yellow Dog or Frontiers. I actually have Cindy's email, but I'm not sure she wants it distributed as I'm thinking their regulars are all they feel they need. I could be wrong about that, but it's time for me to contact her about a return engagement, and I'll try to find out then. Suffice it to say, it will easily be, probably by far, the most expensive Bahamian bonefish lodge you would visit. However, it will probably be totally worth it. It's just so unique. It is remote—only practically accessible by air—it's right next to the honey holes, it's sumptuously luxurious, Charlie and Cindy are a delight…it goes on and on.

FORTY

Prudent and Pithy Piscatorial Precepts

(a.k.a.—Some Nifty Tips for
Fishing the Saltwater Flats)

HOW'S THAT LINE SHOOTING FOR YOU?
There is something that seems to be a blind spot with many anglers and even guides. I have noticed that a number of my angling partners do not clean their fly lines throughout several days of fishing. And most surprising to me is that on many occasions my guide has handed me one of his rods for either fishing or casting practice and I can tell the fly line has not been cleaned in some time.

How can I tell? Because I can't get the line to shoot very well. And why is this? Well, I learned when I first began owning and operating my personal boats that saltwater dries and cakes on any surface and cannot simply be rinsed off. Instead, it must be rubbed off. Which is why each evening I clean and dress the lines I fished with that day. It's a quick, simple, three-step process. First, I simply drag the line through a paper towel that I have soaked in hot water to remove the caked salt. Next, I put some Scientific Anglers fly line dressing on another paper towel and drag the fly line through it (it's not necessary to let the line dry before doing this). Finally, I reel the line back on the reel while dragging it through a clean paper towel to remove excess dressing and keep it from any purpose-defeating extra "goopiness." I hit the flats the next day confident that any difficulty getting line to shoot will be attributed to my sometimes-spotty casting and not the condition of my fly lines. Recalling the butterflies I get with a fly rod in my hand while staring at the eyeballs of a possible double-digit bonefish eighty feet away, I can't imagine not cleaning my lines each night.

Where's Your Thumb?

When out fishing on a skiff it's not uncommon for anglers to pick up each other's rods and sometimes cast them just to see how another brand or rod/fly line combination seems to perform. Guides will also pick up their client's rod for the same purpose.

Almost everybody who picks up one of my rods comments on a modification I make to all my fly rods. It's my "thumb rest."

The cork handle on all my rods has a slight indentation I have installed in the spot where the caster's thumb goes when gripping it. I install this indentation on the cork grip of a new rod by using two types of sandpaper—the first is coarse sandpaper to make the little "well" for one's thumb, and the second is smooth sandpaper to put a nice finish on the result.

Most rave about this little self-installed feature. Only once have I had the technique questioned. It was by someone who mused whether a rod manufacturer would refuse to honor the warranty on a rod that I had "tampered" with. Well, I have returned many a broken rod for repair and never had a problem.

I got the idea from watching a video by someone who is called "The First Lady of Fly Fishing." Her maiden name was Joan Salvato until she married another fly-fishing legend, Lee Wulff (as in the Royal Wulff fly pattern).

Without her dad's permission Joan picked up her dad's fly rod when she was ten years of age and never looked back. By the time she was in her teens and early twenties, she was winning national fly-casting championships against men! Nobody could come close to her in the accuracy division, and her record in the distance division against men was an astounding 131 feet that was later exceeded when a women's division was formed with a cast of an unfathomable 162 feet!

So, it's not surprising that I became keenly interested in Joan Wulff's casting videos. The one that resonated was her power snap, which she says is all about the thumb. She did plenty of casting in the video but she also used a prop. It was an aluminum screen door handle—no door, just the handle. She used it to demonstrate two things. One is keeping your thumb 180 degrees opposite the casting target. The other was pressing down the button on the screen door handle on the forward cast to simulate the power snap.

I bought into her theory, it helped my casting, and it gave me the idea for the thumb rest on my rods. Our fly-fishing legends are indeed a treasure.

Don't Forget Your Gloves...Boxing, That Is

There was once one of those radio personality guys with a comedic schtick that involved calling up folks who had no idea they were on the air. He called himself R. D. Mercer, and his gimmick was to register some sort of trumped up complaint such as, "I got a real problem with you because you sold my wife the wrong size shoes and they're hurtin' her feet real bad." He would purposely escalate the phony beef until he concluded with, "I believe I'm just gonna have to come over there and whup yore ass!"

Well, I have never met anyone toting a fly rod case who was not either a perfect gentleman or lady. But I have witnessed anglers almost come to the point of, like R. D. Mercer, "opening up a can of whoop ass" when discussing a certain topic.

That topic is...maybe you guessed it...whether it's best to crank a fly reel with one's left or one's right hand. It is perhaps more accurate to define the controversial question as whether to wind one's fly reel with the angler's dominant or nondominant hand. But for our purposes, let's say the right hand is dominant.

Now, if you are a right-hand cranker, please don't burn this book in disgust. Because I am in the left-hand cranking camp.

That said, I fully understand the theory behind using the right hand, which is that retrieving line is among the most critical operations of fighting a fish and, particularly with a long, tough fight, one wants the most power and stamina applied to the retrieve.

But I respectfully disagree as follows:

First, many anglers grew up fishing with spinning tackle and are accustomed to holding the rod with the right hand and cranking with the left. I am one of those and firmly believe I can crank just as fast, long, and hard with my left hand as with my right.

Next, if one is right-handed, the rod is held with that hand. So, to me, shifting the rod to one's left hand so the retrieving can be done with the right exposes the angler to the risky circumstance of temporarily losing pressure on the fish.

Finally, I believe it is more important to use one's dominant hand on the rod to maintain constant, maximum pressure on one's hooked fish. And with that I rest my case.

STRIP...STRIP...STOP

We've talked about various stripping techniques for bonefish. There are conflicting opinions on the topic, even among guides. Many will insist on a long, slow strip while others like short strips. I've never heard any guide recommend a vigorous strip unless it's necessary to recover from an inaccurate cast and quickly get the fly where the fish might see it. Why are fast, vociferous strips not favored? Because it can startle the bonefish and spook it into oblivion. Feeding bonefish are in pure predatory mode and prefer to be opportunists happening upon an unsuspecting morsel that is not behaving erratically but rather normally and methodically.

Over the years, I have become persuaded that tiny little strips are advisable if you are presenting to a very big fish. In fact, I have had success in such situations just barely moving the fly while experiencing diminished success when making my fly act too frisky.

But, to me, the most challenging aspect of effective stripping for bonefish is dealing with wind. I know, I know...how does wind affect something that's happening beneath the surface of the water? It doesn't. But wind does very much affect the movement of the skiff. And if the wind is too brisk or the bottom too rocky, the guide will not be able to use his push pole to get the skiff stopped while his angler is stripping on a fish.

This often means the skiff drifts down on the fish and fly at the same speed as the angler's stripping. The result? The fly ends up not actually moving and the fish therefore does not see it, a frustrating and challenging circumstance. It happens because it's difficult for the angler to simultaneously watch the fish he is presenting to and sense the drifting speed of the skiff over the bottom and compensate for that with the proper stripping speed.

It's a dilemma for which I confess to not having a pat answer. I suppose my tip can only be this: Try to be aware of what the skiff is doing as well as your targeted fish. And make sure you're in touch with your fly with your stripping hand at all times and that you feel some resistance as you strip. Hopefully that will make sure your fly is not stationary.

THE LITTLE ONE ATE IT

You may remember the Humble Servant Bonefishing tee shirt and the montage of bonefish guide commentary on the back of it. One of those comments was: "The little one ate it."

Those of you who have fished large or small schools of bonefish with a fly rod know what that means. You also know that it happens with annoying frequency. This phenomenon can be especially maddening when, as is often the case, there are very large bonefish occupying the school along with fish of a size you might not even bother casting to if they were swimming solo. So, is there anything an angler can do about a baby bonefish (sometimes called a "dink") taking the fly instead of a trophy fish? Yes, but it requires keen eyesight and a somewhat sophisticated technique.

A common failing of many anglers is casting to bonefish, stripping the fly, and failing to strip-strike to set the hook because they do not realize the fish has eaten the fly. The verbalization of this goes as follows:

Guide: "Strip, strip, strip. He's got it!"

But no hookup.

Guide: "You didn't strike!"

Angler: "But I didn't feel anything."

The frustrated guide has seen the fish follow the fly, go down on it to eat it, and then spit the fly out because the angler did nothing.

Well, believe it or not, committing this same error ON PURPOSE can be effective in pursuing the larger fish swimming with smaller ones in a school. But the angler must be able to see exactly what's going on to be able to know that one of the juveniles in the school is attempting eat his or her fly whereupon the angler simply DOES NOT STRIP-STRIKE. The goal is for the baby bonefish to spit the fly, therefore allowing the angler to either begin stripping again when larger fish in the school come near his or her fly or pick the fly up and re-cast near a larger fish in the school.

I realize this technique may draw little or no interest from anglers who say, "I don't care how big they are, I just want to catch bonefish!" Anglers who say that likely have far fewer trips under their belts than veteran anglers who have concluded that they don't really need to catch any more very small bonefish from schools.

THE BOW OF THE SKIFF

It was either the Four Seasons or the Ritz Carlton organization that emphasized that they understood the subtle differences that make a guest experience memorable. Well, fly fishing can be very technical, and subtle differences can often define an angler's success.

There are things happening on the bow of a skiff that involve subtle differences.

One of those is the leaning post. For non-anglers reading this, a leaning post is an aluminum or stainless-steel structure on the casting platform (bow) of a flats skiff placed there for the purpose of giving the angler something to lean on when a little weary from a long poling episode over a flat with no fish sighted. Another use is providing safety and stability to an angler when the guide is poling the skiff in a chop.

Now, I'm fine with leaning posts. But only if they are properly located on the bow, otherwise I request they be removed (which is easy). Some lodges make the mistake of placing the leaning post too far forward, causing it to interfere with a long strip of the fly, therefore becoming a "knuckle-buster."

To me, the ideal location for a leaning post is far enough back to avoid interference with stripping—that's obvious. But ideally it will also be far enough back to allow an angler with a bad back to stand, not on the bow, but in the cockpit of the skiff while the skiff is on a plane pounding in a heavy chop and hang onto the leaning post for safety. Now, here's where I get really picky. If the leaning post is also placed so the non-fishing angler can help his fishing partner spot fish by standing on the rear edge of the platform but behind the leaning post...well, that's perfection.

The other thing happening on the casting platform is a key element of saltwater flats fishing, and that's line management. The first step in readying a fly rod to cast to a fish is stripping fly line off the reel. I almost always strip out eighty feet of it. How do I know? Because I make twenty-five pulls of line off the fly reel and know that's what it is from having measured it while practicing casting on my lawn. Where does that line go? Many anglers allow it to accumulate in a pile on the bow waiting for the cast when a fish appears.

Sounds simple but, unfortunately, there is an awful lot that can go wrong. One is a stiff wind that can cause that fly line to be blown overboard and even wrapped under and around the bow before the angler realizes it. Another is, in the absence of good line management, the angler can inadvertently step on his stripped-out fly line in the process of casting, which will abort the cast. Another is the angler can begin casting to an attractive fish only to find that the stripped-out fly line has unknowingly tangled—cast over before it begins.

I never go on a saltwater flats trip without my LineLair. It's a product of a company called Carbon Marine, and it's a rubber casting mat about two feet in diameter with removable rubber "nails" that stick up in the air about four inches. Instead of line stripped onto a smooth deck to be blown overboard, tangled, or stepped on, line stripped onto the LineLair's nails is kept out of harm's way and ready to be casted when that big-un comes along.

But the LineLair is not the only available casting mat or accessory for casting platform line management. Also effective is a stripping bucket. It looks like a skinny trash can, about waist high to the angler with a heavy weight on its bottom to keep it from tipping or blowing overboard. The line gets stripped into the bucket and is then ready to cast with zero chance of being blown overboard or stepped on. These are prevalent on tarpon fishing skiffs.

Finally, there is "the cage." It's a little difficult to describe if you haven't seen one. The cage is a contraption that begins with a little casting stool that is sometimes seen anyway on tarpon skiffs. But up from the stool is an aluminum or stainless-steel cage-like structure that, when the angler is standing on the stool, encloses him or her on all four sides after entering through a removable section of the structure. This provides stability and safety when casting in a chop. The angler is also surrounded on all four sides by a 360-degree stripping basket that is integral to the structure and has a mesh bottom.

Some people hate the cages, but I kind of like them. They are very safe when fishing in a chop, line management is addressed beautifully, and the angler gets some extra elevation—better to see fish and to make a long cast.

Where's My 10-Weight?

The acquisition of my first tarpon fly rod was arranged by the guide who caught me my first tarpon on fly. That was Captain Phil O'Bannon in Boca Grande. Phil was a spokesman for Cabela's at the time and procured for me a two-piece 12-weight Cabela's rod made from a G. Loomis blank. And from Allen Wyatt at Andy Thornal & Co in Winter Haven, Florida., I bought Patti an 11-weight Orvis T-3. Much later, I went to a 12-weight, four-piece Orvis Helios that had a screw-on butt extension that made this nine-foot rod about nine feet, six inches in length.

But I no longer use that rod. When I began to do more tarpon fishing in the Keys and the Marquesas, guides would hand me an 11-weight to fish with. "Just try it," they would say. And I'm glad I did as it was so much easier to cast and fish with. This trend progressed, and I now mostly tarpon fish with my 10-weight Orvis Helios and conservation has much to do with that decision. Here's what I mean.

Unless you're fishing the Gold Cup tournament in Islamorada or going for a class tippet world record, nobody seems to try to land very large tarpon that are well over 100 pounds anymore. The reason is that it takes a very long time, the result being an exhausted fish that becomes easy prey for a shark. Many guides now instruct their anglers to, when a fight with a huge tarpon reaches the hunker-down stage, crank down to maximum on the drag causing the hook to straighten, resulting in a long-range release. So, with that approach adopted, fishing with a 10-weight tarpon rod is far more pleasurable than larger, heavier ones. However, I did land a Keys fish on my 10-weight that my guide estimated at 130 pounds. For some reason, the fight did not last that long, and we did not realize her large size until she was boatside.

I have also caught tarpon on the west side of Andros with my 9-weight as their size is usually agreeable to that. And, to me, an 8-weight is ideal for juvenile tarpon on mangrove banks.

There Oughtta Be a Law

When traveling to a lodge or using an independent guide to flats fish from a skiff there is an important thing I always consider, particularly now that I'm a little longer in the tooth and in a large group of folks who experience some kind of lower back pain.

That important thing is the seating on the skiff.

I sometimes joke that it should be a federal law that all flats skiffs be equipped with a back on all passenger seats. Most skiffs have a seat in front of the center console, and that console serves as a back for that seat. But many aft seats for the guide and the other angler are bench seats with no back. Long boat rides sitting on a bench seat with no back are not kind to either my back or my increasingly aching bones. That said, one of the redeeming aspects of the sport of fly fishing is that, unlike lacrosse, mountain climbing, or even softball, one can be successful at it in one's advancing years.

Therefore, I always make sure I determine in advance the seat details of the skiff from which I will be fishing. If I learn I'll be faced with a bench seat, I promptly cancel the trip. Just kidding, just kidding! What I really do is this: I take with me my Backcountry Cowboy.

I bought mine years ago from a store of the same name in Islamorada, Florida. It's essentially a very lightweight stadium seat made of two connected sections of canvass—one is the seat, the other the back. The two sections are connected with straps so the user can adjust the relative uprightness of his or her sitting experience.

It works beautifully. I could not do without it.

FORTY-ONE
Prudent Pithy Piscatorial Precepts Protracted
(More Handy Tips)

'DEM BUGS

I'll not list them here, but many wonderful books have been written on flies for fly fishing. Some of them feature exquisite photographs of flies, which, taken for their visual pleasure, are truly works of art and often present kaleidoscopes of dazzling colors that rival the beauty of exotic tropical birds. Other such books concentrate more on the technical aspects of tying the flies as they explore the pedigrees of varieties of animal hair and feathers used along with precise techniques for getting a newly tied fly just right.

I'm not going into any of that.

Instead, I'm just going to tell you what I do about flies for my own fishing in the hope that, particularly with less-experienced anglers, I can be of some help. One thing I do NOT do about flies is tie them. Two reasons: One is my lack of patience. The other is, as the country boy would say, "I ain't too good at that close work." Consequently, I am a purchaser of flies from fly shops and individuals who tie.

Here are my go-to saltwater flats flies:

For tarpon, I like purple and black streamers in the morning or in low light. As the sun gets higher, I go to brighter colors, starting with tan and sometimes going to bright green, yellow, or orange. In fact, I have a green tarpon toad fly attached to the frame of a photo hanging in my den of a 100-pounder taken from the oceanside at Islamorada. Palolo worm flies? You bet. Guides are widely using them even when there is no chance of a hatch.

Over the years, I have fished with a wide variety of bonefish flies before settling on three that are my old reliables.

Despite Mr. McVay inventing it almost fifty years ago, the Gotcha still gets regularly snarfed by hungry bonefish. I like the orange-and-tan color and prefer a barred tail (has stripes on it). And the Enrico Puglise Spawning Shrimp pattern, in almost any color, rarely gets refused. Finally, the Mantis Shrimp, a beige-colored fly with rubber silly legs, is always dependable.

Most of my bonefish flies are tied on a #4 hook and have bead chain eyes (a small, lightweight fly) as I aim to fish in skinny water whenever possible. When targeting larger fish in deeper water, I love fishing with a white-and-tan Gotcha Clouser fly. But I carry a wide selection of bonefish flies in both bead (light weight) and lead (heavier to sink better in deeper water) eyes.

Permit flies? I have a variety of crab patterns but in recent years have become persuaded that permit will eat a bonefish fly as quickly as anything else (not that they EVER eat a fly quickly, if at all). In fact, I also have a fly attached to a photo of a permit I caught. It was an olive-green, lead eye Enrico Puglise spawning shrimp pattern.

So, what to do if a bonefish refuses a fly you have expertly presented? The first thing is to keep fishing with it in case that fish was an outlier. If refusals continue, you change flies. But change to what? Interestingly, in his book on bonefishing, the legendary Chico Fernandez recommends first changing the size of the fly rather than the pattern or the color.

OUCH!

Know what a doctor fly is? It's a jumbo horsefly high on a cocktail of performance-enhancing drugs. Or maybe a creature from a horror movie. The Bahamians gave the name doctor fly to these mean-as-Nurse Ratchet bloodsuckers because their bite feels just like being on the business end of a hypodermic needle. And they visit you out on the flats in groups of four or five, executing controlled dive-bombing maneuvers that would put a Naval aviator to shame.

A fascinating fact about these diabolical critters is that they only bite one's lower extremities. I don't recall ever having been nailed on my face or arms. But the legs? Ouch, ouch, and ouch!

Although in recent years they don't seem nearly as bad, Andros Island has always been the doctor fly capital of the universe. Don't tell my dermatologist, but I prefer fishing in shorts rather than long, quick-dry flats or wading pants. But Andros? Nope. I break out the long pants.

So, you ask, what's my tip?

Sadly, I don't have one. I've had no luck with any of the repellant products, and long pants and socks are the only feeble defense.

There is one thing, however. On one of my mothership trips, the captain had the niftiest little sawed-off fly swatters with handles just like a bait-casting rod. Really clever. I've tried to find where to buy them without success.

A NATION OF BONEFISH

I see anglers just learning about fishing for bonefish on the flats plagued by the same problem I wrestled with until I finally got it through my thick skull what to do about it. I'm talking about wading a vast flat fishing very large schools of fish that are staying tightly together as they swim to and fro.

When the dream shot occurs (they're coming right at you), the temptation is to cast the fly just a foot or two in front of the lead fish with the expectation that an immediate hookup will result. It doesn't work out that way. You'd think safety in numbers would make a large school oblivious to possible perils and therefore unwary. Not the case. Instead, and inexplicably, they are spookier than cruising singles and doubles along a mangrove shoreline.

The only way I've found to successfully fish the schools I'm describing here is to try to anticipate the path of the school and cast the fly twenty feet or more in front of them and let it sit. Then, the tricky part is sensing as closely as possible the moment they have arrived at your fly, whereupon you VERY GENTLY move it. Bingo—hookup!

In the Bushes Again

Mangroves. I won't attempt a primer on them as there are many fine books available covering these fascinating aspects of nature. Mangroves are both beautiful and important to our ecosystem and to fisheries that hold bonefish and related species. But hooked bonefish have a maddening habit of bolting into the mangroves and doing their best to wind your leader, fly line, and backing around countless leaves and roots as though each were an individual yo-yo.

So, what to do?

First, try to keep the hooked fish out of the mangroves by lowering your rod and pulling in the direction opposite their intended path to the mangroves.

Next, if this fails, immediately (but gently to avoid a backlash) put your reel in total free spool. When bonefish no longer feel pressure from the angler, they will often simply either completely stop or slow their speed to a crawl, perhaps believing they are free. This allows the guide the chance to advance the skiff on the stopped fish while the angler retrieves as much of his line possible while still not putting any pressure on the fish (which may make him run again).

Then the fun begins. It's usually necessary for angler, guide, or both to pull on their wading boots and exit the skiff to begin the tedious process of, branch-by-branch, root-by-root, untangling the line and hopefully coming upon a still-hooked fish that can be landed. Sadly, quite often this process results in the angler or guide holding the tag end of the leader that is minus both the bonefish and the fly he ate.

If there is any doubt that free-spooling causes a hooked bonefish to feel free and stop swimming, once when I found myself disconnected from my hooked bonefish, it was because the fly line became separated from the backing. We were able to pole up to my fly line lying still in the water and hand line the fish in!

An Accident Waiting to Happen

Sometimes I still see anglers do something that only invites trouble. When reeling up to move to another spot, they will sometimes hook the fly, not on one of the all-metal guides on their fly rod, but on one with the ceramic ring inside. I learned the hard way not to do this as I found that it can, over time, cause the ceramic ring to loosen and fall out.

READY, AIM, FIRE!

On one of our mothership trips to Moore's Island off Abaco I was wade-fishing with guide Town Williams on the west side of Mangrove Cay, which is the part of the Moore's Island area closest to the ocean. For some reason I cannot recall, I was fishing solo that day. After wading for a while and not seeing fish, Town instructed me to continue wading in the same northerly direction while he fetched the skiff and made a big circle around in front of me to pick me up for running to the next flat.

I nodded and continued to wade in almost perfect conditions—bright sky and light winds. Perhaps ten minutes into my wade without Town to help spot fish, I saw in the distance a single shark swimming slowly directly toward me. It was not a large shark; I judged it to be maybe two to three feet in length. Even if it had been a six- or seven-footer, my reaction would still have been one of nonchalance as sharks in ankle-deep water will not bother you unless you bother them.

So, I continued wading, constantly scanning the water in 180-degree sweeps of my vision looking for bonefish. I was on high alert in doing so as the ocean-side flat I was wading had, on previous trips, held some monstrous bones.

Meanwhile, that shark kept coming on its same path toward me, and I continued watching it while still performing my visual sweep of the entire flat. It wasn't long before the only thing that drew my eye was that approaching shark, as he was now much closer as his track toward me had continued.

Dear readers, to this day I am still chagrined to tell you this: That shark got less than twenty feet in front of me before I realized it was not a shark but a bonefish that could have been as large as fourteen or fifteen pounds!

By the time I began false casting, the gap between this career fish and me had closed, and what might have been the trophy of my years of fly fishing the flats spotted me. With a couple of kicks of its substantial tail, it bolted past me and streaked off.

So, you ask, what is my tip?

It's very simple: "Shoot first and ask questions later!"

Forty-Two

Save Me a Spot

Although that first fishing trip with my Sunday school teacher resulted in a paltry tin can's worth of measurable results, I felt the same exhilaration that has kept me on the water for many decades. Important elements fuel such a compulsion: the proclivity of our human nature to hunt, our satisfying immersion in the tedium of careful preparation, and the delicious combination of fear and optimism.

In the absence of those last two, anglers would not pick up a rod because those two very human emotions are concomitant residents of one's psyche. Those two emotions alternate their emergence as they fuel the angler's obsession. Some anglers fear stormy weather or perhaps a shark or bear attack, but almost all feel that familiar and basic human emotion—fear of failure. It's why optimism pervades the being of almost every angler. Fear of failure motivates the angler to carefully prepare. Optimism takes over as the mission unfolds. If the mission is a dud, it's optimism that puts the angler on the water the next day effervescing with enthusiasm.

In addition to optimism, there's something else that sustains the angler when fear of failure is realized—gratitude. A thankfulness for the experience of just being there to give it a shot and a serenity that overcomes an angler's core in recognition of the privilege.

That serenity is more easily achieved the more experienced and successful the angler becomes. When I was learning to fly fish, I was an abysmal caster. So, the fear part of the couplet dominated the optimism part, all sustained by a strident competitiveness.

The more proficient one is at something, the more one wants to do it. When some of my angler buddies struggled at times, they began to regret invitations to go on some of my trips. However, when they decided to work on their casting and had more success fishing, they began inquiring with regularity about the next destination.

Fanatic that I am, I was largely immune to the kind of discouragement that would give rise to my standing down. I just kept on keeping on and finally reached a place where, with my fly line stripped out and staring down a fish, I had at least a vague idea of what might happen with my cast. When I began to get enough memorable trips under my belt, the emotions of serenity and gratitude began to displace the ever-surfacing frustrations experienced by all anglers.

Perhaps emotion is not the apt term. Emotion is what a disappointed angler experiences. Serenity and gratitude are perhaps intellectually derived from mining the depths of one's being.

All I know is that the more I fish, the more grateful I am for just being able to do it. When I began, I would count every fish and, when the number was high, way too pridefully recite it to fellow anglers when returning to the lodge. I would not dream of doing that now even if I still counted my fish, which I do not. Do I still get skunked or have a lousy day? Extremely rare on the former, occasionally on the latter. But I no longer wind myself up like a pretzel in frustration or despair. Instead, I find myself treasuring just being in the midst of the intricate splendor God created for us and embracing the peace it brings.

I find I now take even greater pleasure in the success of my angling partners. This is in contrast with the early days when my greatest catches were still in front of me. Then I would sometimes begrudge the fact that my angling partner lucked out with the dream shot. Have I become more mellow? Sure. But I will tell you this: Even now, when staring at a tailing bonefish in the eight-pound class with his wagging tail seeming to be the size of an American flag at a car dealership, my heart rate and blood pressure would break the machines that measure them.

By now, non-angler readers will know this about fly fishing: It ain't easy, brother. Indeed, it is challenging, frustrating, heartbreaking, and glorious all at the same time. Many, including me, wrestle with the question: Why in God's name do we do it? Why torture ourselves for a few moments of glory? (Does that sound as if I could be writing about golf?)

One answer may be the same given by mountain climbers—because it's there. Surely there is something to that. I believe there is likely something in good men and women that not only relishes a challenge; they simply must have it.

This takes us back to those two emotions: fear and optimism. I can't think of the latter without recalling the old joke about the supremely optimistic farm boy who ran outside on Christmas morning to see what his present was only to be confronted by a huge pile of horse manure. Without hesitation, he dove into the pile and, industriously digging toward the bottom, exclaimed, "There must be a pony in here somewhere!"

The question then remains: Why do anglers subject themselves to the time, expense, frustration, and toil required to pursue mere moments of piscatorial glory?

The best job of nailing the answer may have come from a wonderful friend of mine who is a real-life embodiment of the Dos Equis beer TV commercial character—"the most interesting man in the world." He is a Hall of Fame angler, a business titan, an accomplished author, and a movie producer named Bob Rich.

In his outstanding book *The Fishing Club: Brothers and Sisters of the Angle*, something famous angler Andy Mill said to Bob caused him to do some research that resulted in a "voila!" moment. Bob uncovered a quote from a chap named John Buchan, the Earl of Tweedsmuir, and used it in his book. With kind and full attribution to my fine friend Bob Rich, I will gratefully repeat it here:

"The charm of fishing is that it is the pursuit of what is elusive but attainable, a perpetual series of occasions for hope."

So, while I have written of optimism, perhaps a more apt descriptor is what it really comes down to—*hope*. Going further, is that not what almost everything in life comes down to?

Accordingly, I tell you this: I sincerely *hope* you have somehow been enriched by this book.

And something else:

I *hope* to see you on the flats with your line tight, your rod in a curve, and a smile on your face.

Save me a spot, won't you?

Acknowledgments

Many years ago, my sweet wife gave me a very classy and well-organized fishing logbook. Each blank page was perfectly organized with places to record location, weather, tides guides, and details of the day's catch.

So, what did yours truly do with it?

Unfortunately, nothing. Which is a ridiculous oversight, particularly for a writer. Consequently, everything in this book is straight out of my memory.

For this acknowledgments section, I put that memory to work to recall and write down the name of every guide I have fished with around the world over the years. While probably missing some, I came up with a total of 151 of them, 106 on the saltwater flats and forty-five in rivers and streams.

Although not by name, I recognize them here because this book would not have made it from my memory to the page were it not for the rich experiences, instruction, and fellowship these fine people afforded me. I thank them with all my heart and salute their skill and professionalism.

To me, guides are a special breed of people. Almost all are at the highest level of dedication and competitiveness. This may be underscored by the fact that when most of them go on vacation, guess what they do? They go fishing!

But perhaps what I treasure most about guides is the personal relationships I have formed with them, many of these resulting in close, long-lasting friendships.

After having four novels published, this is my first work of nonfiction. That meant navigating a brand-new array of potential publishers, editors, and literary agents. That would not have happened were it not for my two champions—my great friends Bob Rich and Paul Dixon, who went the extra mile to connect me with the best editor I've ever worked with, the marvelously talented Jay Nichols of Stackpole Books. My heartfelt gratitude to you all.

Index

Abaco, 42, 130, 170, 198, 211, 224; Bight of Abaco, 39, 125, 160; Great Abaco, 39, 60, 69, 123–124, 129, 203; Little Abaco, 97, 162; Marls of Abaco, 125–129, 131–133
Abaco Bonefish Lodge, 131–132
Adams, Aaron, 56, 63, 66, 222
Adams, Paul, 38, 39, 104
Adderley, Kiki, 176
Adderley, Ramon, 10, 59
Adderly, Perry, 62, 141
air charter companies, 194
Alphonse Island, 189–191
Alphonse Island Lodge, 191
Ambergris Cays, 58
Andrews, Sean, 213–214
Andros Island, 114, 116, 174, 180, 187; archipelago, 113, 147; doctor fly problems on, 235–236; east side, 32, 120, 221; Middle Bight, 175, 178, 179; North Bight, 32, 115, 119; north coast, 117, 121, 122, 130, 146, 148; South Andros, 105, 106, 111–112, 168, 206; west side, 18, 33, 34, 56, 106, 121, 153, 155, 156, 158, 162, 164, 175, 221, 224, 233. *See also* Joulters Cays

Andros Island Bonefish Club (AIBC), 30–37, 46, 153
Angling Report (newsletter), 96–98
Ashcraft, Randy, 166, 167
Avalon (company), 182–184

backcountry; backcountry fishing boats, 87–89; of Boca Grande, 82, 85; of Isla Holbox, 134–135; redfish found in, 80–81; Yalahau Lagoon, 138
Backcountry Cowboy (stadium seat), 233
backing. *See* fly line
Bahamianese, 60
Bain, Alton, 174, 176
Bain, Elizabeth ("Miss Liz"), 174–176, 178
Bain, Simon, 154, 155, 157
Bain, Stanley, 174
Bair, Andy, 105
Bair, Stanley, 105
Bair's Lodge, 105–107, 110–112
Bang Bang Club, 113–115
Bannerot, Rick, 196
barefoot fishing, 57, 98
barracuda, 9–10, 64, 160, 161, 166, 188, 218–220, 223
Bayless, Tom, 155–157, 159, 160, 204

Index

Bazo, John, 93–94
Bean, Andy, 74
Beavertail skiffs, 98, 101
Berry Islands, 3, 10, 53, 57–58, 71, 76, 162, 187
Bethel, Charles B. M., III, 221–222, 224
billfishing, 9–10
Bimini Island, 9–10, 204
Bishop, Bill, 82–83
Bishop, George, 73, 75
Black Fly Lodge, 205, 224
Blackwood Creek, 64, 69, 141
blue heron walk, 54–55
bluewater fishing, 9–10
Boca Grande, 3, 83, 135, 167, 232; Boca Grande Channel, 82, 163; Boca Grande Pass, 79, 80; *Brittania* visit to, 173; Bush family stays in, 86–89; permit as rare in, 81, 85; phosphate discovery at, 78–79
Boca Moon (Foster), 79, 86, 89, 98
Boca News (Foster), 79, 86, 89, 98
BogaGrip, 66, 71, 76, 106, 161, 222
Bonefish & Tarpon Trust (BTT), 24, 27, 30; board members, 30, 56, 63, 164, 177, 196; BogaGrip, discouraging use of, 66, 71, 76; mangrove restoration and, 41–42; scientific research of, 66, 183, 222
Botting, Cecelia, 106–107, 111

Botting, Nicolas, 106–108, 110–111
Brittania (royal yacht), 173–174
Broadshad Cay Lodge, 115–117, 119
The Brown Trout (fly shop), 210
Buchan, John, 242
Buffet, Jimmy, 80, 106, 178, 194
Bully (guide), 102–104
Burke, Monte, 91, 92
Burnt Store Marina flats, 82
Burrows, "Graveyard", 61
Burrows, Monique, 60, 61, 70
Burrows, Ricardo, 59–62, 64–70, 140, 167, 168, 199
Bush, Barbara, 87, 88
Bush, George H. W., 30, 80, 86–89
Bush, Laura, 90

Cabbage Creek, 34
the cage (fishing tool), 231–232
Capone, Al, 115
Captiva Pass, 82
Cargill Creek, 37, 154, 174, 221
Cargill Creek Bonefish Lodge, 174–175
Carreras, Fernando de las, 105, 132
Carters Cays, 162, 168
casting, 5, 7, 10, 42, 143, 229; accessories for casting platform, 230–232; backcasting, 28, 47–48, 208; barefoot casting, 57, 98; for barracuda, 219; blind casting, 59, 135–136,

247

207, 209; for bonefish, 11, 14, 33, 56; casting range, being out of, 54–55; distractions while casting, 8; double haul, 47–48, 75, 171; either-handed casting, 20, 157; false casting, 47–48, 167, 168, 239; grand slam, casting for, 158; initial challenges of, 13, 26, 67, 80, 240–241; from the leeward shore, 27; lessons and tips, 19, 20, 34–35, 82; power snap, 20, 226–227; presentation, 34–36, 47, 56, 208–209; rubbing of fly in mud before casting, 126; to schools of fish, 236; second cast, 208, 210; shark, casting to, 64; strong wind, casting into, 116; successful casting, 8, 13, 68, 81–82, 117, 139–140; tarpon, casting to, 36, 81, 163

Catch a Falling Knife (Foster), 89

Causey, Don, 96–98

Cayo Romano, 184–185

Chalks Airlines, 204

Charlotte Harbor, 78–79, 85

Christmas Island, 58

Chub Cay, 145, 187, 193; double-digit bonefish of, 33, 71, 75–76; as a private club, 76–77; receivership status, 73, 74; Sand Bank flat, 74, 141; spinning rods, fishing with, 11, 13; Tongue of the Ocean, proximity to, 10, 72

Clark, Ron, 124, 127, 129

cobia, 81, 85

Cochran, Vaughn, 205

Conch Republic, 170–171

conservation, 22, 27–28, 71, 76, 222, 232

crabs, 7, 76, 102

Cross Harbour, 62, 69

Crossing Rocks, 62, 133, 203, 205

Cuba; Cuban flats, 2, 56, 183, 184; single-file skiff, fishing from, 181–182; stripping for barracuda in, 219–220; tarpon as plentiful in, 180, 184

Cuban yo-yo, 24, 129, 180

Curtis, Bill, 195–196

Daniel, William, 197

Danylchuk, Andy, 76

D'Arville, Percy, 54–55, 62, 161

Davenport, Cameron, 61

Davis, Terrence, 126, 128–130, 132, 160–161

Deep Creek flats, 112

Deep Water Cay Club, 16, 19, 43, 97, 99, 200, 202; Club owners, 21–22; David Senior as guide, 23–29; famous visitors, 20–21; as granddaddy of bonefish lodges, 2, 4, 40; Hurricane Dorian damage to, 39, 40; McClean's Town and, 17, 19, 21, 25, 38; spinning rods, use of, 13, 15

Delfin, Eusebio and Hilda, 204

Index

Delphi Club, 58, 60, 131–133, 203, 205
Diana, Princess of Wales, 174
Dixon, Paul, 196
doctor flies, 235–236
Dolphin skiffs, 106, 127
Dombrowski, Chris, 20
Dora, Dennis, 195–196
Drake, Gil, 2, 20, 21, 25, 28–29
Drake, Gil, Jr., 2, 202
Drake, Tommy, 2
Dry Tortugas, 163, 171, 173
duck walk, 54–55, 62, 161
DuPont family, 79–81, 86

East End Lodge, 38, 40–45, 105, 168
Eleven Experience, 61, 164, 165
Elizabeth II, Queen, 173–174
El Saltamontes Lodge, 142–143

Fairbanks, Cole, 3, 28, 85
Fairbanks, Deanna, 3, 13, 16, 28
Fernandez, Chico, 235
Finchem, Tim, 17
Fish Cay flat, 71, 74, 75
The Fishing Club (Rich), 242
fishing hours, 17–19, 101, 112
Flamingo Cay Rod & Gun Club, 221–224
flies; algae flies, 191; Bonefish Special, 145; cicada-patterned flies, 211, 215; colored streamers, 219, 234; Crazy Charlie, 26, 113, 119; double-hook flies, 219; dry flies, 107, 202, 208; the Dumpster, 202; Gotcha, 26, 31, 44, 235; mantis shrimp flies, 65, 66, 235; Meko Special, 19; Merkin Crab, 158; mouse flies, 215; palolo worm flies, 83, 235; permit flies, 43, 158, 235; Pink Puff, 26; polecat flies, 3; popping bug flies, 81, 219, 223; Puglisi spawning shrimp, 99, 145, 168, 235; tarpon flies, 34, 36, 81, 82, 93, 164, 234–235; topwater flies, 81, 102, 219
fly boxes, 44, 140, 211
fly dryer, 44
fly line, 7, 13, 28, 241; backing, 20, 52, 65, 68, 71, 129, 140, 142, 157, 237; butt of rod, line catching on, 169; casting with either hand, 20, 157; cleaning and dressing lines, 225–226; corrosion and limp lines, 44; in double haul technique, 47–48; hand line, 24, 25, 129, 180; leader, 13, 68, 108, 118, 137, 218, 237; left-hand drag prior to clearing line, 33; line management, 223, 231; line retrieval as critical, 227; palming the reel and, 52; sink line, 81, 82, 135–136, 147; stepping on fly line, 8, 57, 98, 144; stripping techniques and, 83, 84; strong wind, casting

entire fly line into, 116; test line for impaled hook removal, 109; tippet, 44, 93, 109, 118, 218, 232

fly reels, 11, 14, 33; Billy Pate reels, 30; free-spooling in mangroves, 237; fresh water rinsing after use, 44; Orvis reels, 71, 93, 117–118; palming the reel, 51–52; sound of surrendering the line, 8, 68

fly rods, 47, 169, 211, 218, 237; bonefishing, rods used for, 7, 32, 42, 75, 229; Cabela's rod, 232; Orvis Helios, 93, 232; spinning rod *vs.* fly rod, 14–15, 26; stripping techniques and, 36, 83, 84, 219, 231; tarpon rods, 34–35, 81, 88, 93–94, 157, 171–172, 190, 232–233; thumb rest modification, 226–227; thunderstorms, graphite fly rods reacting to, 69; transitioning to fly rods, 13–15, 30; for walk-and-wade fishing, 110. *See also* casting

The Fly Shop, 138, 184

Foster, Frank, 98–102

Foster, Matthew, 42, 117, 201

Foster, Patti, 59, 118, 127, 172, 181, 209; Captain Phil, fishing with, 81–82; mangroves, fishing success in, 140–142; permit, elusive for, 12, 142, 182; Princess Diana, encounter with, 174; river-crossing in New Zealand, 212–213; tarpon fishing at Flamingo Cay Club, 223; wade-fishing, preference for, 139, 143, 215

Foster, Skip, 42, 48

Foster, Will, 42, 44, 117

Frazier's Hog Cay, 74, 145

Frey, Lou, 89

Frontiers (outfitters), 138, 191, 214, 224

Fulton, Rich, 42–43, 149–150

Funk, Fred, 16–17, 21, 30

Gardens of the Queen flats, 56, 183

Gasparilla Inn, 79–81, 85–87, 89

giant trevally (GT), 189, 190

Glinton, Omeko (Meko), 19–20, 23, 38

Gorda Cay, 62, 67, 68, 140

Gowdy, Curt, 21, 46

Graham, Karen, 46–48, 50–51, 60

Grand Bahama Island, 45, 114, 126, 141; clubs located on, 2, 98, 102, 105; Freeport, on north shore of, 200; Hurricane Dorian as ravaging, 38–41; Water Cay, off north shore of, 97. *See also* McClean's Town

Grand Cay, 114, 162

grand slams, 85, 157, 158, 182, 184

Great Harbour Cay, 53–55, 57–58, 62, 161

Great Sale Cay, 162
Griffin, Elias, 147, 149, 152
grouper, 3, 81
Grove Isle Club, 155
Gutermuth, Bill, 65, 66

Hawkins, Mason, 21
Hells Bay skiffs, 22, 101, 222
Helwig, Grif, 163–164, 171–172
Hemingway, Ernest, 9, 114, 115
High Rollers (Bishop), 82–83
HM Paraiso del Mar, 135
Home Waters Club, 201
Hommel, George, 30–31, 34
Homosassa, 82, 91–95
hooks; #4 hook for bonefish flies, 235; bare hook fishing with meat, 14, 15; hook corrosion, 44; impaled hook incidents, 26, 108–111
Horn, Bill, 82–83, 177–178
Hughes, Bumpy, 162, 168
Humble Servant Bonefishing, 12, 144, 229
Hurricane Dorian, 45, 103, 104, 128, 131; Deep Water Cay Club, damage to, 21; Grand Bahama Island, as ravaging, 38–41; McClean's Town as hit by, 28, 39
Hurricane Matthew, 148–149
Hurricane Mitch, 200–201

In Search of Fly Water (television series), 46–50

Isla Holbox, 134–138
Islamorada, 30, 232, 233, 235

Jackfish Channel, 106, 112
Josie Cay, 147, 149
Joulters Cays, 116, 122, 130, 146–149, 152

Kamalame Cay Resort, 150
Kempt, Clint, 205
Kennedy, David, 124, 147, 149, 166
Kennedy, Jay, 124, 147, 149, 164, 166, 184
Key Point flat, 67
Key West, 163, 170–172, 192
Kreh, Lefty, 21, 31, 91
Kresge, Cary, 168
Kunio (guide), 212–213

lady-friendly lodges; Bair's Lodge, 112; Delphi Club, 203; East End Lodge, 45; Mangrove Cay Club, 178; Prescott Smith's Lodge, 120; Ricardo's Tailing Bones Guest House, 70; Soul Fly Lodge, 58; Water Cay Bonefish Club, 99
Land of the Giants, 18, 33, 120, 175, 177, 179, 223
Leadon, Brian, 33
Leadon, Dennis, 46, 56
Leadon, Rupert, 156; as AIBC owner and guide, 31–32, 36, 153; carpenter's saw, playing,

32, 37; casting advice, 34–35;
Karen Graham and, 46–48,
60; Land of the Giants and,
33, 223; palming the wheel,
cautioning against, 51–52
Leadon, Rupert, Jr. (Nick), 46
Leadon, Shawn, 36
leaning posts, 230–231
Leathen, Cecil, 40–41, 44, 45
Leonard, Lenny, 172
Lewis, Justin, 42
Lightbourne, David, 10–11, 59,
71, 73, 141, 145
lightning strikes, 68–69
LineLair, 231
lobster; diving for lobster, 117,
126; lobster as Bahamian fare,
70, 99, 205; lobster fishing, 32,
174
Locklear, Mike, 92–93
Long, Jimmy, 93, 94
Lords of the Fly (Burke), 91, 92
Louis, Joe, 71
Love, Davis, III, 16–17, 19–21,
30
Lowe Sound, 148–149, 151

Mangrove Cay, 166, 206, 238
Mangrove Cay Club, 174–179
mangroves, 102, 138, 183,
233, 236; of Andros Island,
156–157; fishing around
mangroves, 108, 140–142,
237; of Joulters Cay, 146–147;
mangrove restoration

project, 41–42; of Sandy
Point, 61–62
Mantle, Peter, 203
Marquesas Keys, 61, 158, 162,
163, 172, 232
Marsh Harbour, 39, 70, 130,
161, 170, 203; conch salad
food stand in, 128–129;
Foster Family holiday at,
175–176; Great Abaco Island,
located on, 60, 123–125;
Marsh Harbour airport, 69,
131, 132; Spring City as a
suburb of, 126
Maverick skiffs, 106, 121
McClane, A. J., 2, 28, 31
McClean's Town, 40, 41, 45,
97; Deep Water Cay Club, as
across from, 17, 19, 21, 25, 38;
Hurricane Dorian damage to,
28, 38–39; as Pinder family
home town, 24
McClelland, Mike, 214
McCreery, Rick, 61
McCrickard, Alex, 108–110
McCrory, Walt, 72–73
McGuane, Thomas, 196
McVay, Jim, 31, 235
Melvin, Sandy, 80, 85
Menocal, Luis, 183
micro skiffs, 176–177, 179
milkfish, 189–191
Mill, Andy, 35, 82–84,
242
Monroe, Marilyn, 171

Moore's Island, 8, 65, 70; flats, 63, 160, 166, 199; mothership trips to, 129, 160–162, 199, 238; mutton snapper fishing, 166–168
Moore's Island Bonefish Lodge, 199
mothership trips, 61, 129, 168, 183, 236; to Great Harbour Cay, 53, 58; on the *Hi Hatter*, 154–155, 161; to the Marquesas, 163, 172; May, trips during the month of, 186; to Moore's Island, 160–161, 238; on *The Outpost*, 149, 161–162, 164, 165, 172; to Williams and Billy Islands, 153–159, 222

Nauheim, Bob, 119
Neher, Robert, 40–41, 44, 45
Nervous Waters, 105–107, 131–132
New Zealand; Best of New Zealand Fly Fishing, 214; clarity of water in, 207; Over the Top Helicopter services, 210; Poronui Lodge, 211–213, 215–217; presentation, opportunities to focus on, 208, 209
Nicholls Town, 148–151
Nicklaus, Barbara, 74–75
Nicklaus, Jack, 53–54, 72, 74–75, 117, 123
North Andros Bonefishing, 150–151

North Riding Point Club (NRPC), 20, 38, 39, 102–104

O'Bannon, Phil, 81–83, 85, 88, 232
Oklahoma flat, 91–93
On the Bow (Horn), 82, 177
oolite, 147
Orvis (company), 119, 132, 196; Orvis apparel, 48, 57, 111; Orvis gear, 43, 71, 93, 118, 137, 232; Orvis stores, 15, 124, 138, 142, 215

palolo worms, 83, 235
Panga boats, 135, 137
Park, Willie, Sr., 23
A Passion for Tarpon (Mill), 35, 82
Pate, Billy, 30, 31, 91
Pelican Bay Hotel, 200
Perkins, Dave, 13, 57
Perkins, Leigh, 57, 119, 132
permit, 54, 62, 105, 125, 147, 163, 167; at Billy Island, 158; at Boca Grande, 81, 85; at Christmas Island, 58; Cuba, surfeit of, 180; as elusive, 12, 142, 158, 182, 184; at Moore's Island, 166; mothership trips to fish permit, 153, 160; permit flies, 43, 158, 235; in the Seychelles Islands, 189; at Water Cay Bonefish Club, 98–102
Pete and Gay's Guesthouse, 61

Index

Pickford, Nigel, 143
Pike, Chad, 61, 164
Pinder, David, Jr., 26, 200
Pinder, David, Sr., 19, 23–29, 59
Pinder, Jeffrey, 26
Pinder, Joseph, 26, 200
Pinder, Paul, 211
Pindling, Lynden, 113
Pink Elephant (restaurant), 85, 89
Poronui Lodge, 211–213, 215–217
Pot Cay, 113, 115
Puglisi, Enrico, 99, 145
Pyrenees Mountains, 203–204

Red Bay Sunset Lodge, 115, 121–122
redfish, 80–81, 85, 87, 93, 94
Renaud, David, 73
Ricardo's Tailing Bones Guest House, 69–70
Rich, Bob, 242
Richmond, Ed, 134–137, 155, 160
Rickmon Bonefish Lodge, 61
Riley, Shawn, 116–118, 152
Robby's Place, 149–152
Rolfing, Mark, 17, 21
Rolle, Mark, 151
Rolle, Philip, 59, 147–151
Rubin, Robert, 38, 103
Russell, Keith, 149–150, 152
Ryan, Andrew, 204–205

Saban, Nick, 80
Sailflow (weather forecasting site), 187

Salvelinus (company), 203
Sandy Point, 133, 141, 203; five diverse fisheries of, 61–62; Moore's Island, accessing from, 160, 199; Ricardo Burrows as guide, 59–60, 64–65, 67; Ricardo's Tailing Bones Guest House in, 69–70
satellite phones, 158–159
Schwarzkopf, Norman, 173
Sea Bear (yacht), 74, 75
Seeber, Santiago, 105
Seminoles of Red Bays, 121–122
September 11 terror attacks, 197
Seychelle Islands, 188–191
Seymour, Louvan ("Skeemer"), 148–149
shark, 66, 172, 238; bonefish skiffs, hovering around, 26, 209; bull shark at Marquesas Keys, 163–164; at Deep Water Cay, 26, 28; lemon shark, 43, 64, 65, 141, 178; shark-fishing contest, Fred Funk holding, 16–17; tarpon as prey for, 166, 232
Sharp, Bayard, 81
shrimp, 3, 11, 14, 25, 26, 76, 84, 147
sight-fishing, 8, 59, 82, 107, 196, 207, 209
Simeon (guide), 141–142, 168
Smathers, George, 78
Smith, Andy, 113–117, 119–120, 157
Smith, Benry, 114–116, 121–122

Smith, Charlie ("Crazy Charlie"), 113–116, 119, 162
Smith, Diane, 122
Smith, Prescott, 115–116, 120–121, 150
Smith, Stacy, 116, 120–121
snapper, 7, 81; mangrove snapper, 3; mutton snapper, 44, 62, 160, 162, 166–168, 200; yellowtail snapper, 130
snook, 3, 88, 95, 190; backcountry snook, 87, 134, 138; at Boca Grande, 81, 85, 167; Everglades snook fishing, 74, 202
Soul Fly Lodge, 55, 57–58
Spanish Wells, 175, 179
spinning rods, 11, 13, 26; bonefish, using to catch, 3, 25; left-hand cranking, 227–228; Mangrove Cay Club as providing, 178; meat fishing with, 218; spinning-to-fly-rod transition, 14–15, 30
Stafford Creek Lodge, 115, 120–121, 150
Stamps, Roe, 30
starfish, 8
St. François Atoll, 189, 190
stingrays, 168
stopwatch use, 143
Strangers Cay, 162
striped bass, 196
stripping, 33, 36, 56; in double haul drill, 47; fast strip not favored, 228; guides advising on, 60; long and slow strip, 83, 84; proper execution of, 7, 34–35; stripping basket, 232; stripping bucket, 231; strip-striking, 33, 229–230; in a strong wind, 116; sunscreen as interfering with, 125; tick-tick-tick method, 83, 84; two-handed stripping, 83–84, 219
sunglasses, 110
sunscreen, 57, 125–126
Swinney, Dabo, 80

Tagini, Claudio, 96–97
Tailing Bones Lodge, 61, 70
tarpon, 12, 121, 125, 147, 179, 220; at Billy Island, 157–158, 223; at Boca Grande, 3, 79–85, 88; Cuba as abundant in, 180, 184; daisy-chaining tarpon, 36, 84, 93–94; on fly, 30, 81, 83, 85, 88, 91, 171, 172, 232–233; at Homosassa, 91–94; in Key West, 171–172; at Marquesas Keys, 61, 162–163, 232; May as a prime month for tarpon fishing, 186; in Mexico, 134, 135, 137, 138; striking the tarpon, sin of, 35; stripping for tarpon, 219; tarpon-fishing books, 82–83; tarpon flies, 34, 36, 81, 82, 93, 164, 234–235; tarpon rods, 34–35, 81, 88, 93–94, 157, 171–172, 190–191, 232–233

Tarpon Club, 135–138
Tarpon Hole, 164
Thomas, Sidney, 97–104, 162
Thorne, Hank, 115
Thrift Harbour, 27, 43, 141–142
thunder storms, 68–69
tiger fish, 188
timekeeping with stopwatch, 143
Toney, William, 93, 94
Tongue of the Ocean, 10, 72, 130, 147, 149, 175
Treasure Cay, 60, 124, 129
triggerfish, 189, 190
trolling, 9, 10, 82
trout; brown trout, 209–211, 213, 214; at Home Waters Club, 201; in Ireland, 204–205; Karen Graham as a trout angler, 46–47; in New Zealand, 207–212, 215; rainbow trout, 107, 209, 213; river trout, 199–200, 219; sea trout, 85, 94; in Slovenia, 202–203
trout set, 33, 83, 144
trout strike, 83–84
Trudeau, Pierre, 113, 119
Trump, Donald, 193
Turner, Dick, 154, 155, 161
Turtle Sound, 117

Vaiden, Philip, 124, 128, 134, 136, 137, 153–157, 160

Valdène, Guy de la, 2, 20
Valdiek, Paul, 21–22
Vega Cruz, Alejandro, 134–138

wade-fishing, 19, 71, 101, 106, 141; duck walk for shallow wading, 54–55; at low tide, 62–63; at Mangrove Cay, 166–167; at Marls of Abaco, 125; sharks, encountering, 64, 66, 238; spooking fish when wading, 145; at Strangers Cay, 162; wading boots, 45, 214–215; wading *vs.* poling, 139, 143; walk-and-wade fishing, 5, 110, 207, 212; at Whidden's Creek, 80–81
Walkers Cay, 114, 162
Wardlow, Jeff, 170–171
Water Cay Bonefish Lodge, 97–104
water clarity, 6, 7, 11, 72, 82, 138, 207
water temperature, 186
weather forecasting, 187
Weeks, Jim, 123–125, 127–131, 134, 136, 147, 193
Wheeler, Fred, 149, 161, 164
Wheeler, Penny, 149, 161, 164
White, Oliver, 132
William, Edmund ("Town"), 126–129, 131, 132, 160–161, 238

Williams and Billy Islands, 153–157, 159, 222, 223
Windfinder (weather forecasting site), 187
Wood, Dave, 213
Wulff, Joan, 20, 226–227
Wulff, Lee, 115, 226
Wyatt, Allen, 124, 219, 232

Yalahau Lagoon, 138
Yellow Dog Fly Fishing, 138, 214, 224

www.ingramcontent.com/pod-product-compliance
Ingram Content Group UK Ltd.
Pitfield, Milton Keynes, MK11 3LW, UK
UKHW041821310326
5020IPUK00001B/8